NUCLEAR INSECURITY

_____

NUCLEAR INSECURITY

*Understanding the Threat from Rogue
Nations and Terrorists*

JACK CARAVELLI

PRAEGER SECURITY INTERNATIONAL
Westport, Connecticut • London

Library of Congress Cataloging-in-Publication Data

Caravelli, Jack, 1952–
  Nuclear insecurity : understanding the threat from rogue nations and
terrorists / Jack Caravelli.
    p. cm.
  Includes bibliographical references and index.
  ISBN-13: 978-0-275-99746-5 (alk. paper)
  1. Nuclear terrorism—United States—Prevention. 2. Nuclear
nonproliferation—Government policy—United States. 3. Nuclear
substances—Security measures. 4. National security—United States.
I. Title.
  HV6433.86.C37 2008
  363.325′570973—dc22   2007029127

British Library Cataloguing in Publication Data is available.

Library of Congress Catalog Card Number: 2007029127
ISBN: 978-0-275-99746-5

First published in 2008

Praeger Security International, 88 Post Road West, Westport, CT 06881
An imprint of Greenwood Publishing Group, Inc.
www.praeger.com

Printed in the United States of America

∞™

The paper used in this book complies with the
Permanent Paper Standard issued by the National
Information Standards Organization (Z39.48–1984).

10 9 8 7 6 5 4 3 2 1

To my parents, Victor and Harriet Caravelli, my family, Kathy, Chris, and Artyom Caravelli, and Dr. John W. Jayne

Contents

Acknowledgments

FOR ANY FIRST-TIME book author there are many solitary moments in bringing to life a set of ideas through the written word. My experience was no exception. However, throughout this process I was buoyed by the unstinting support of colleagues and friends whose encouragement has been invaluable and for which I am most grateful. In this respect I am particularly indebted to John Wood, Duncan Wood, Derek Robinson, Mike Coffey, Ruth Kempf, Phil Hutchinson, and Dave Martin. I was supported in exemplary fashion by Hilary Claggett at Praeger International Security. I hasten to add that I am solely responsible for the book's contents.

Introduction

Acquiring nuclear weapons ... is a religious duty.

Osama bin Laden, 1999

The gravest danger our nation faces lies at the crossroads of radicalism and technology. Our enemies have openly declared that they are seeking weapons of mass destruction, and evidence indicates they are doing so with determination. The United States will not allow these efforts to succeed.... History will judge harshly those who saw this coming danger but failed to act. In the new world we have entered, the only path to peace and security is the path of action.

President George W. Bush, September 17, 2002

SINCE THE EARLY days of the Cold War, America and its allies have lived under the specter of nuclear attack. The 1962 Cuban Missile Crisis demonstrated the potentially catastrophic consequences of political miscalculation, but in its aftermath the United States and the Soviet Union continued for more than two decades an aggressive nuclear arms race. Concurrently, both sides also came to understand that nuclear arms were too dangerous to serve as useful tools of policy and, as a result, albeit in fits and starts, undertook arms control agreements designed to reduce their vast nuclear arsenals.

Perhaps most importantly, the superpowers came to realize that the utility of nuclear weapons was in their threatened, rather than actual, use. Thus was born the declaratory or official American and Soviet policies of deterrence through mutual assured destruction by which a nuclear attack by one side would be met by an immediate and overwhelming response by the other. At least one U.S. president—Ronald Reagan—found the concept of mutual assured destruction immoral, leading to his proposal of a missile defense system for America that today is in its embryonic stages. Nonetheless, for the most part, deterrence served to stabilize the superpower rivalry until the breakup of the Soviet Union in late 1991.

The effectiveness of deterrence was a direct result of each side believing the other had the will and means to respond with overwhelming force to a nuclear first strike. This was a contemporary version of the classic balance of power theory of politics in which the actions of each side were constrained and moderated by their assessment of the capabilities of the other.

One of the most far-reaching outcomes of the September 11, 2001, terrorist attacks is that the United States and its allies confront a new type of threat where our previous understandings about defense and deterrence no longer fully apply. Just as past generations confronted Hitler's demonic visions of a new world order, so today are we challenged by an individual and movement imbued with an unrelenting commitment to force radical change on the world. Islamic fundamentalism, whose most recognized advocate is al Qaeda leader Osama bin Laden, has chosen by a series of deadly acts to declare war against the United States and its allies. Since the early part of the twentieth century the American public, for the most part, has supported the political decisions and resulting sacrifices made by its armed forces in such far-flung places as fields in France, islands in the Pacific Ocean, the frozen landscape of North Korea, and the desert in Kuwait. Even in America's arguably most controversial wars, Vietnam and the current hostilities in Iraq, the American public gave the governing administrations the benefit of the doubt for lengthy periods of time. Albeit painful, generations of Americans are familiar with their sons and daughters fighting and dying in distant lands. They were not prepared to see their fellow citizens leaping out of buildings in New York City in final acts of desperation or their being crushed when the buildings collapsed. That is the new world and new type of warfare they were thrust into on September 11, 2001.

The writings and pronouncements of bin Laden and his followers indicate that Islamic fundamentalists have a long-term messianic vision to restore a caliphate or region governed by the Islamic fundamentalist interpretation of the Koran across a wide expanse of the Middle East and South Asia. As the major Western power in the region, and as the supporter of both Israel and the relatively moderate Arab nations in the region such as Saudi Arabia and Egypt, the United States, referred to as the "far enemy" by Islamic fundamentalists, stands in the way of this radical political agenda. Regardless of how one views the long and painful U.S. military involvement in Iraq or how that conflict is resolved, the goals of Islamic fundamentalism have not and are unlikely to abate absent sustained defeats, politically as well as militarily. Even victory in Iraq—however unlikely that outcome appears as this book is being written in early 2007—will not end the threat of Islamic fundamentalism. The reality is that a continuing and evolving threat is likely to dominate U.S. national security planning for years to come. Part of that threat comes from the potential use of nuclear or radiological weapons against the United States and its allies.

The emergence of Islamic fundamentalists capable of and willing to carry out conventional attacks on American soil, as well as in such diverse locations as London, Madrid, Egypt, Russia, and Indonesia demonstrates a collective vulnerability that to most Americans is and should be deeply unsettling. As of early 2007 there had been no subsequent terrorist attacks in the United States, but no U.S. government official or expert can assess whether this current situation is the result of good fortune, skill in preventing such attacks, or some measure of each.

What we can conclude with unassailable confidence is that Islamic fundamentalist groups such as al Qaeda embrace a continuing commitment to imposing vast destruction on American society. Osama bin Laden's professed intention to acquire and possibly use nuclear weapons was confirmed by former Central Intelligence Agency (CIA) director George Tenet in 2004 when he acknowledged at a Senate Intelligence Committee hearing that al Qaeda sees the use of nuclear weapons against the United States as a "religious obligation."[1] Consistent with Tenet's assessment are the apparently unsuccessful efforts by al Qaeda operatives through the 1990s to acquire highly enriched uranium in Russia, Europe, and elsewhere. In August 2001, just one month prior to the attacks against New York and Washington, bin Laden met in Kabul, Afghanistan with Sultan Bashiruddin Mahmood and Abdul Majid, former employees of Pakistan's atomic energy program. The meetings lasted several days, covering various aspects of nuclear weapons technology.[2]

Tenet's assessment also is consistent with a windfall of documents recovered by the Western media, including CNN, the *Washington Post*, the *New York Times,* and the *Wall Street Journal* in Afghanistan after the defeat of the Taliban in mid-November 2001. Several documents reportedly describe the manufacture of nuclear weapons and their effects. Perhaps the most dramatic was the discovery by CNN journalists at the home of Abu Khabab, a senior al Qaeda official, called the "Superbomb" that contained substantial technical information about nuclear weapons. Based on handwriting analysis, Khabab almost certainly wasn't the author of the work, but it may have been the product of an Arab (possibly Egyptian) scientist.[3] In another find, CNN correspondent David Ensor reported on the uncovering of a design for a "dirty bomb."[4]

Islamic fundamentalists fuse religion and politics and extend that philosophy to the use of nuclear weapons. In the wake of the September 11, 2001, attacks, bin Laden was criticized in some quarters of the Arab world, including moderate clerics, for the brutality of the attack that occurred without adequate warning.[5] To give any future attacks of similar or even larger magnitude an air of legitimacy, bin Laden required a fatwa or religious ruling. In

1998, bin Laden had issued his own fatwa, "Urging Jihad Against Americans." While bin Laden's lack of religious authority to issue a fatwa didn't slow his supporters from carrying out the September 11 attacks, the al Qaeda leader clearly had more ambitious plans in mind in seeking the fatwa.

Bin Laden received his much-desired religious stamp of approval with the May 23, 2003, publication of a fatwa titled, "A Treatise on the Legal Status of Using Weapons of Mass Destruction against Infidels." The author, Sheikh Naisr bin Hamid al Fahd, was among a small group of clerics later arrested in Mecca by Saudi authorities for actively supporting terrorist activities. Sheikh Fahd's twenty-five page fatwa is nothing less than an elaborate attempt to bestow on bin Laden and his followers the moral authority to use nuclear weapons. For Fahd, his interpretation of Islamic law takes precedent over any man-made laws. From that perspective Fahd addresses, and dismisses, any notion that the use of such weapons can't be justified because children and Muslims could be killed or injured. He claims that there exist estimates of ten million Muslims killed by various U.S. weapons and that an attack that killed an equal number of Americans would be permissible. As Fahd writes, "If the unbelievers can be repelled only by using weapons of mass destruction, then their use is permissible, even if you kill them without exception."[6]

This intellectual foundation demonstrates that Islamic fundamentalists understand clearly that possession of even one nuclear weapon can serve a larger political purpose. Setting aside for the moment the inflammatory nature of Fahd's rhetoric, the only way that deaths of that magnitude can be inflicted on America or its allies is through the use of nuclear weapons. Biological and chemical weapons, albeit terrifying in their own right, provide any would-be user with much less assurance of inflicting mass casualties.

Nuclear and radiological threats to U.S. security could take various forms, including the illicit theft or diversion of nuclear materials, detonation of an improvised nuclear device or a nuclear device stolen from a nuclear state's existing inventory, capturing a nuclear reactor and threatening its destruction, or the use of a radioactive dispersal device or so-called "dirty bomb."

There is no reliable way to predict the future likelihood for any of these scenarios. Neither complacency nor panic is warranted by our current understanding of this panoply of threats but deep concern is fully justified. For example, the devastation wreaked by even a small, crude nuclear device used against a population center would be horrific. When the first plane hit the World Trade Center (WTC) on September 11, there were about 30,000 people in the building and many of them escaped. As devastating as the events were, the death toll at the WTC would have been far greater if the weapon had been a crude nuclear device. Many variables would affect the yield or destructive force of such a device, including the presence of large buildings such as those in Manhattan that act to somewhat attenuate the blast's effects. However, even with a blast yield about one tenth of the yield from the detonation over Nagasaki, Japan, in 1945 (about 21 kilotons derived from about 6 kilograms of plutonium), there is no doubt that the WTC towers would have been destroyed instantly and probably everyone in the buildings killed.[7] Radiation would have covered a large portion of lower Manhattan and the resulting electromagnetic pulse would have wreaked havoc on unprotected electrical equipment throughout the region. The cost of the cleanup alone would have been even more staggering and widespread than what New York City experienced after the attack on the WTC.

A U.S. government study titled the "National Planning Scenario" came to many of the same conclusions in assessing the effects of an improvised 10-kiloton nuclear weapon detonated on the ground near the White House in Washington, DC. More than 200,000 immediate deaths are projected and another 25,000 people would succumb to various cancers in ensuing years. Approximately 90,000 citizens would be injured or become ill. Radiation would contaminate a 3,000-square mile area. The costs of the cleanup would be astronomical. These figures don't begin to capture the resulting disruption to critical governmental functions or the emotional and psychological costs to the area and the nation.[8]

The apocalyptic goals and ambitions of Islamic fundamentalists like bin Laden can be ignored only at our peril, but it still is appropriate to inquire whether their capabilities match their dark vision. To steal or otherwise acquire a fully assembled nuclear weapon is a daunting challenge and there is no reason to believe that Islamic fundamentalists have done so. Strategic weapons such as those used by the United States or Russia weigh hundreds of pounds (tactical nuclear weapons are somewhat lighter) and are well protected by their respective military organizations. Even if such a weapon somehow was acquired, its undetected transport over probably large distances would be a logistics nightmare. Finally, the unauthorized detonation of many, but not all, nuclear devices in the United States, Russia, and the other nuclear powers is virtually impossible due to the incorporation of sophisticated permissive action links.

Other scenarios are more troubling. Could a terrorist group fabricate and detonate its own crude nuclear device if the fissile materials needed, probably 8 to 12 kilograms of plutonium or 25 to 50 kilograms of highly enriched uranium (HEU), depending on the sophistication of the design? Considerable and intense debate has swirled around those issues for decades among Western scientists and other experts. As far back as 1977 the U.S. government's Office of Technology Assessment (OTA) reached the troubling conclusion that only two highly skilled people—a machinist and a physicist—would be required to make a simple nuclear device, assuming the availability of the fissile material.[9] Other highly respected physicists such as Theodore Taylor, a weapon designer from Los Alamos National Laboratory and Nobel laureate Luis Alvarez reached a similar conclusion.[10]

There are other reasons for concern as well. Information about nuclear devices is widespread, the product of mankind living with and learning about the myriad aspects of nuclear technology for over sixty years. Fabricating a nuclear device is not as simple as reading about how to do so from a textbook. Ultimate success can't be accomplished without various types of technical and scientific know-how, including the intricacies of fusing the device. As one example, albeit available in many universities, sophisticated machinery would have to be used to fabricate with exacting precision the component parts needed for the weapon and complex calculations carried out to ensure its detonation. Even the (relatively) simple and most reliable method for a making a nuclear device, the so-called gun assembly method in which two pieces of fissile material, each subcritical, are brought together at very high speed to cause a chain reaction and detonation, requires sophisticated knowledge of various scientific disciplines.

As Pluta and Zimmerman point out, the critical mistake, however, would be to impose on terrorist organizations the same exacting scientific standards as used by nuclear scientists in the United States or elsewhere in attempting to judge the capabilities of terrorists to make even a crude nuclear device. They argue that when national authorities have developed nuclear devices they have sought to make them reliable, predictable, and safe.[11] According to Pluta and Zimmerman, "A bomb built by a terrorist need not be especially reliable, and it certainly need not be particularly predictable."[12] Their conclusion is that, "We assume that the terror cell will be concerned with its own safety while assembling the device and transporting it to target, but we do not believe that any terrorist group would or could even attempt to reach the safety levels demanded of an American weapon."[13]

The good news, if it can be so described, is that terrorist organizations, however heinous their ambitions and intentions, do not have direct access to the weapons or materials needed to carry out such attacks independently and no known indigenous capability to make fissile material. This is underscored by past but unsuccessful efforts by al Qaeda operatives to acquire highly enriched uranium from South Africa or to acquire a nuclear warhead from Chechen terrorists.[14] At the moment, the gap between terrorist aspirations and capabilities is the primary barrier protecting the West. Islamic fundamentalists need a fissile material supply source that, to date, they have not been able to access. Unfortunately, there remain multiple sources of nuclear material in many parts of the globe, including substantial quantities which are in the hands of national governments with their own hostile intentions toward the United States and the West.

What narrows the gap and fans the flames between nuclear ambition and nuclear capability for Islamic fundamentalists is the presence of a small number of nations such as North Korea, a proven nuclear power, and Iran, whose own nuclear program almost certainly includes a military component, that have pursued this goal aggressively for several decades. North Korea and Iran may harbor their own plans for using their current or future nuclear capabilities for political or military advantage, but the expertise and materials developed in those national programs could be transferred to and used by sub-national groups such as al Qaeda. Such assistance is not assured as various rivalries and mistrust could conspire to stifle such cooperation. For example, there seems little but enduring enmity between al Qaeda, a Sunni-dominated organization, and Iran's Shiite ruling theocrats. Nonetheless, it would be fool-hardy in the extreme to ignore the wider potential for cooperation between rogue nations and terrorist groups. Patterns of cooperation are always in a state of flux in the international system. For example, we do not fully under-stand how or whether nations with nuclear capabilities might assist other non-nuclear states desiring to "join the club." Statements from Iran regarding its possible willingness to assist Venezuela underscore this dimension of the non-proliferation challenge.

There also are other potentially available sources of nuclear materials and expertise from nations who do not actively cooperate with terrorist organiza-tions. Here are two of the most prominent examples. When we add to the mix of North Korean and, possibly within a few years Iranian development of fis-sile materials, the vast quantities (about 300 metric tons) of poorly secured nuclear materials at official nuclear storage sites in addition to large quantities of radiological materials in Russia, the potential for Islamic fundamentalists to obtain the materials to attack America or its allies becomes frighteningly real.[15]

There have been numerous documented cases, some discussed herein, in which Russian insiders have stolen or diverted nuclear materials, primarily for financial gain. As recently as early 2007 various reports as well as reporting from the International Atomic Energy Agency (IAEA) surfaced claiming that in late 2006 a Russian was arrested in a sting operation by Republic of Geor-gia authorities for allegedly trying to sell a small amount of weapons-grade uranium to an agent posing as a foreign buyer with the promise of access to more of the same material.[16] The material in question seems to have been of proliferation concern as confirmed by Igor Shkabura, deputy director of the Bochvar Inorganic Materials Institute, a leading Russian nuclear facility, who claimed that the uranium sent by Georgia for analysis, "could be used for military productions, including nuclear weapons."[17] Adding an air of interna-tional intrigue to the case was the vehement reaction of senior Russian offi-cials, including Foreign Minister Sergey V. Lavrov, who claimed that the sting operation was an unjustified attempt by Georgian officials, long at odds politically with their former Russian masters, to embarrass Moscow.[18] No evi-dence exists to support that charge but Western concerns about the security of Russia's vast stock of nuclear materials again bubbled to the surface through a series of comments from officials and expert commentators.[19]

Terrorist organizations may be attempting to exploit these vulnerabilities. According to two U.S. commentators, Russia is the only country where se-nior officials have confirmed that terrorists "have carried out reconnaissance at nuclear weapons storage facilities."[20] In late 2005, according to the commentators, Russian Interior Minister Rashid Nurgaliev, whose organization is responsible for guarding most of the Russian nuclear sites, said the purpose of the surveillance was to plan attacks to seize nuclear materials.[21]

Similarly, the situation in Pakistan, another nuclear power, is at once fragile and alarming. Pakistani President Pervez Musharraf has escaped at least two assassination attempts and the widely held view of U.S. government officials and academics is that elements of the Pakistani security and military elite embrace, at least privately, the views of radical Islamic fundamentalists. What happens to Pakistan's nuclear arsenal, estimated at fifty nuclear weapons and a large amount of fissile material if the current relatively moderate government is overthrown or replaced? Can we have confidence that nuclear weapons or fissile materials—the building blocks for making a nuclear device—wouldn't fall into the hands of Islamic fundamentalists?

The result is that there exist myriad possibilities for terrorists to acquire nuclear weapons, materials and expertise. As pointed out by Harvard professor Graham Allison and others, if such materials or weapons are denied to terrorists they cannot use them. As Allison notes, it's that simple.[22] As we have seen, the other inescapable truth is that multiple paths by which terrorist organizations today can acquire the means to attack the West with nuclear or radiological materials. In this environment the overriding challenge is for the United States and the international community to harness the will, resources, and leadership to deny them these materials. Failure to do so—and in significant ways we are failing today—can lead to devastating and unprecedented consequences for America. The Cold War has ended but we live in a new age of nuclear insecurity.

The capability of the American government to deter future terrorist nuclear attacks is open to serious question. It is possible but far from assured that the U.S. military's nuclear posture, and what may prove to be a modest missile defense capability, will deter the governments in Pyongyang and Tehran from overtly threatening America or its allies. In this sense the previous notions of deterrence may yet have some value in the new international order because we can "hold hostage" to overwhelming attack the populace and military forces of those nations, assuming a modicum of rationality on the part of their leadership.

Nonetheless, the fundamental reduction in the efficacy of deterrence as a strategy, however, quickly becomes apparent when it is understood that the United States has little or no capability to respond in kind to the terrorist use of nuclear weapons. In the event of such an attack who would we retaliate against and where? It is unlikely that there will be a "return address" in the event of a terrorist attack. Islamic fundamentalists have no cities or critical infrastructure to protect. Similarly, the current U.S. government's capability to detect the illicit transport of nuclear materials into the country is almost nonexistent, according to the Government Accountability Office, the congressional investigatory authority.[23]

Moreover, even if the leaders of North Korea and Iran chose to refrain from cooperating with subnational terrorist organizations, their own nationalist nuclear ambitions greatly add to the nuclear insecurity of the United States and its allies. In 2007 it appeared likely that both nations were on a trajectory that would result in the emergence of capabilities every bit as threatening as nuclear weapons in the hands of radical fundamentalists. The bilateral relationship between the United States and Iran, for example, remains mired in mutual suspicions and enmity. Iranian support for Hezbollah in Lebanon and Tehran's scarcely camouflaged activities in Iraq, coupled with the forward movement of the Iranian uranium enrichment program in the face of U.N. sanctions imposed in December 2006 and March 2007, could set the Bush administration and Iran's theocratic regime on a collision course. Are the storm clouds of war gathering with the decision by the Bush administration in early 2007 to send a second carrier battle group, with its immense air power and missile capabilities, to patrol the waters off Iran? For the scientific community, the sum total of nations and terrorist organizations seemingly intent on acquiring nuclear capabilities has prompted the first symbolic movement forward in twenty years of the hands of the "doomsday clock."[24]

As a result of these diverse and troubling developments, we must return to the question of how we keep such weapons out of the hands of terrorists and, ideally, those nations who would develop them in opposition to the will of the international community. The problem is not abating; the IAEA reported that in 2006 there were 149 documented cases of nuclear smuggling. Many of those involved low-level radioactive sources of limited proliferation concern, but about fifteen of the cases were described as involving more serious seizures of nuclear materials or radioactive sources.[25]

During both the Clinton and Bush administrations, policies and programs have been developed with the goal of preventing the spread of nuclear weapons and materials and radiological materials. Congress, for the most part, has done its job in unusually bipartisan fashion by providing substantial amounts of funding since the early 1990s for various program initiatives that fall under the rubric of threat reduction programs; Congressional figures show that by 2007 at least $9 billion were appropriated for them. In some critical areas the U.S. government's policies and programs have achieved notable successes, making significant contributions to American and international security. Nonetheless, those successes exist against a broad canvas littered with myriad examples of policy failures, bureaucratic ineptness, and insufficient congressional oversight, resulting in frequent missed opportunities and needless compromise to our security. Despite the resources and expertise available to safeguard our nation, the threat of nuclear or radiological materials being used against America or its allies remains dangerously and unacceptably high. The Cold War vulnerability to nuclear attack has been replaced with a new vulnerability to rogue states and Islamic fundamentalists that is every bit as dangerous to American society.

This book recounts the U.S. government's successes and failures since the 1970s in curbing the emerging nuclear threats from rogue nations and Islamic fundamentalists. Parts of the narrative draw heavily from my professional experiences as a CIA officer who managed one of the Agency's first nonproliferation organizations, as a member of the White House National Security Council staff, as a director for nonproliferation during President Clinton's second term, and as one of the senior managers at the Department of Energy in George W. Bush's first term, directing the department's efforts to secure nuclear materials and radiological materials at dozens of sites in Russia and other parts of the former Soviet Union as part of the U.S. government's threat reduction program. During the same period I also had oversight of the department's efforts to assist Russian authorities in interdicting sensitive materials being smuggled across Russian borders. It is the insights garnered from an unusual combination of experience in the intelligence, policy, and program sides of the U.S. government's efforts to staunch the spread of nuclear weapons that I share with the reader to illuminate our government's actions against an unsurpassed threat.

This journey through the bureaucracy introduced me to many talented and dedicated officers at both senior and junior levels. They are unsung heroes, often putting their nation ahead of personal comfort or gain. Conversely, I also encountered a small number of officials whose persistent incompetence, crippling caution, and unethical conduct betrays the public they have sworn to protect. Ultimately, it is this mix of the dedicated and incompetent officials who shape America's response to the threat of nuclear terrorism and our nuclear insecurity.

I have endeavored to present my understanding of these issues in a manner as politically neutral as possible. After thirty-seven years of living in Washington, DC, I have some appreciation of the profound differences in philosophy and approach that underpin many of the foreign policy priorities of the Democratic and Republican parties. As a career federal officer for much of my professional life my duty was to work with those in elected office from both political parties. I number among my closest colleagues foreign policy experts from both sides of the political aisle. Against the backdrop of often intense and at times rancorous policy debate stands the overwhelming consensus among liberals and conservatives, Democrats and Republicans, that America's vulnerability to nuclear and radiological attack is real and that much more needs to be done. To be sure, profound differences often exist between them over questions of approach and tactics, but their underlying assessment of the challenge posed to U.S. security by nuclear weapons in the hands of rogue nations or terrorist groups is fundamentally the same.

Before proceeding, a scope note is in order. Some thirty programs fall under the rubric of "international threat reduction programs" within the United States government. Space limitations make it impractical to discuss or assess each of those. I have chosen to focus most of my commentary on those programs whose size and mission have made them the most prominent, beginning with the nuclear weapons elimination and security work undertaken by the Department of Defense and the nuclear and radiological material security programs managed at the Department of Energy.

Another section of this book presents two country case studies, Pakistan and Iran. Not only do they constitute continuing and significant security problems for the United States but they also provide valuable insights into the successes and failures of U.S. nuclear nonproliferation policies. In turn, assessment of these successes and failures leads into a discussion of ways to develop a new strategic framework for nonproliferation that will reduce America's nuclear insecurity.

I have not endeavored to address in this book, but will do so in a separate work, the fledgling nuclear security programs administered by the Department of Homeland Security to protect the United States domestically. The United States has more than 19,000 miles of borders and hundreds of places of entry by sea and air. Defending all of them against, for example, the illicit smuggling of a crude nuclear device is a monumental task and still beyond the current reach of U.S. government programs. As such, I begin from the premise shared by many colleagues that the success or failure of the U.S. government's international threat reduction programs and its nonproliferation policy choices tells us more than anything about the state of America's nuclear insecurity.

PART ONE

Securing Nuclear and Radiological Materials

1

The Clinton Years: Where Are the Nukes?

THE END OF the Cold War, whose date we can set at December 1991 with the resignation of Soviet President Mikhail Gorbachev, was one of the twentieth century's most positive developments. Decades of confrontation in which hundreds of millions of citizens living in Russia, on its periphery, and in Eastern Europe were enslaved under the communist yoke, while trillions of dollars were spent by the United States and its allies on the development of military capabilities to deter Soviet aggression, concluded without a direct clash of the superpowers. This propitious and historic outcome that was widely expected to yield a "peace dividend" was soon overtaken by a new set of security problems. In the wake of the Soviet Union's breakup there trailed a series of looming consequences that seized the attention of the Clinton administration from its first days in office. Concerned about the vacuum caused by the political chaos resulting from the collapse of the authority that had ruled the Soviet Union since 1917, Clinton administration officials, for example, focused on the financial stability of Russia, the largest and most important nation to emerge from the breakup of the Soviet empire.

Worries about Russia's deepening financial instability also spilled over into the security arena, becoming linked to Washington's concerns about the security of Russia's vast nuclear arsenal. Throughout the Cold War, the Soviet military and its vaunted and dreaded security services, the KGB and its military counterpart the GRU, had maintained iron-fisted control over Russia's nuclear assets. As a result, through the Soviet era security for the most part was robust at nuclear storage sites, nuclear institutes, operational military bases, and border crossings. Outsiders could not easily penetrate that closed and tightly monitored world while insiders with access to materials that could be sold for quick profit—a situation that would soon become a major security threat—were intimidated from doing so. Albeit sorely deficient by Western standards in some fundamental areas of jurisprudence, Soviet justice was swift and sure.

The security situation changed dramatically and quickly after the Soviet Union's breakup. The reliable and established elements of the layered physical security system that includes guards, gates, fences, and sensors proved vulnerable to the general chaos that ensued throughout the newly emerging states of the former Soviet Union such as Russia, Ukraine, and Kazakhstan. Discipline among site guards, other soldiers, and institute workers with direct access to nuclear materials eroded as the new Russian government that emerged in the aftermath of communist rule struggled to pay salaries in many industries, including the nuclear industry, and prevent general social collapse. Desperate people will do desperate things and the Clinton administration had ample cause for worry about the security of Russia's nuclear materials. Financial resources previously committed to maintaining the security of sites eroded, resulting in a commensurate erosion of the physical security infrastructure. Gaping holes in fences and locks and alarm sensors that didn't work became pervasive features of Russia's nuclear security landscape.

The fracturing of the Russian nuclear establishment's security system, combined with growing recognition of the potential of other nations to develop nuclear weapons, resulted in a series of actions by the Clinton administration. On December 14, 1994, President Clinton declared a national emergency to address the "unusual and extraordinary threat to the national security, foreign policy, and economy of the United States by the proliferation of nuclear, biological and chemical weapons and the means of delivering such weapons."[1] On that same day Clinton issued Executive Order 12938, organizational changes at the Pentagon and Central Intelligence Agency (CIA) placed greater resource emphasis on collecting information on and assessing nonproliferation issues.[2] As they pertained to Russia, these measures were designed to answer two overarching policy questions: where are the nuclear weapons or "nukes" and are they secure.

Russia's emerging political and security problems were exacerbated by a set of supply side numbers that painted an equally alarming picture. The first set was the vast quantity of nuclear weapons and nuclear materials in Russia. Published estimates stated that more than 25,000 strategic and tactical nuclear weapons were stored in a combination of operationally deployed and reserve sites.[3] The amount of stored nuclear or fissile material, the highly enriched uranium (HEU) and plutonium (Pu) used to make a nuclear device but not in existing warheads, was much harder to estimate. No precise figures were available, but the working estimate assembled by U.S. Department of Energy (DOE) program experts was that some 600 metric tons (MT) of materials probably were stored throughout institutes and other facilities under the control of Russia's Ministry of Atomic Energy or Minatom, later renamed the Federal Agency for Atomic Energy or Rosatom. (Other civilian sites also contained substantial amounts of material requiring security.) The 600 MT estimate was almost wholly the product of the DOE experts because no reliable evidentiary base existed to provide U.S. policymakers or program managers with a high confidence estimate of Russia's stored fissile materials. As U.S. experts would later discover, even Russian knowledge of the amount of nuclear materials under its control was highly suspect because almost every Russian storage facility kept its records on index cards usually written in pencil. In addition, at almost every nuclear site some material would be held back from official accounting by plant managers who wanted to ensure their production numbers would meet established quotas even if some of that material was lost or used in experiments. The integrity and accuracy of that system didn't, and shouldn't, inspire much confidence in the West.

The second set of numbers that concerned policymakers was the small amount of fissile material needed to make a nuclear device. Unclassified figures published by the International Atomic Energy Agency (IAEA) set the figures as approximately 25 kilograms for highly enriched uranium and approximately 8 kilograms for plutonium. Most competent Western and Russian nuclear scientists would confirm that even smaller quantities can produce a self-sustaining chain reaction or nuclear yield, although a crude or improvised device almost certainly would require larger quantities of fissile material because those designs would not be as efficient as those developed by experienced bomb designers. Nonetheless, even the diversion of small amounts of fissile material from Russia's vast stocks could wind up in the hands of nations or terrorist organizations that could threaten America or its allies.

The Clinton administration's assessment of the dangers posed by this emerging situation proved to be highly accurate. From 1992 through 1998, a series of smuggling cases demonstrated that the vulnerability of Russia's fissile materials to theft or diversion was real, not hypothetical.[4]

- 1992—In Podolsk, a technician stole 1.5 kilograms of HEU.
- 1993—In Murmansk, a Russian naval officer stole 4.5 kilograms of HEU.
- 1993—The German Magazine *Stern* reported a Russian counterintelligence officer admitted that North Korea had smuggled 56 kilograms of plutonium from Russia, enough fissile material to make seven to nine nuclear devices. The report remains unconfirmed.
- 1993—A thief stole 1.8 kilograms of HEU from a naval facility.
- 1994—A small amount of plutonium that had been produced in Russia was seized at the Munich Airport.
- 1994—In Prague, police seized 2.7 kilograms of HEU that had been produced in Russia.
- 1998—The Russian foreign intelligence service, the FSB, uncovered and interdicted a plot at Chelyabinsk, one of Russia's premiere nuclear weapons laboratories. Russian authorities acknowledged that the material involved in the plot, about 18.5 kilograms of HEU, was sufficient to make a nuclear bomb.

These incidents provided important insights to Western experts attempting to work cooperatively with Russian counterparts in developing effective security countermeasures. The first lesson was the undeniable and widespread vulnerability of Russia's nuclear and military establishments to the illicit diversion of materials from what should have been secure facilities. In each of these cases it was fissile materials, not nuclear weapons, which were the targets of criminals. The ease of transporting small amounts of these materials, compared to the logistical challenges posed by first stealing and then transporting an unwieldy nuclear weapon inside a warhead weighing perhaps one thousand pounds (for strategic warheads) doubtless goes a long way to explaining this phenomenon. In one of the most succinct but descriptive assessments ever offered on this problem, a Russian prosecutor judged that "potatoes were guarded better" than the nuclear material at Murmansk.[5]

The second lesson was that the smuggling cases were the product of insider actions, mostly with either a single perpetrator or a few trusted accomplices. For example, in the 1993 case at the Sevmorput Shipyard in Murmansk, retired Russian navy officer Alexei Tikhimirov, working with Oleg Baranov, broke into one of the shipyard's unprotected areas. Tikhimirov's brother, Dmitry, worked at the shipyard and assisted him. A back door was forced open in a building containing fresh nuclear submarine fuel. Alexei Tikhimirov and his accomplice removed 4.5 kilograms of uranium enriched to 20 percent U-235 and escaped. The thieves were bold but sloppy as they left open the door they entered, triggering rapid discovery of the theft. However, Tikhimirov and Baranov escaped capture for six months until Tikhimirov's brother tried to enlist the help of a fellow officer in selling the merchandise. The three defendants were put on trial; Alexei Tikhimirov and Baranov received prison sentences of several years while Tikhimirov's brother was freed.[6]

The Tikhimirov case underscores that one of the predominant features of smuggling during this period was greed, rather than ideological or political motives, or as part of an organized crime operation. In this latter regard, Russia's ongoing organized crime problem had become well-documented, seemingly beyond the capacity or willingness of Russian law enforcement authorities to control. But organized crime is about making money, preferably with limited risk, through virtually any available means. During this period, it appeared that organized crime figures felt they could make more money with fewer concerns, more reliably through other illegal methods than nuclear smuggling. As a result, there is no evidence of systematic efforts by organized crime groups to engage in nuclear smuggling activities. Similarly, there is little credible evidence that other nations or subnational or terrorist groups attempted to acquire fissile materials through smuggling.

Other smuggling cases also demonstrated the ease with which illicitly acquired fissile materials could be transported, not only from remote facilities in Russia, but across Russia and into Europe. Ideally, nuclear materials and warheads were fully protected at their locations but, as we have seen, the practical reality, particularly for materials, was rather different. The Russian Customs Service, like its counterparts in the West, had a long history of focusing attention and resources on preventing the illicit transport of materials into Russia as much as worrying about smuggling from Russia. Perhaps that approach was appropriate in the Soviet era when officials worried about the penetration of Russian borders as part of its overall security mind-set, but it was rapidly becoming outdated by the early 1990s as demonstrated by the May 1994 smuggling case in Tengen, Germany.

It was entirely by happenstance that German law enforcement authorities in Tengen discovered 5.6 grams of plutonium in the garage of Adolf Jaekle who was under investigation for counterfeiting.[7] Different theories exist regarding the original source of the material but one plausible opinion is that the material came from a Russian nuclear weapons laboratory, possibly the vast complex east of Moscow then known in the West as Arzamas-16. The uncertainty of the material's point of origin notwithstanding, the case demonstrated clearly the challenges confronting Russian security officials both at sensitive sites and at border crossings. Nikolai Kravchenko, a senior Russian Customs official and a respected colleague, told me in 2003 that in the year 2000 some 500 incidents of attempted illicit transport of nuclear and radiological materials had been recorded by his colleagues. Most of these materials posed no direct proliferation threats but his point to me was clear: Russia's border security and export control system was under considerable and constant stress.

It would be inaccurate to conclude that only Russian materials were the source of concern to the West or that Russian officials were indifferent to the problem. On both counts the evidence points in a different direction. The Russian Ministry of Atomic Energy was the governmental authority charged with protecting most nuclear materials. Minatom had a long record during Soviet days of providing adequate security for these materials. What had changed was the critical lack of resources given it by the new Russian government in the 1990s to carry out this critical mission.

The U.S. government's response to this deteriorating security situation was a mixture of enlightened policy and often clumsy implementation. One of the best examples of bipartisan cooperation on a critical national security issue was the work of former Senator Sam Nunn and Senator Richard Lugar. Nunn and Lugar, two of the senate's most respected voices on international affairs, concluded that Russia's emerging security problems posed a direct threat to U.S. interests, just as President George H. W. Bush had judged during the end of his administration and as the Clinton administration would conclude shortly after coming into office. For Senators Nunn and Lugar the challenge was the development of a new type of program that would work cooperatively, rather than in competition, with the Russian government. In so doing, the Cold War's habits and security culture developed in Washington over fifty years would be changed radically. As even the most casual observer would attest, change does not come easily in Washington and as Senator Nunn recounted years later, many Senate colleagues from both political parties had deep reservations about a new cooperative approach. Nunn and Lugar remained undaunted, successfully pushing through the Senate and then the House of Representatives one of the most important pieces of national security legislation in the post-Cold War era.

Known officially as The Nunn-Lugar Program or the Cooperative Threat Reduction Program, it began in 1991 after Soviet President Mikhail Gorbachev requested assistance in dismantling Soviet nuclear weapons from outgoing President George H. W. Bush.[8] The Nunn-Lugar Program is actually an amalgam of thirty programs, some with annual funding in the hundreds of millions of dollars and some with a much smaller funding profile, administered by the Departments of Defense, Energy, and State. Although focused mainly on Russia, the Nunn-Lugar Program has carried out work in other parts of the former Soviet Union, including Ukraine and Kazakhstan, and the program's scope of work has included various programs to reduce the threat posed by biological and chemical weapons. Through the 1990s about $400 million annually was appropriated for the U.S. government's overall program activities.[9] The focus and emphasis of the various constituent programs often differs, but the overall mission and goals set out by the Nunn-Lugar legislation falls into five broad categories:[10]

1. Stabilizing, transforming, and downsizing the Russian nuclear weapons complex
2. Securing Russian nuclear materials, warheads, and technologies
3. Limiting the production of fissile material
4. Disposing of excess fissile material
5. Establishing transparency in the nuclear weapons reduction process.

Flushed with Congressional support that set in motion the creation of a new set of government programs, the Department of Defense, soon to be followed by the Departments of State and Energy, began a series of engagements with their Russian counterparts. A bilateral or "umbrella" agreement had been set in place by which the U.S. and Russian governments agreed formally to allow the work called for under Nunn-Lugar to be carried out at sensitive Russian sites. That agreement, signed in September 1993 by senior representatives from the Department of Defense and the Russian Ministry of Atomic Energy, was important for symbolic as well as substantive reasons. The political environment and atmospherics at the time were heady, filled with the enthusiasm emanating from the prospect that the two formerly bitter rivals could undertake cooperative engagement in such sensitive areas.

Initial optimism soon gave way to a series of mutual recriminations fueled by suspicions and blunders on both sides. The Russian security services could muster scant enthusiasm for allowing U.S. technical experts to visit and conduct work at many of their most sensitive facilities. One of the first program requests, to conduct work at Sverdlovsk, was rejected by the Russians out-of-hand. Conversely, a number of U.S. officials, contractors, and laboratory experts, particularly from DOE, had the attitude that they were the saviors of "impoverished and backward" Russia. This attitude was reflected in what Russian officials would later describe as the condescending tone of many U.S. technical experts who were perceived as making endless requests for visits to sensitive sites without producing much substantive work. Some Russian experts privately branded DOE's style of engagement as "nuclear tourism" which did little to demonstrate the U.S. government's commitment to rapidly improving the security of Russia's nuclear materials. The predictable result was that scant progress, measured in the amount of fissile material receiving security upgrades, was made in this part of the Nunn-Lugar Program through the 1990s.

The parlous security situation at many Russian nuclear sites underscored the necessity for rapid and more focused U.S. cooperation. Numerous eyewitness accounts described in vivid and troubling detail the security lapses and problems infecting Russia's nuclear establishment. Perimeter security fences were found to have holes large enough for people to walk through. Guards manning external security checkpoints or conducting perimeter patrols were often found asleep or lacking adequate clothing to properly withstand the rigors of Russia's often brutal winters. They also often lacked weapons and ammunition to ward off any determined attackers, a situation of considerable concern as many of these sites were in remote locations, making it unrealistic for the guard force to expect timely external assistance in the event of an incident. Intrusion detection sensors often either didn't work or were missing and there were inadequate security cameras at most sites to carry out adequate remote monitoring of the facility.

Physical security problems weren't the only vulnerabilities in Russia's ability to protect its fissile materials. Few, if any, programs existed to monitor the activities or reliability of insiders with direct access to sensitive materials. Given this extensive list of security shortcomings it was small wonder that the nuclear smuggling incidents described above were carried out with such success. Why were these pressing needs so slowly addressed by U.S. programs that were well-funded by Congress and politically supported by the administration?

It is instructive to dissect the reasons for DOE's failures as they hold lessons for other similar programs. The first problem was the lack of qualified program leadership. The senior career officer overseeing all DOE's threat reduction work, Ken Baker, was a retired Air force officer with little, if any, technical expertise to develop, or managerial experience in making, complex international programs work. One of Baker's subordinate program managers, Ken Luongo, the Director of the Material Protection, Control, and Accounting Program whose mission was to secure Russia's nuclear materials, was a political appointee and former congressional staff member, highly dedicated to the program's mission and widely respected for his substantive knowledge. Luongo also was not by inclination or training a hands-on manager and his critical mistake was in the development of a managerial model for the program in which he surrounded himself with DOE laboratory officials for advice on program implementation. The conflict of interest inherent in allowing personnel with vested interests in the U.S. government's financial decisions and resource allocations was a far-too-frequent aspect of program management throughout DOE's international programs. As a result, a large percentage of the funding appropriated by Congress and intended for work in Russia began flowing back into the DOE laboratory complex. More than 50 percent of the funding for virtually every DOE threat reduction program was flowing into the labs, not Russia. The threat reduction work envisioned by and fought for by Senators Nunn and Lugar to address a pressing national security problem was starting to look like another set of federal jobs programs.

The results of DOE's emphasis on allowing laboratory personnel to oversee critical elements of the program were predictable. Most laboratory employees doubtless are excellent scientists but their years of scientific training often left them poorly prepared to be program managers capable of advancing critical national security work in Russia's complex political and bureaucratic environment. For example, a plasma physicist from Los Alamos National Laboratory was appointed to manage the installation of security perimeter equipment such as fences and sensors in suburban Moscow at Kurchatov Institute, one of Russia's most prestigious scientific centers. It was a terrible waste of a scientist's specialized expertise to assign him the task of overseeing the installation of fences, alarms, and sensors. In an era when the U.S. laboratories were trying to reinvent and find new missions, perhaps that mismatch is in one respect understandable. However, the national interest and the program's mission suffered. In this case the project would run years behind its scheduled completion and millions of dollars over budget.

Neither Baker nor Luongo evinced much interest in sorting out and taking managerial actions to address such problems. Until 2000, the situation described at Kurchatov was mirrored by other parts of the program. Nonetheless, Luongo's energy and dedication to the program stood in marked contrast to other DOE program managers and programs suffused with little sense of urgency. With the backing of Energy Secretary O'Leary and Deputy Secretary of Energy Charlie Curtis (who would go on to work with former Senator Nunn at the Nuclear Threat Initiative), Luongo was able to establish from ground zero a program, albeit flawed in its initial management model, with considerable potential to make a direct contribution to the nation's security.

The approach and results of DOD's Defense Threat Reduction Agency, by contrast, were far more positive. Through agreement between the departments, DOD had agreed to work primarily with the Russian Ministry of Defense (MOD), its natural counterpart, in disposing of nuclear weapons, leaving the nuclear material security work to DOE and Minatom. There was a higher level of respect between DOD and the Russian MOD than existed between their technical counterpart organizations, resulting through the 1990s in a lengthy period of cooperation that produced tangible results. In addition, DOD took a more rigorous approach to its financial accounting practices than did its DOE counterparts, instituting a sweeping audit program that identified problems before they became embedded in program practices.

The State Department, traditionally the center of U.S. diplomatic activity, also became involved in nonproliferation program work. One example, which grew out of the 1992 Freedom Support Act, was the establishment of a Nonproliferation Disarmament Fund (NDF). NDF was not heavily funded when it began operation in 1994; its initial annual funding levels were well under $50 million. Nonetheless, the NDF mission which was to commit funds rapidly to unanticipated or high priority requirements to halt or neutralize the proliferation of weapons of mass destruction or conventional armaments was well-conceived and the program was well-managed.[11]

From a broader perspective, the administration's strategic approach reflected awareness that even if the security programs at nuclear sites had been universally well-managed, they could not fully address the scope of Russia's proliferation challenges. As a result, at the Department of State a program through the International Science and Technology Center (ISTC) was developed by which Russian scientists were provided opportunities to pursue scientific but nonmilitary work as a way to keep them from selling their expertise and services to nations of proliferation concern in the Middle East and Asia. Anne Harrington, an exceptionally dedicated and energetic career officer, was the guiding force in infusing into the program a sense of mission that resulted in employment for hundreds of Russian scientists. At DOE, two comparable programs also were established, the Initiative for Proliferation Prevention and the Nuclear Cities Initiative. Few efforts were expended to coordinate the priorities or resources of the three programs.

Shortly thereafter, the DOE also initiated a program in conjunction with the Russian Customs Service to install portal monitors at Russian border crossings and airports. These monitors were designed to detect the illicit transport of nuclear and radioactive materials and reflected the now-unassailable reality that security measures had to extend beyond what was being done at the nuclear sites. A nation's border and customs services can be a powerful force for protecting the national interest through vigorous enforcement measures. Conversely, they can serve as a focal point for graft and corruption because of the many organized crime factions, individuals, and, at times, nations, who want to carry out all forms of illicit smuggling activities.

Russia's reputation as a nation fraught with corruption in many parts of both the civilian economy and government was a direct concern to DOE officials (and elsewhere by their DOD counterparts) cognizant that funds for the fledgling program would have to be monitored closely. Only about $2 million were appropriated for the program's start, but it didn't take much imagination to realize that Russia's vast borders, combined with equally vast nuclear, biological, and chemical industries where former insiders already had proven an interest in profiting from their access, were a troubling combination. Under these circumstances the opportunity for program growth would be considerable if measurable results could be demonstrated. Those results were not forthcoming immediately.

Much of the criticism for the delays and problems in the programs can be traced to gaffes by various U.S. government actions. Nonetheless, there also existed the concurrent reality that dealing with Russian officials was time-consuming and at times frustrating. In addition, all the threat reduction programs begun in the 1990s were dependent, by necessity, on the goodwill of the rank-and-file Russian workers. Russian President Yeltsin could issue endless proclamations of cooperation but there was a larger reality underlying all the photo opportunities and convivial political rhetoric. Corruption and attitudes borne of deeply ingrained suspicions had become an endemic part of the Russian landscape and there was no reason to believe that workers at sensitive sites were immune to that phenomenon. Did a nuclear site security manager really want to work with U.S. experts? Would a world-class scientist accept money from the State Department or DOE to abide by its program's rules not to work with rogue nations? The answer to these and related questions remained not far from the thoughts of all U.S. program managers. It was the wholly appropriate policy of the U.S. government to take all reasonable measures to ensure that the funding it was providing for the threat reduction program was used properly. Various programmatic audit mechanisms were installed, particularly at DOD and State, to carry out that policy guidance. What everyone inside the process fully understood, however, was that there existed no foolproof way to ensure that some Russians at some of the sites weren't misusing the resources provided. The administration accepted this reality, sometimes against skeptics in the opposition party in Congress and in the intelligence community, in the belief that the programs, albeit far from perfect in concept and execution, were in no way a gift to Russia but rather were serving U.S. national security interests.

One of the more creative elements of the Clinton administration's foreign policy approach was the creation of a process of semi-annual meetings of senior officials from the United States and Russia under the auspices of the Gore-Chrnomyrdin Commission, named for the second-ranking officials at the time in the U.S. and Russian governments. Under this policy umbrella senior officials established useful bilateral dialogues, discussing everything from health and agricultural questions to the security of nuclear materials and regional proliferation problems such as Iran's nuclear ambitions. The Commission also served as a mechanism to bring forward new initiatives, such as the administration's proposals for a shutdown of Russia's three plutonium-producing nuclear power plants. The Commission's existence did not guarantee results, and in some areas such as the Iran problem, the results of the bilateral dialogue were meager and highly disappointing. Nonetheless, under such skilled hands as Leon Fuerth, Vice President Gore's trusted and highly respected national security adviser, there existed for much of the 1990s a reliable mechanism to focus high-level attention on issues of mutual concern to the two former antagonists.

It would be entirely misleading to conclude that the problems of nuclear material security were limited only to Russia. In the 1990s, perhaps the most dramatic and successful example of U.S. government action to secure nuclear materials occurred in 1994 in Kazakhstan, a former Soviet republic. In 1992, Vladimir Shkolnik, the Kazakh Atomic Energy Director, was caught totally unaware of a looming security problem of vast proportion when during a visit to the Ulba Metallurgy Plant he stumbled across some 600 kilograms of HEU that, depending on enrichment level, could be used in the production of more than twenty nuclear devices.

Shkolnik's discovery triggered a major political debate within Kazakhstan President Nursultan Nazarbayev's government over the long-term disposition of the material. A number of options were put on the table. On the one hand, the Kazakh government could maintain possession of it as some of Nazarbayev's advisers advocated, citing the value of deterring the nuclear powers that surrounded that mountainous nation, Russia, China, India, and Pakistan. Other governmental officials recognized, however, that the long-term security of such a large amount of material was far from assured. Kazakhstan's neighbor, Iran, with its suspicious nuclear activities, almost certainly would have coveted even a small amount of the fissile material and in the often lawless conditions of the Soviet Union's breakup, criminal attempts at theft, perhaps aided by insiders, was another possibility.

Given this set of unpalatable outcomes, Nazarbayev's government decided to relinquish control of the HEU. It first turned to Russia with an offer to sell the material to the Russian government. For reasons not fully understood in the West, the new Yeltsin government declined the offer. The Kazakh government then approached U.S. Ambassador William Courtney. By any measure Courtney, a reserved but friendly man who engendered great loyalty from his staff, was one of America's most talented diplomats. Courtney would become my colleague and friend on the National Security Council (NSC) Staff in the late 1990s. Courtney contacted Washington immediately, beginning a lengthy process involving the Departments of State, Defense, and Energy in what was called Operation Sapphire.

Operation Sapphire had all the ingredients of a popular spy novel.[12] After considerable debate within the U.S. government over how to act on the information received from Courtney, the NSC decided that the only sure way of keeping the material away from undesirable elements was for the U.S. government to conduct a clandestine operation to remove it in its entirety. Time and secrecy were of the essence. A tiger team was formed with the State Department responsible for negotiating with the Kazakh government the terms of the removal, DOD responsible for the transportation, and DOE responsible for technical oversight and preparation of the material for transport. Each department was eager to help, as well as more than willing to lead the operation, doubtless for reasons of perceived bureaucratic prestige. Nonetheless, no department was willing to contribute the funding required to compensate the Kazakh government for the material and to pay for the considerable logistical requirements of moving about one ton of some of the most dangerous material on the planet safely from Kazakhstan to the United States. For example, DOE manager Ken Baker reportedly told his junior managers that DOE refused to contribute to the funding for the operation. This squabbling lasted nearly four months, slowing the mission and possibly jeopardizing its success. The impasse was broken only when it was agreed that Nunn-Lugar funding, to date used primarily for work in Russia, would serve as the funding base to support the operation.

The wholly unnecessary delay caused by the bureaucratic dispute over funding was not the only domestic issue to plague Operation Sapphire. The Clinton administration understood that bringing a large amount of fissile material into the United States could touch off a fire storm of protest from environmental groups with whom the administration was working to establish good relations. It was left to Vice President Gore to work the political issues in his home state of Tennessee, where the Y-12 Oak Ridge plant, part of the DOE complex, was chosen to receive the material.

Adding to the Clinton administration's political problems was a set of technical challenges that slowed the start of the operation. Given the weight of the cargo, it was decided that the U.S. Air Force's enormous C-5 transport aircraft would have to be used to remove the HEU. What had to be determined was whether the aircraft could safely land on Kazakhstan's short, poorly maintained, and icy runways. Once these calculations were made and the final political approvals received, the operation commenced and was successfully completed at the end of November 1994. In the end, the combination of Courtney's persistence and the cooperation of the military and technical elements of the operation proved the right mix to remove a very dangerous proliferation problem.

It was not long after the completion of Operation Sapphire that I joined the NSC Staff as a director for nonproliferation. I had been serving at the CIA since 1983 in various analytic, managerial, and staff capacities with my last assignment as the chief of the group that followed proliferation issues involving Russia. As recounted in myriad books, CIA is an organization that because of the controversy surrounding many of its activities builds love or loathing within its ranks. Through my years working at the Agency's headquarters in Langley, Virginia I had developed many strong professional relationships and, in general, had positive feelings about the skills and dedication of my colleagues. Nonetheless, the inescapable judgment is that in recent years the Agency made several critical blunders related to its failures to predict or interdict the September 11, 2001, al Qaeda attacks or accurately assess Iraq's largely dismantled weapons of mass destruction programs. The long overdue 2004 reorganization of the intelligence community mandated by Congress that resulted in a diminution of the Agency's role as the lead analytic component in the intelligence community was necessary and the direct result of poor leadership by some at the CIA's highest managerial levels, particularly on the analytic side. According to many friends and former colleagues, the past years have taken a heavy toll on morale and that surely does not serve the national interest. The recent arrival of a new director and new deputy director present a badly needed opportunity for renewal.

The opportunity afforded me to join the NSC Staff was impossible to resist. Located in the imposing Eisenhower Executive Office Building next to the White House West Wing, the NSC since its creation in 1947 had served as the focal point for the formulation of U.S. foreign policy. The NSC staff is not large in number, drawing on many parts of the bureaucracy for its personnel, particularly from the Department of State, where numerous NSC "alum" would go on to serve in various ambassadorial appointments. The pressure can be intense and the hours grueling, but for those interested in the policy-making process there is no better opportunity than the NSC. After a long interview process, I was hired into the NSC Staff in the first part of 1996.

From my first days at the NSC until my departure nearly four years later, the management style of Sandy Berger, the National Security Adviser to Bill Clinton, seemed worthy of emulation. With an office only steps from the Oval Office, the position provided virtually unlimited access to the president and was one of enormous influence. The Clinton-Berger relationship had extended to at least the McCarthy campaign in the early 1970s and it was apparent that Clinton trusted Berger implicitly. By any standard Berger was not and did not advertise himself as a "grand strategist" in the mold of Henry Kissinger who served as National Security Adviser to Richard Nixon. An attorney by training, Berger took a different approach to the job than his Harvard-educated predecessor. With consistent and quiet competence Berger always looked out for the interests of his one client, the president of the United States. In practical terms this meant management of the interagency policy-making apparatus, including directing the actions of senior cabinet members when necessary, in a way that largely has escaped Condoleezza Rice and Stephen Hadley, President George W. Bush's two national security advisers. Berger also recognized and didn't attempt to compete with the expertise, particularly in Russia policy questions, of Vice President Gore's talented security adviser, Leon Fuerth, who was the driving force behind the Gore-Chernomyrdin Commission. Berger was unstinting in his support of the NSC staff, a significant advantage given the inevitable policy disputes that arise across the U.S. government's often unwieldy bureaucracy.

Consistent with my interest and expertise in Russia and the former Soviet Union, I was asked by Dan Poneman, a highly regarded and long-serving NSC Senior Director for Nonproliferation, to serve in the nonproliferation directorate and follow nonproliferation issues in Russia and its activities in the

Middle East. That substantive assignment also brought me into direct contact as the NSC officer with oversight of the U.S. interagency's Nunn-Lugar Threat Reduction Programs that had been demonstrating a mixed record of success.

I set out to glean any available insights into the reasons for the successes and failures of the various programs. It did not take long for some of the problem areas to be clarified. One of the more interesting aspects of any NSC assignment is the opportunity to work with different elements of the interagency. As the "new kid on the block" in this policy arena, my telephone log was filled with calls from various parts of the bureaucracy seeking to meet me and lobby, directly or indirectly, for their favorite projects. After about two weeks of these conversations, I could readily identify two trends. The first was that the interagency rivalries were as intense as anything described to me by Poneman or his successor, Gary Samore, another talented and experienced officer. In our introductory conversations, few opportunities were passed up by line officers at the Pentagon, for example, to criticize counterparts at the State Department or for State Department officers to criticize the CIA.

The second insight that emerged from my initiation into the ways of the bureaucracy was the realization that most in the interagency actually had one thing in common—the low regard in which it held DOE and its senior career officers. I was taken aback by this and probed deeper. Many viewed DOE as notoriously hermetic, dominated by its national laboratories with limited influence in the interagency processes and passing observance of national rather than departmental priorities. On closer examination it appeared that much of the distrust and enmity toward DOE was engendered by senior career officer Ken Baker and several of his personal associates who were the mainstays at many interagency meetings. In virtually every conversation on the workings of the interagency, I was told that Baker lacked the substantive and leadership skills expected of senior managers and that he almost certainly was the source of a steady stream of reporting on the workings and plans of a Democratic administration to staffers working for Republican Senator Pete Domenici of New Mexico. As a senior career officer, Baker's duty was to serve the administration in power but by all accounts he seemed just as committed to simultaneously helping the opposition party. These negative observations also seemed in accord with the emerging critique of the reasons behind the failure of DOE's work in Russia.

As the 1990s came to a close and the Clinton administration prepared to give way to the Bush administration, the record that emerged from nearly a decade of effort to secure nuclear materials was decidedly mixed. On my arrival at the NSC I set out to develop with interagency counterparts a series of measures to accelerate the threat reduction work but those plans were never carried out because of my unexpected assignment in 1997 as White House representative to negotiations with senior Russian officials regarding Iran. Those negotiations are discussed in a forthcoming chapter. During the Clinton administration the threat reduction programs had been established with bipartisan support and generously funded. The programs scored some early successes, both in Russia where the DOD threat reduction program was dismantling many threatening weapons and in Kazakhstan where Ambassador Courtney's skill and persistence was the impetus for the successful Operation Sapphire which removed a significant amount of HEU from possible theft or diversion. However, that record of success was marred by the chronic problems arising from the bureaucratic missteps at DOE. As a result, by the end of the decade most of the estimated 600 metric tons of Russian fissile material at Minatom sites remained poorly protected, an unenviable record of modest accomplishment that, while recognized by some, troubled few in the department. This lack of a sense of urgency within the department and its associated laboratories seemed to some as business as usual but events soon would conspire to show the recklessness of that attitude.

The Bush Years: Securing Nuclear Materials in an Age of Terrorism

AS THE 1990s gave way to the dawn of a new century I was about to embark on a new assignment as director of the Department of Energy's (DOE's) Office of International Material Protection and Cooperation, the "umbrella" name for several distinct but related programs that included the troubled nuclear materials security program previously managed by Ken Luongo, known as the Material Protection, Control, and Accounting Program or MPC&A; the Second Line of Defense export control program; and, later in 2002, the new radiological security program. By the time of my departure from the National Security Council (NSC) I acquired an informed understanding of the problems and personalities infecting the department's threat reduction work. I also saw the potential inherent in a young and talented staff in need of an outside perspective from someone not beholden to the entrenched DOE powers and willing to address some of the underlying problems.

The challenge of trying to move an important but struggling set of programs forward intrigued me when Rose Gottemoeller, the political appointee who oversaw the department's threat reduction work until the end of the Clinton administration, approached me with this offer. Over the past few years I had attended meetings and worked with Gottemoeller on various projects, judging her to be a person of considerable integrity and professionalism and highly qualified for her job. Working with her would be easy, but her deputy, Ken Baker, would serve as my immediate supervisor; the overwhelmingly low opinion in which he was held across the bureaucracy gave me great pause before accepting Gottemoeller's offer.

In the first week of 2000 I assumed responsibility for the program. In doing so it became apparent quickly that the challenges before me were a managerial Rubik's Cube in that myriad problems that had festered for so long all clamored for attention. Ongoing Russian suspicions, gaining the trust and confidence of my staff, and establishing the program's priorities after years of underperformance were at the top of the list. I was fortunate in that my deputy, Ken Sheely, had been with the program for several years and knew its strengths and weaknesses well. A young, talented, and energetic type with a quick wit and propensity for thinking creatively, Sheely also had the distinction of being loathed by Baker, who on several occasions pressed me to replace Sheely but I would have none of it. Sheely's experience and knowledge of the people and problems were critical to setting the program on a productive path quickly.

Sheely confirmed my suspicions, first seen at the NSC, that the program had never developed a strategic plan. Lacking this basic planning mechanism which my predecessor and Ken Baker had resisted developing, it was evident why the program had struggled. We set about to fixing this gap immediately but not without considerable assistance. By undertaking courtesy calls in Congress, the executive branch, and among the nongovernmental organizations (NGOs) who tracked the threat reduction programs, I developed a picture of the perceived strengths and weaknesses of the program. In my judgment, it also was important to infuse the program with a greater sense of urgency.

In this regard a significant political boost was presented by the January 2001 publication of the bipartisan Baker-Cutler Task Force Report, named after the former senator from Tennessee, Howard Baker, and a former White House Counsel and Democratic Party activist, Lloyd Cutler. Their key judgment could not have been clearer as it mirrored the concerns espoused by many observers that critical DOE threat reduction programs were moving too slowly. According to the Task Force Report, "The most urgent unmet national security threat to the United States today is the danger that weapons of mass destruction or weapons-usable materials in Russia could be stolen and sold to terrorists or hostile nations and used against American troops abroad or citizens at home."[1]

The Baker-Cutler Report sounded a clarion call that I was determined to answer through the MPC&A program at every opportunity. Because there was no strategic plan on my arrival there also was no planned timeline for the completion of our work. Several of the department's more grizzled and perhaps cynical members opined that this situation served well the interests of those organizations and individuals who had a vested interest in a nearly endless stream of congressional funding as a means of job security. This perspective could never be proved or disproved but it was a disturbing reminder of the attitudes that might be infecting the threat reduction programs.

The Baker-Cutler Report called for an eight to ten year completion goal for the security upgrade work at Russian nuclear sites. Working with Ken Sheely and our small coterie of federal managers, a plan was developed that nearly matched this recommendation, setting a 2008 completion date for the program's main work. We anticipated and planned for a longer time frame, for example, to continue the program's project to train Russian technicians

THE DOE APPROACH TO SECURING NUCLEAR MATERIALS OVERSEAS

For decades DOE has been responsible for providing security for nuclear weapons and materials located in the United States. The establishment in the early 1990s of the Nunn-Lugar Program to commit U.S. resources to upgrading the security of nuclear weapons and materials in Russia and other former Soviet states such as Ukraine presented a unique set of logistical and legal challenges compared to carrying out similar work in the United States. However, there also were many insights gleaned from DOE's domestic experiences that were readily applicable to those countries. Most of those lessons involved using the U.S. domestic model in which Nunn-Lugar resources would address both threats from outsiders such as terrorist organizations who might forcibly attempt to steal or divert sensitive materials as well as insiders, a security threat that became acute in Russia during the 1990s.

There are three overarching elements to the DOE nuclear security model applied to work at Rosatom and Russian Navy facilities:

1. Physical protection systems, include fences around buildings storing nuclear materials and video surveillance systems
2. Material control systems, such as installing seals on nuclear material containers and implementing a badge system for personnel to reduce the threat from insiders
3. Material accounting systems, such as implementing computerized data bases that would address one of the first identified security problems under the Nunn-Lugar Program, the lack of a precise inventory of Russian nuclear materials.

These security upgrades normally are carried out in two phases. In the first, which usually takes six to twelve months to complete, rapid upgrades such as improved perimeter fencing are carried out. In the second phase—comprehensive upgrades—often requiring an additional eighteen to twenty-four months to complete, involve the installation of more sophisticated electronic equipment such as closed circuit television and motion detectors.

There also are other aspects to DOE's security work. The human element of any security program is paramount; the most sophisticated systems in the world are worthless without adequate training for Russian personnel in using those systems properly and maintaining them. DOE has invested considerable program resources since the 1990s in various training and educational programs for their Russian counterparts, seeking to develop a culture of security awareness that will be maintained after the program's work is completed. Other program resources have been expended to ensure that guard forces at nuclear sites are adequately trained and equipped.

and experts in various areas of nuclear security. We deemed it essential to do as much of this work as the Russians and program resources would permit to ensure that our established panoply of security upgrades—including better fences, better equipment for security forces, and better overall security practices—were sustained after the program's core work had been completed. Simply put, it would at best have been a Pyrrhic victory to reach our goals if the Russians reverted to the past practices and insufficient resources commitment that had plagued their previous efforts.

Drawing on my experience at the NSC, it was evident that even the best-laid plans in Washington would never reach fruition without the active cooperation of our target audience, in this case Russia's nuclear security establishment. As noted, that cooperation could not be taken for granted. Shortly before my arrival the Ministry of Atomic Energy had appointed Vladimir Limonayev, an experienced staff member, to manage the Russian part of the program. I set out to meet Limonayev to assess if it was possible to engage him in a genuine partnership that would serve the interests of both nations.

In summer 2000, I brought a delegation of program managers to Moscow to meet my new counterpart. Limonayev was a cautious, but highly competent, professional and friendly individual, clearly trying in our initial meetings to assess me and the American team. He appeared to share my view that there were compelling reasons to move the program forward at an accelerated pace, but it became apparent immediately that there was a significant obstacle.

For at least the past eighteen months there had been an ongoing set of negotiations at the end of the Clinton administration that continued into the start of the Bush administration over the procedures for U.S. experts to gain access to Russia's sensitive nuclear sites. This was the central issue for the program because our government would not commit funding to projects without verifiable proof that those resources were being used for their intended purposes. Because my focus and energies at NSC had been on the negotiations with Russia over the Iran weapons of mass destruction (WMD) problem, I had not followed as closely as I would have preferred the protracted negotiations over access that had been stalled at the departmental level. On my arrival at DOE I learned that the negotiations were being carried out by a State Department Foreign Service officer on assignment to DOE who knew little about nuclear security work and the DOE Office of General Counsel whose staff was not familiar with the program. It seemed odd and rather disconcerting that there was little involvement from any of the MPC&A program managers—those with the greatest equities—in the negotiations.

Limonayev appeared sincere in describing his support for the program and its new and clearer set of objectives and timelines but warned me bluntly that the goals of our strategic plan would never be achieved without the access agreement. Of course he was right. When I returned to Washington I set out to discover where and how things had bogged down on the U.S. side. The bad news was that progress indeed had ground to a halt in bureaucratic wrangling.

The good news was that the State Department officer was departing DOE for a more appropriate assignment, presenting an opportunity for the program to take over this work in which it had direct interest. By fall 2000, my office had assumed direct responsibility for the negotiations and we made an overture to Limonayev to join in moving forward the stalled negotiations. The offer was not only the most practical thing to do given existing problems, but it also was a mechanism for assessing Russian intentions. Removing impediments to progress in the United States was important but we didn't know if the Russians were prepared to take their own set of positive steps.

The Russian reaction was immediate and positive; Limonayev committed to assembling a delegation with authority to move the talks on access forward. For the next several months U.S. and Russian delegations met on several occasions in London, doubtless raising some questions from British officials about the purpose of U.S. and Russian officials cloistered together for days in a London hotel. Progress came in fits and starts as both sides from time to time would feel the need to contact their respective capitals for advice or concurrence on controversial or complex items. By early summer 2001, the delegations had reached a tentative agreement and my staff began to breathe a sigh of relief with the prospect in sight that we would achieve a program breakthrough.

The Washington bureaucracy once again proved true the old adage that it's not over until it's over. Armed with a draft agreement, Dave Jonas, a former Marine lawyer and the new Deputy General Counsel for the fledgling National Nuclear Security Administration (NNSA) (of which my programs were part), a semiautonomous subsidiary of DOE created in 1999 to 2000 by Congress primarily to address chronic security problems at the DOE national laboratories, was tasked to gain the concurrence of his counterparts in the legal departments at the Pentagon and State Department. Jonas had an affable personality and was easy to work with in many ways. Unfortunately, he lacked the gravitas or willingness to engage his more experienced counterparts in the give and take necessary to secure their support. While interagency concurrence was not formally required, it was a desirable political commodity. Months slipped by as the Washington bureaucracy debated the nuances of seemingly every sentence. In the process, the Russians became increasingly impatient by what they perceived as stalling. Limonayev had been authorized to make some important concessions in the London talks that, if formally agreed to by the United States, would enable us to carry out our mandated oversight duties, freeing up the flow of resources. Once it became apparent that the U.S. government could not reach internal agreement on a final draft, Russian authorities very quickly took an increasingly tough stance, allowing virtually no forward progress on various projects that already had been underway.

This impasse persisted until September 11, 2001. On that beautiful, sunny, late summer day I was in my office when the first reports were broadcast on

CNN detailing attacks on the World Trade Center (WTC) in New York City and then at the Pentagon in Arlington, Virginia, right across the river from the DOE's Washington offices. In the immediate chaos of the first hours, DOE, along with the rest of the federal government in Washington, evacuated its offices. Vehicular traffic in the city became gridlocked as thousands of motorists jammed the streets. The heavily used Washington Metro subway system was closed as a precautionary measure by local officials unsure of whether more attacks would be carried out against public transportation nodes. I had little choice but to begin walking toward my home in suburban Virginia. As I did so the flaming ruins of the Pentagon were within easy sight, chilling proof that the United States had entered a new and dangerous era.

The emotions of those in Washington and New York who witnessed the attacks doubtless are indelible but even those can't compare to the agonies suffered by the victims and their families. One of the victims of the attacks on the WTC was my boyhood best friend, John O'Neill. When we were ten years old, John told me that he would work for the FBI. He had recently retired from the FBI as its lead counterterrorism expert, having been involved in chasing and warning of Osama bin Laden for years. John was the lead investigator of the terrorist attack on the USS *Cole*, one of the precursors of the September 11 attacks, and widely respected in the law enforcement community for his untiring devotion to duty. In what can only be described as a terrible irony, several weeks before the attacks, John had joined the private sector, becoming director of security at the WTC. He had no time to settle in the job. When the attack occurred John was in his office on the thirty-fourth floor in the north tower. After the initial attack, he managed to evacuate the building, calling his son to say that he had not been injured.

John was never one to shy away from duty's call. He returned to the building to help with the evacuation of its trapped occupants and was killed when the building collapsed. His body was recovered several weeks later and the funeral was held in Atlantic City, NJ, and was attended by an overwhelming crowd of family, friends, and law enforcement officers. *New York Post* reporter Murray Weiss captured John's life and death well in his "The Man Who Warned America."

In the dark days following the attacks no one really knew what might happen next. From my perspective the possibility could not be dismissed that even more deadly attacks might be planned against the United States. I resolved to use the one means at my disposal, the programs under my authority, as a modest contribution to reducing this possibility. To do so would first require that the bureaucratic impediments to completion of the access agreement had to be removed. I informed Limonayev that it was my intention to sign the access agreement at the earliest possible opportunity with or without the concurrence of the bureaucracy. Limonayev expressed heartfelt sympathy for the losses and devastation inflicted on America. He also welcomed my decision to press forward, saying that on September 10 he had been in the

Caucasus in a mock exercise to test Russian reaction to an attack against a nuclear power plant. The Russians clearly had their own fears about nuclear terrorism. We scheduled a meeting in Washington for late September.

In anticipating the meeting, there was the all too familiar hand-wringing at DOE. I informed Baker of my plans to sign the agreement, eliciting from him a list of objections but, finally, what might be characterized charitably as a neutral stance. My response was simple; I informed him that by the end of September I would put my signature on either the access agreement or my resignation.

Never one to make a controversial decision if he could avoid doing so, Baker sought the advice of Linton Brooks, the incoming political appointee who would directly oversee DOE's international threat reduction work before becoming administrator of the entire NNSA. Brooks had been another midrank military officer, a retired Navy captain, with a reputation for decency but indecisiveness. Because Brooks had not yet been confirmed for his position, I had no obligation to consult with him on this question but chose to do so out of courtesy. I explained my reasoning and intentions, emphasizing that without the agreement the U.S. government's lead program for securing Russian nuclear materials would be stalled indefinitely. Brooks was unmoved, stating his opinion that more time should be spent working to secure interagency consensus on the access agreement. The time for needless hesitation, in my mind, had long passed as a result of countless months of delay.

I honored my commitment to Limonayev in late September 2001 by signing the access agreement in Washington. Brooks was irate by what he saw as an act of defiance but, ironically, I heard from various officials in other parts of the interagency that there was overwhelming support for my decision. No criticisms of any consequence arose against the agreement either within DOE or by the interagency, and with the stroke of a pen we were able to accelerate the work entrusted to us by the Congress and expected by the administration.

From a broader perspective, the Bush administration, like the American public, was in an understandable state of shock from the attacks. In the wake of the attack, President Bush's strong moral tones of indignation and refusal to bow to coercion were well received around the nation and the world. In December 2002, the Bush administration published National Security Presidential Directive (NSPD)-17, the "National Strategy to Combat Weapons of Mass Destruction." NSPD-17 provided the intellectual framework for the administration's approach and priorities to countering the WMD problem. This strategy rested on three pillars: counterproliferation, which emphasized interdiction and deterrence to combat WMD use; strengthened nonproliferation to combat WMD proliferation, including multilateral cooperative efforts and domestic programs such as DOD's Cooperative Threat Reduction Program and DOE's MPC&A and border monitoring work; and consequence management to respond to WMD use.[2]

Programmatically, the administration, initially skeptical to some degree about the effectiveness of the threat reduction programs with Russia, supported increased funding for them after a thorough interagency review of each. In the MPC&A case, with administration support annual funding levels rose from about $130 million when I arrived in early 2000 to nearly $250 million by early 2002. DOD's program work in Russia also received administration endorsement and subsequent funding increases.

The rapid expansion of the program's funding provided its own set of managerial challenges. The first involved the lack of trained and experienced federal managers to oversee the program's expanding directions. As with other parts of DOE as well as many large programs throughout the federal government, the MPC&A program from its inception had been too heavily dependent in some respects on contract employees and also, in our case, laboratory employees. I hasten to add that in countless ways the program's contractor and laboratory personnel provided invaluable services. Nonetheless, in my judgment it was inappropriate to ask contract or laboratory employees to make program decisions, including those on funding issues, as had been the case previously, given the inherent conflict of interest raised by allowing such decisions to be made by those whose parent organizations had a vested interest in the outcome. The program received assistance from Ken Baker who worked with congressional staffers to allow some of the new congressional funding to be used for hiring federal staff that was not provided for in the initial Congressional rush to draft and pass the appropriations legislation.

We also needed to ensure that the quality of our rapidly expanding work was not being compromised by our desire to move the program forward quickly. In this respect I relied heavily on the work of the program's technical survey team (TST), an internal program element comprised of six highly experienced personnel, all with extensive technical backgrounds. Led by Dr. Ruth Kempf, a respected scientist from Brookhaven National Laboratory, the team carried out intensive reviews of our major program initiatives and reported the results directly to me and my deputy. Because of the integrity of Kempf and her team, I viewed the TST as a most effective way to receive quick and unbiased assessments of the progress being made on the range of projects encompassing more than sixty Russian nuclear sites. Some in the program resented the independence of the TST while others from time to time would attempt to deny TST full access to various projects. Those attempts almost always failed. The TST reviews were integral to our attempts to manage the program properly and I urged in vain my colleagues within DOE's managerial ranks, beginning with Ken Baker, to adopt this useful managerial tool for other programs working in Russia.

Perhaps the most controversial element of the MPC&A program was its work with the Russian Navy. In the 1990s, the U.S. government received a series of reports detailing cases of stolen nuclear fuel and fuel rods used by the Russian Navy. These reports, later confirmed by Russian officials, had shaken the Navy's most senior officials, including its commander, Admiral Kuryedov, who would deal with other serious problems on his watch, including the tragic sinking of the submarine Kursk. Before my arrival at DOE a program initiative began, with Congressional approval, to assist the Russian Navy in developing the same type of security procedures—better fencing, alarms, and sensors—that were being installed with our counterparts at Minatom.

Any type of U.S. government funding that assisted an element of the Russian military—even for the program's national security objectives—was controversial and looked askance by some in the intelligence and civilian defense policy communities. Nonetheless, for unknown reasons, U.S. military officers never voiced concern about the program. Perhaps because of their military training they recognized that security threats change over time as do the required responses to them. As a former intelligence officer who had spent years studying the Soviet military, I also was struck by the irony, to say the least, in working cooperatively with the Russian military. There was no secret about my past employment—I had traveled to Russia on official business as a CIA officer in the mid-1990s—but it never was an issue working with Russian officials. My Russian counterparts apparently shared my view that past career assignments couldn't be allowed to compromise the solution to current problems of great concern to both sides. I was treated with considerable respect by my Russian counterparts and always tried to accord them the same courtesies.

Working with senior Russian Navy officials had its challenging moments. Their program leader was Admiral Nikolai Yurasov, a short, barrel-chested officer with a direct, no nonsense manner. I respected Yurasov's ability to make things happen in a rigid and at times slow-moving system. As with other elements of our program work, access to sensitive Navy facilities was something that some in the Russian Navy or Russian intelligence services were not eager to grant visiting Americans. This caused some problems for the program. There were occasions where we refused to commit program funds to Navy projects because of this lack of access which we required to verify the integrity of our security upgrades. We were usually able to work with Yurasov to gain the desired level of access without compromising Russian security standards. He always appeared to act in Russia's best interests and with the behind-the-scenes but considerable support of Russian Navy Commander-in-Chief Vladimir Kuryedov. Yurasov's untimely passing in 2007 at age fifty-nine saddened many of his colleagues.

The seriousness of the work on occasion was interrupted by some unintended embarrassment. During one visit to Moscow I was accompanied by Ken Baker who wanted to see the progress being made by the program. One item on our itinerary was a meeting with Admiral Yurasov and his senior staff to address several thorny problems. About half way through the meeting Baker heard through the U.S. interpreter that Yurasov was celebrating a birthday. Baker immediately jumped out of his chair and began singing "Happy Birthday," as Yurasov, his subordinates, and the U.S. delegation sat in silent embarrassment. The rest of the meeting didn't go very well and I later apologized to my Russian counterpart for Baker's gaffe.

The program's work with the Russian Navy was overseen by two federal managers, Garry Tittemore, the division director and Bruce Pentola, Tittemore's de facto deputy. The program's work with the Russian Navy had benefited considerably from the technical skills of several mid-level employees such as Byron Gardner from Sandia National Laboratory as well as several of his colleagues from Los Alamos National Laboratory. Gardner's dedication, expertise, and credibility with his Russian counterparts were instrumental in much of the progress achieved during this period. Things became muddled at the more senior laboratory and program oversight levels. Tittemore and Pentola had become, in my judgment, too heavily dependent on their laboratory counterparts to make decisions related to the direction and funding priorities for Navy projects.

To confirm or refute my suspicions, I asked Kempf and her TST to independently review the work being done by Tittemore's division. According to the TST briefing, progress was being made but there also was deeply disturbing news in some of their other findings. It appeared that $750,000 in federal funding had been approved by my staff for landscaping the top of a Russian Navy storage bunker. At first I thought the report was a prank given its bizarre content but the TST was quite serious in its finding. I was livid as that work and the expenditures for it had no proper place in the program and I told Tittemore and Pentola in no uncertain terms. These unjustified expenditures were precisely the type that would undermine the program's credibility in the eyes of its skeptics.

My refusal to turn a blind eye to this activity generated resentment by Sandia National Laboratory manager Dori Ellis who tried to argue that such work helped build rapport between the U.S. and Russian program teams. Program direction, oversight, and accountability for federal officers were not job requirements in her mind-set. Over time, Ellis became so frustrated by my insistence on accountability for the program's work and its financial expenditures that she went directly to Baker with a fatuous proposal to remove the Navy work from my purview. I appreciated that Baker told me about this immediately and he discounted her proposal.

Ellis's attitude was the exception as most of the other managers from other DOE laboratories with personnel assigned to various aspects of the program were, in the main, professional. They continued to compete for program dollars, including the use of such tactics as occasional attempts to discredit the work being done by other national laboratories and private contractors, a practice that was de rigueur in other parts of DOE. However, they also understood the importance of working cooperatively with federal staff and to respond to their directions and priorities. That was a substantial change from past practices. Nonetheless, what was as important to me as addressing the particular problem in the Navy work, and the view I held throughout my tenure at DOE, was that I failed to convince two of my federal managers the importance of their maintaining firm managerial control over the most controversial element of the program. In my judgment they had become advocates for the equities of the labs, not the program. Shortly after the incident Tittemore was replaced by John Gerrard, another experienced manager, who proved to be as ineffective as his predecessor in enforcing that part of his managerial duties. Near the end of my tenure I was particularly distressed to overhear a representative from one of the laboratories brag how Gerrard was "in their back pocket."

On a more positive note, these managerial shake-ups within the Navy Division brought to my attention the exceptional talents of Nicole Nelson Jean, a young federal officer working in Tittemore's division. Often twenty years younger than most of her Russian counterparts, Jean would become a major contributor to our work with the Russian Navy as some of her more experienced U.S. federal counterparts were failing to carry out program direction. She was entrusted with leading several sensitive negotiations, consistently delivering impressive results, while demonstrating the young managerial talent that existed within the department.

From a broader perspective, the managerial problems encountered within the program in no way should detract from recognition of the staff's overall exceptional dedication. Most of the Russian facilities visited throughout the program were in inhospitable and sometimes dangerous locations and our federal, contract, and laboratory personnel traveled there routinely and without complaint. For example, visiting Russian Navy facilities on the Kola Peninsula in winter was enough to test anyone's fortitude. The area was dubbed the "land of the flying dogs" because small dogs were known to have been blown off cliffs by the frequent gale force winds often present in the area. Leaders and managers should, as one of their primary duties, motivate their staff. I have no hesitation in acknowledging that my staff motivated me every bit as much as I may have motivated them.

Other parts of the program began to move forward quickly. Pat Cahalane and his deputy, Greg Slovik, were two of the program's most capable managers and I entrusted them to oversee our work at Minatom sites. In all, they managed projects at about fifty Minatom sites, a substantial increase from the program's first days of cooperative work in Russia. Under their leadership we succeeded in enhancing the security of about 250 metric tons of nuclear materials. Although it was protecting some of the world's most deadly materials, there was nothing particularly sophisticated about this work. In keeping with the program's model, we built more secure fences, installed more reliable sensors, and worked to enhance the capabilities of the Russian response forces guarding these materials than at any time before in the program's history. We also continued our efforts, led by John Boyd, a Vietnam War veteran whose heroism there was totally disguised by his casual demeanor and gentle manner, to train workers at these same Minatom sites on the "best practices" for the long-term maintenance of the security enhancements being installed. If the primary mission of the expenditure of large sums of U.S. funds was to improve the security of Russia's vulnerable nuclear materials, we wanted to take every reasonable precaution to ensure that those security upgrades were sustained after our departure. The work done by Boyd's division was integral to the program's comprehensive approach to security upgrades in Russia.

As DOE's threat reduction programs in Russia expanded, it became increasingly obvious that it was necessary to have full-time, permanent representation there to support the department's equities. One of the best decisions made by DOE management during this period was to work with the State Department and the respected U.S. ambassador in Moscow, Sandy Vershbow, another NSC veteran, to establish a full-time DOE office located in the U.S. embassy. In the past, DOE had established a similar permanent official presence in other embassies, although usually on a smaller scale. Perhaps the best model for this was the consistently high-quality work performed by Lisa Hilliard at the U.S. Mission to the International Atomic Energy Agency (IAEA) in Vienna. As Russia was the host nation where most of DOE's international program dollars were spent, it was appropriate as well as overdue for DOE to have permanent representation in Russia. DOE's first Moscow office director, Cindy Lersten, did an excellent job in developing a new staff and working with both her U.S. and Russian counterparts. Lersten's skills received deservedly high marks from her counterparts and were instrumental in helping to resolve a number of problems that inevitably arose from working in Russia.

In Washington, working with a young and inexperienced federal staff had its share of frustrations but it also had many satisfying moments. Because staff training was accorded a low priority by senior management as well as the administrative side of DOE's new NNSA, the senior managers in my program joined with me in expending considerable discretionary time in developing and carrying out various intraprogram training activities. If the first duty of federal senior managers is to advance their program's mission, the second priority is professional staff development. This lesson was instilled in me years earlier as a junior CIA officer. In comparison to the NNSA approach, CIA's commitment of time and resources to staff development could serve as a model for other parts of the U.S. government. Many of the skills I applied in the latter half of my career can be traced to the training I received at the Agency. I regret that I had little success in convincing DOE senior management of the value of investing more time and resources in staff training. Such investment is fully justified.

Nonetheless, we had some success in our go-it-alone approach. A concerted effort was made to provide many of the staff with exposure to the interagency process, for example, and the results were positive. This approach was at considerable variance with the established culture in some other DOE programs. Several of my counterparts in other programs felt the safest way to avoid potential problems at interagency meetings whose purpose often was to establish a common approach to looming issues, given DOE's already modest reputation, was to refrain from exposing their junior officers to the occasionally contentious give-and-take interagency process. That low risk strategy missed the point entirely; our young officers could have no better training than to interact with their counterparts from State, CIA, and DOD. With a modicum of encouragement, in many cases junior officers such as Harvard-educated Ann Kohnen quickly emerged as the substantive equals of DOE officers in other organizations with much greater experience, mostly as a result of a willingness to accept such opportunities. In Kohnen's case, she also distinguished herself by undertaking a sensitive mission to the Republic of Georgia where she was instrumental in negotiating and reaching agreement with senior Georgian officials regarding the security of some radioactive sources. The positive results were important for the program but I was equally pleased to have given Kohnen the opportunity to take on such a challenging assignment that DOE's often calcified personnel system probably would have given to a more senior officer, regardless of qualifications.

The program's momentum was palpable with tangible progress in many areas, but even our best efforts could not dispel the feeling I and others held that the scope of the security problems in Russia, not to mention similar problems in other nations with nuclear materials, was far too large for any program to undertake alone. At the Pentagon, the Defense Threat Reduction Agency had been doing an excellent job in securing and destroying Russian warheads but they were fully occupied with other work and lacked the personnel and financial resources to take on significant parts of our work. This realization led me to seek external partners to assist us in accelerating our nonproliferation work. My first port of call was the United Kingdom, America's stalwart ally and whose government held views similar to those of the Bush administration regarding nonproliferation.

For reasons that weren't entirely clear to me as well as several British counterparts, the Blair government had invested lead responsibility for nuclear security work in an unlikely bureaucratic home, its Department of Trade and Industry (DTI). I met with several senior managers at DTI in mid-2002 and they seemed keen to undertake their own projects in Russia. I described in detail extant MPC&A projects in Russia as well as looming opportunities for new initiatives where British assistance would be invaluable. As I would come to learn from this and a subsequent meeting, there were only two "small" problems with this overture. The first was that DTI lacked the financial and personnel resources to carry out any substantial work in Russia. The second, as confided to me by Limonayev, was that the Russians did not want the British there. The access granted by the Russians to the United States was, in part, a reflection of the considerable resources we could bring to various projects that the United Kingdom's budgetary constraints could not match.

Realizing that cooperative efforts with the United Kingdom at best would yield limited results, my focus turned to developing a multilateral approach to securing nuclear materials in Russia and beyond. The idea of bringing together in one place the international community to discuss these ideas held great appeal. A proposal was developed and sent to Brooks and Baker to hold an international conference. Brooks evinced little enthusiasm for the idea, questioning why the department would want to take the time required for such a purpose. My relationship with Brooks had been lukewarm from the start of his tenure and, in the aftermath of the September 11 attacks, he opined that the work done by the program to secure nuclear materials had little to do with combating terrorism. I found this attitude inexplicable as well as entirely inconsistent with what President Bush declared as one of his administration's most pressing concerns. One thing was certain about the NNSA; it was never far from the center of the bureaucratically inane.

After extensive and protracted wheedling and cajoling on my part, Brooks and Baker relented and approved the idea for an international conference. They refused my request, however, to invite Secretary of Energy Spencer Abraham, apparently fearing that he would be embarrassed if the conference was unsuccessful. Holding a conference was hardly an innovative idea. What I wanted to accomplish, however, was something more than what often characterizes most conferences. The goal for this conference was to establish a forum for ongoing discussion with those from other countries with nonproliferation policy and program objectives similar to those of the U.S. government. My rationale was to position DOE as an international leader in this area by showcasing the many things it was capable of accomplishing, not only through its own resources but by working cooperatively with others. The conference also was a way to advance the program's goals indirectly in that work done by other nations, even if modest by U.S. government standards, would reduce existing problems of nuclear insecurity resulting from still vast quantities of unsecured nuclear materials.

Planning and executing an international conference of the desired size outside Washington—about 250 to 300 attendees—was the sizable challenge that would require considerable assistance. In this regard I turned to John Wood, a highly accomplished Oxford-educated U.S. businessman who ran the Trilateral Group, an established and successful consulting business in London. I met John during my tenure at the NSC when he came to my office to describe his various cooperative commercial projects in Russia. That work included interactions with many senior Russian scientists, such as Dr. Yevgeny Velikhov, a nuclear physicist and director of Moscow's well-known Kurchatov Institute and Dr. Nikolai Plate, one of Russia's most respected chemists. Ably assisted by his partner, Derek Robinson, John possessed the experience, vision, and sophistication the program required to organize and bring to London the senior participants needed to make the conference a success.

My trust in John and his organization was amply rewarded. In late September to early October 2002, the conference was held at London's Intercontinental Hotel. In addition to participation from serving senior U.S. officials such as then Undersecretary of State John Bolton and U.S. Ambassador Ken Brill who was posted at the IAEA, Leon Fuerth, Al Gore's former national security adviser was in attendance, as well as senior governmental representatives from twenty-six nations. The IAEA sent senior representatives such as Kenji Mura-kami, who still heads the Safeguards Division and is one of the IAEA's most respected figures. NATO sent representatives as did Interpol. It also was important to me that the United States show solidarity with the Russians in this area of cooperation on nuclear nonproliferation, and the Russian Ministry of Atomic Energy supported the conference fully, sending a large delegation led by my counterpart Vladimir Limonayev, and agreeing to serve as the conference co-sponsor.

The highlight of the three-day gathering was a stirring speech given by former British Prime Minister Margaret Thatcher. John Wood had enjoyed a long friendship with one of Britain's most storied political figures and he was most generous in using that relationship to secure Mrs. Thatcher's participation. What made Mrs. Thatcher's appearance even more gratifying was that her health was fragile and we would have been grateful if she had made only a brief appearance at a reception and exchanged pleasantries with some of the conference participants. On the conference's final evening John and I greeted her at the hotel entrance; Mrs. Thatcher inquired immediately if "we would mind" if she made a few remarks. We assured the political icon that her willingness to do so was most generous and that the audience would keenly welcome any thoughts she might wish to share.

Few predictions could be easier to make. Thatcher's speech enthralled the audience, particularly the Russians, whose previous form of government for so long had been the target of her withering criticisms about its repressive domestic and aggressive foreign policies. During her speech the aging but indefatigable dowager seemed to gain strength and energy as she proclaimed that the end of the Cold War had given way to a new era of global threats from rogue nations and terrorist organizations. Consistent with her reputation for eloquent but direct language, Mrs. Thatcher's words were pointed and concise when she spoke of countries seeking to bring harm to others. "Our first line of defense," she declared, "must be to deter or to stop such countries from obtaining weapons of mass destruction."[3] The audience's response was immediate and overwhelmingly positive. The speech also was a great triumph for the program and its work. My only regret was that Brooks, who stayed at the conference for only a few hours on the first day, was nowhere to be seen when one of the political titans of the twentieth century extolled the importance of the work being done by the program.

Thatcher's speech stirred the conference attendees, capping three days of remarkably open exchanges of the international community's problems, vulnerabilities, and opportunities against the spread of nuclear weapons. Many new and lasting relationships were developed. Most importantly, the conference's objective to make the gathering in London the first act in an anticipated long run of cooperative efforts was realized with the establishment of separate working groups focusing on nuclear and radiological security, a working group on technical approaches to carrying out nuclear material security work, and a fourth working group on ways to meet the challenges of enhancing export control and protecting borders from illicit smuggling.

After my departure as program director, DOE canceled abruptly a planned follow-up conference, completely abdicating its opportunity to develop a position of international leadership in nuclear nonproliferation issues. Funding to continue the work was ample and no one could criticize the conference's value. For this reason I could only conclude that the decision to terminate this successful initiative was made for personal or political reasons by NNSA management. Fortunately, DOE's profligate obtuseness became irrelevant when several other important supporters from outside DOE stepped forward to continue sponsorship of the working groups established in London.

From 2001 to 2003, DOE's work with the Russian Customs Service to enhance the security of Russia's borders also began expanding rapidly and developing a new momentum. The border security program, known as the Second Line of Defense (SLD), had been placed under my authority in 2001 as a logical extension of the MPC&A work at the Minatom sites. The program's work benefited considerably from the partnership established with Nikolai Kravchenko, a senior official on the Russian Customs Service. Kravchenko accepted the daunting challenge of securing thousands of miles of borders with a resolute and professional demeanor. Because we had no reason to believe that Kravchenko was engaged in illicit activities or otherwise abusing his position—which would not have been surprising given the scope and nature of his duties—I decided that he was exactly the type of official we needed to develop a long-term partnership. The program's annual budget had increased in the late 1990s from an insignificant $2 million to over $20 million by the first part of this decade. As with the MPC&A work, the challenge for the SLD program was to locate, train, and support the individuals who could move the program forward along the lines I deemed appropriate. I found that individual in Dave Martin, a young but talented federal officer who combined solid technical skills with ability, not always demonstrated at DOE, to work productively with foreign counterparts. In turn, Martin was assisted by Mike Coffey, a veteran officer with his own impressive technical skills and countless hours of interaction with Russian officials.

The partnership between Kravchenko and my officers yielded tangible results almost from the start. As with other similar programs, the challenge was to at once develop a set of priorities for the use of program resources that reflected the U.S. government's best understanding of the situation while being receptive to the views of our counterparts on resource prioritization since their understanding of the "ground truth" was always superior to what any outsider might hope to achieve. Martin and Coffey demonstrated considerable skill in this area. Kravchenko respected them and believed his views were taken into consideration when we were deciding which of the regions and border crossings should receive priority funding. Because there were about three hundred sixty such border crossings, it was important to ensure that we used available funds to enhance Russian capabilities at crossings of greatest concern or vulnerability. With Kravchenko's help we began to assemble such a list to ensure they received priority attention.

Our greatest compliment came in 2002 from the Government Accountability Office (GAO), the congressional investigatory arm. Through the years many of the DOE international programs had been found frequently to be poorly managed, resulting in accomplishments far more modest than what should have resulted from available funding levels. On my arrival at DOE I sensed a near paranoia from Baker who feared another poor report card when the GAO announced plans for an investigation of one of the programs for which he had general oversight. The one constant through years of turnover among political appointees and career officers who came and went at DOE was Baker's involvement in these programs. He told me several times "as one career officer to another" that he held everything together because he knew DOE's intricacies and that some of the political appointees like his immediate supervisors, Joan Rohlfing and Rose Gottemoeller, were weak managers, who were easily outmaneuvered or manipulated. That attitude was just one example of a climate of distrust that permeated the international programs. Baker's skewed views notwithstanding, in my observation, the truth was radically different; many of the DOE programs suffered because of Baker's poor leadership and countless reviews by the GAO that painted a consistent and damning picture of chronically ineffective management, poor strategic planning, and missed opportunities. GAO reviews were important because of their thoroughness—some inspections could last months—as well as the close reading their reports often received on Capitol Hill. On close examination the case can be made that through all the years of political appointees who came and left DOE regularly, the one constant overseeing the programs so routinely found lacking by the GAO, was Ken Baker.

From my first days at DOE I made every effort to establish a positive relationship with him and there were periods of good working relations. There also were growing signs of merging problems. During my first eighteen months at DOE I sent Baker various memos on program problems and opportunities. This was done not only to keep him informed, which was appropriate, but to solicit the input of my immediate supervisor. I came to realize that for every positive step or direction that was being pursued that there were a dozen others that needed to be pursued. Any assistance in addressing those would have been well received. I don't know if Baker read the memos and papers sent from the program but his responses often demonstrated questionable judgment. For example, I had been approached by officials of the Israeli government inquiring about the possibility of bringing the SLD border monitoring program to Israel. As one of America's stalwart allies, and given Israel's location in one of the world's most unstable and dangerous regions, I was fully prepared to agree to the Israeli request. It would have been a pleasure to again work with Israeli officials. Baker wouldn't respond to the request, giving no answer for weeks. He finally turned down the request to assist Israel without any explanation when I pressed him on it. The Israeli government was less than satisfied. Fearing political criticism, I later learned that DOE began a minor series of substantive exchanges on export control issues with the Israelis, exactly what they did not want.

The climate of distrust swirling around the international programs extended outside departmental walls. I was determined to modify the way the programs under my purview dealt with the GAO, and with the assistance of Martin and Coffey took on the challenge of assisting the GAO in its review of our border monitoring program. I had been at DOE long enough to know that the standard if unofficial guidance from Baker was to stonewall GAO investigators and tell them nothing more than was absolutely necessary. I found that attitude tactically short-sighted, highly unprofessional, and probably unethical. Resolving to take a different tack, Martin and I agreed that we would share with the GAO the strengths as well as the warts—which surely existed—of the SLD work. In short, I didn't want the GAO to think they had uncovered anything negative about the program that we didn't know existed already.

Once their review was underway, the GAO investigators respected that we weren't trying to play a shell game with them. As a level of mutual respect emerged it became clear from our conversations that the GAO auditors knew well Baker's standard guidance for working with them and confided that it just made them work harder to find the flaws in other programs. Confident that they had received our cooperation in their investigation of the SLD program, the GAO's main conclusions were a programmatic triumph, the first one being that our work was a model for similar government programs.[4] It didn't take much knowledge of past GAO assessments of DOE's work to know that was a description seldom used for the threat reduction programs.

The GAO review was instrumental in establishing the program's credibility but it was only one part of the program's challenges. By far the largest programmatic challenge was implementing the strategic plan presented to me by Martin and Coffey. As the world's largest country, Russia had thousands of miles of borders, now poorly protected in the wake of the resource problems resulting from the Soviet Union's collapse. As with the approach taken by MPC&A work at nuclear facilities, Martin and Coffey agreed it was critical to establish a prioritization for our SLD resources, most of which were dedicated to installing portal monitors at borders, airports, and seaports that would monitor attempts to smuggle various types of fissile materials. Consultations with Kravchenko yielded some important insights as to how to use our resources most efficiently, but to ensure that our funding decisions were supported by the best available evidence, we also drew on input from the interagency, including excellent support from the intelligence community. As a result, the strategic plan was shaped and prioritized by our understanding of those smuggling routes that for various reasons seemed most likely to be used for the transport of illicit goods and materials. Particular attention was paid to smuggling routes through southern Russia and toward the Middle East. The strong cooperation we received from Kravchenko and his staff of Russian Customs Service officials, who knew those issues and problems intimately, along with the interagency support, demonstrated how threat reduction programs could make rapid progress when they leveraged existing capabilities. During my tenure at DOE, if there was any approach to program management worth touting it simply was recognition of and willingness to use our resources in a way that built on existing expertise wherever we found it.

For the SLD program, of almost equal importance to our strategic approach was selecting the right equipment for the task, a seemingly mundane but vitally important decision for a mission whose success or failure was heavily dependent on the technical detection of illicit trafficking. Different U.S. and Russian commercial vendors, as well as technical experts working at the DOE national laboratories, had the skills to develop equipment for monitoring various types of nuclear smuggling activities. In most cases their products worked as claimed in laboratory settings. However, the remote and often environmentally harsh Russian border post hardly replicated such favorable testing conditions. Martin and Coffey to their considerable credit understood the requirements for installing sensitive equipment that could function under adverse conditions. Those decisions, and others like them, were what convinced the GAO in its 2002 judgment that the program was on a solid foundation. During this period more than seventy border posts and several airports and seaports were equipped with DOE portal monitoring equipment. The work done during that period by the SLD team made a direct contribution to U.S. security.

Both the MPC&A and SLD programs took a decidedly negative turn by late 2002. The mutual distrust Baker and I had for each other spilled over very publicly. One of the last straws occurred when Baker directed his factotum, Cherie Fitzgerald, to probe into whether the funding for the London conference represented a good use of resources and whether the contract was written properly, notwithstanding the fact that before the conference we sent Baker memos detailing all we were trying to accomplish and how we planned to do so. I didn't work for Fitzgerald but knew she almost certainly was inquiring on Baker's behalf. The irony is that I had nothing to do with negotiating the contract or its amount, my contract administrators took care of those details, which was wholly consistent with their responsibilities as well as federal contracting practice. I was confident that the contract administrators had considerable integrity and that the conference's contract was proper. To my knowledge no impropriety was ever uncovered although there was talk for months that Fitzgerald was trying to uncover some such impropriety although she had no official standing to do so. I also knew how much had been accomplished for the national interest by the London conference from the overwhelmingly positive feedback received from many attendees. Unfortunately, it was consistent with Baker's approach to put senior staff on the defensive when he himself felt pressure. He had demonstrated the same tactics against former DOE Intelligence Director Notra Trulock during the infamous scandal over possible Chinese spying at a DOE laboratory.[5]

Baker's conduct over many years had become sufficiently troubling that several congressional staffers compiled a lengthy dossier detailing his managerial abuses toward a number of DOE officers. The report circulated among several DOE senior managers in early 2003, including Linton Brooks and Deputy Secretary of Energy Kyle McSlarrow. As far as I know neither McSlarrow nor Brooks ever investigated the allegations. Baker had paranoid insecurities that I, like others who had worked for him, wanted his job. Did Baker believe that the success of the London conference as well as the GAO praise for the SLD program would be stepping stones I would use to advance my career? As a lover of ancient history I wondered if the political intrigues of twenty-first century DOE were becoming faintly reminiscent of ancient Rome in the first century where career and character assassination were all in a good day's work. In actuality, I harbored no longing for Baker's job; I found my own duties wholly rewarding and far more satisfying than the administrative matters that occupied much of Baker's day.

The interactions with Baker became so difficult that in mid-2002 I sent Brooks an e-mail saying that an unhealthy environment permeated the organization. I didn't think that was an exaggeration as other senior managers had made similar remarks to me. One of my counterparts, Steve Black, had been telling me for months that he realized that Baker liked to pit senior managers against one another, while other counterparts said they tried whenever possible to work around Baker. Brooks responded to my e-mail with a curt reply, convincing me that he was unprepared to look closely at this situation. In response, new charges of contract violations in the MPC&A program surfaced. I left the program in late November 2002 in favor of a staff assignment elsewhere in the department, although one DOE staff member took it upon himself to spread a rumor that I had resigned. Some six months later and after the allegations of contract impropriety had been disproved, I was offered the opportunity to return to the program and I declined.

During my three-year tenure at the helm of three DOE's threat reduction programs, considerable progress was achieved in carrying out key mission objectives. About 250 metric tons of Russian fissile material received security improvements, a radiological security program, the first of its kind in the U.S. government, was initiated, and our border security work in Russia expanded exponentially. Just as important, in the main, the program staff demonstrated that this work could be carried out with proper federal oversight that simultaneously drew on the considerable talents of laboratory and contractor personnel. The program had been placed "on the map" with such entities as the U.S. Congress and the IAEA and, albeit far from perfect, the staff endeavored to keep faith with the responsibilities entrusted to it by the American public.

One of the classic mistakes made by senior managers in government and probably the private sector for that matter is to believe that they are

irreplaceable. I tried not to labor under that illusion. At the time of my departure there were many talented people throughout the interagency who could
have made excellent contributions to the program if given the opportunity to
lead it. In addition, there would have been considerable merit in bringing into
the program's leadership a talented person from outside the government or to
call on the services of my recently departed deputy, Ken Sheely. Unfortunately, Baker's selection of David Huizenga, an insider from the environmental management side of DOE, set off a firestorm of protest. The sad irony was
that Huizenga, an affable and experienced domestic program manager, also
was in a sense a victim in that he was placed in the wrong job. I wanted him
to succeed and build on the momentum that had been established. I offered
my thoughts on how to keep the program moving in a forward direction but
my offer was never acted on. Unfortunately, his background as a modestly
successful manager in DOE's domestic work, which requires in some critical
respects different managerial and substantive skills than required by the work
of the international threat reduction programs, hardly prepared him for managing highly demanding and politically charged work that had many moving
parts. Many believed that Baker achieved what he wanted, placing someone
in the job who would be a compliant caretaker rather than a risk taker or
problem solver.

The results were predictable. Many of the program's most talented managers who had made important contributions left in disgust, creating a sizable
leadership vacuum. The departures of Cahalane and Martin transpired in short
order. That was followed by the departure of Greg Slovik, a senior technical
expert and manager and Gerald Backen, the program's most experienced contracts officer. In the aggregate, these losses accounted for much of the program's managerial energy, experience, and relationships with Russian
counterparts. By the time of my departure, Sheely already had taken another
job within the department, primarily because of Baker's refusal to promote
him to the senior executive ranks despite my repeated endorsement for that
promotion.

As a result of the chaos roiling the program's ranks, mission performance
fell dramatically. As I had learned during my tenure, the program's progress
was tied directly to our ability to write contracts that committed funding to
our various projects. Contracts enabled the program to move forward; it was
that simple. Suffering from chronic personal indecision and with few experienced advisers to rely on, Huizenga set the program onto a drifting path as he
refused to take on the difficult decisions of a senior manager.

Because of Huizenga's inability to make programmatic commitments, the
congressional funding appropriated for the work began to pile up. After about
two and one-half years, reports surfaced that nearly $700 million of funding
given the program had not been spent.[6] These "uncosted balances" were staggering in size; DOE may have been the only department in government that
didn't know how to spend money for its programs! Adding to the irony was

that this funding would have been used on established projects that were proving to government auditors and most outside observers to be effective and in the national interest. That financial mismanagement did not prevent the department from requesting budgetary increases for the program in the ensuing years. In fiscal year (FY) 2006 the MPC&A budget exceeded $300 million and in FY 2007 was about $350 million but the departmental leadership, in the mistaken belief that the program would begin winding down, has requested about $280 million for FY 2008.

DOE was slow to inform Congress of the scope of the program's financial debacle or the underlying reasons for it, but the congressional hue and cry that resulted on learning the true state of affairs caused considerable embarrassment within DOE managerial circles. Reverting to old habits, according to program insiders, Baker, sensing a looming political problem, ordered Huizenga to spend the accumulating funds as quickly as possible, even if it meant going after what Baker called "low hanging fruit," projects of dubious value but for which contracts could be written easily. As a result, important but complex core projects in Russia and elsewhere slowed while the program negotiated new agreements to spend money in second-order locations that posed little or no threat to the United States such as establishing cooperative programs for export control in the Bahamas. Unlike Russia where negotiating and implementing projects was time-consuming, many smaller nations were eager to receive any type of U.S. assistance as their easy negotiating process often demonstrated.

While most senior administration officials outside DOE had little awareness of the underlying causes for the precipitous drop in pace of the nuclear material security work, they were prepared to give it a political boost. At a 2005 summit meeting in Bratislava, Slovakia, Presidents Bush and Putin reached agreement on the importance of accelerating nuclear material security work in Russia. Broad principles of mutual support to govern future work were reiterated, but no agreement was reached on key specifics. For example, access that would have enabled security upgrades to proceed at Russian nuclear warhead assembly and disassembly plants, also known as serial production facilities, where vast quantities of fissile material is processed, was not negotiated. In the ensuing years, even impetus from the highest levels of the U.S. and Russian governments have not been enough to fully restore the momentum to DOE's threat reduction work.

The core mission of securing Russia's unprotected arsenal of nuclear materials has slipped badly over the past few years. According to analysis performed by credible observers, the numbers paint a sobering picture of mediocre performance. By the time the program's leadership changed hands in late 2002 substantial progress had been made in the core mission, represented by the 250 metric tons of fissile materials that had received security upgrades. That figure was the product of assessing completed security upgrades, conversations with Russian experts, and the work of our TST.

Nonetheless, an element of imprecision in the estimate has to be acknowl-edged given the scope of the problem and Russia's inherent penchant for se-crecy. Although using a different metric for measuring progress, in the ensuing years progress in completing security upgrades has slowed to a crawl. According to one outside expert, by 2006 upgrades had been completed at 54 percent of former Soviet buildings containing nuclear materials.[7] Since the program's inception it has received over $2 billion from Congress, enjoyed broad and sustained bipartisan political support, and has had about fifteen years to carry out the program's critical and time-sensitive mission. Yet, with all these resources, political advantages, and time, only about half the mission of securing some 600 metric tons of nuclear materials has been accomplished and most of that progress occurred during the first part of this decade. This can only be construed as a significant programmatic failure and a major con-tributor to the American public's nuclear insecurity.

Even fewer buildings—about 40 percent—containing nuclear warheads such as at Russian Navy sites have received security upgrades. These numbers are not only disappointing but perhaps also even worse than imagined. Several years ago the new DOE program management changed the way it described the program's progress from one based on amount of fissile material secured, represented by the previously cited total of 250 metric tons of material secured up until late 2002, to an accounting method based, as described above, on the number of buildings secured with program money. The differ-ence is far more than mere semantics. What DOE will not acknowledge is that it seldom knows how much material is contained in any building. As a result, it may claim to have secured a large number of buildings but without knowing what or how much is being stored in the building it is impossible to assess the amount of material being protected. The Russian nuclear storage com-plexes under Rosatom authority are not just single buildings or a small cluster of buildings, but rather sprawling facilities, encompassing many buildings spread over, in some cases, tens of miles. In some instances there are ways to be confident that a particular building is being used to hold nuclear materials but, again, confidence in the actual amounts held within any building is often low. Moreover, for various reasons Russian experts may move some of the materials from time to time. Are current DOE officials playing a shell game with American security to make its program look better than what it is actually accomplishing in Russia?

Compounding the problem is that current DOE managers have been less than honest in keeping Congress informed about their strategic planning and timelines. The program's original strategic plan to finish the security upgrades by 2008 is still espoused by DOE as the program goal, chanted as a mantra whenever senior managers are questioned about those plans and timelines. The cynicism of this answer becomes apparent when compared to the internal program deliberations that now acknowledge privately that this critical goal will not be reached until 2012 or 2013 at the earliest. As a result, for at least the next four or five years the American public will remain at an unnecessary risk of nuclear terrorism as large amounts of nuclear materials that could be better protected languish in poorly protected locations for lack of program leadership. They deserve better from their public servants.

As MPC&A's core work in Russia was slowing precipitously, the department began searching for new missions outside Russia. As described previously, a crude or improvised nuclear device can be fabricated from highly enriched uranium or plutonium but for various technical reasons the path to such a weapon is much easier if HEU is used. Albeit vast, Russia's supply of poorly secured HEU was far from being the only source of this dangerous material. By some informed estimates, there were about 50 to 60 metric tons of HEU in several hundred civilian power and research reactors in at least forty nations. Ironically, large amounts of this HEU were supplied in the 1960s and 1970s by the United States to support cooperative research efforts in various countries. About 128 of these facilities hold at least 20 kilograms of HEU, almost enough material to make a nuclear device. DOE experts claim that they have a broad understanding of the location and amounts of material at these facilities, but as with the estimates involving Russia's nuclear materials, most independent experts question whether DOE fully understands the scale of the problem or has an adequate plan to address it in a timely way.[8] What does not appear to be in dispute is that most of this material also is poorly secured. According to a report issued by the IAEA after its experts visited one such site, the HEU "was observed to have essentially no physical protection."[9] Compounding the security challenges, much of this material is located in university or other types of public settings easily accessed by the public. Under these circumstances it often is unrealistic to try to install the type of MPC&A layered and extensive perimeter security upgrades used at Russia's sensitive sites. As a result, the best option is simply to remove the material, the sensible approach being taken by DOE's new program called the Global Threat Reduction Initiative (GTRI).

GTRI's self-professed objective is to reduce and over time eliminate the civilian sector's reliance on HEU.[10] By early 2006, the department was claiming that progress had been made at 45 research reactors by either converting them to more proliferation-resistant fuel or shutting them down.[11] However, the department's credibility again has become subject to scrutiny and skepticism. A January 29, 2007, investigatory article written by Sam Roe of the *Chicago Tribune* concluded that "the U.S. Department of Energy is exaggerating its progress in securing tons of nuclear weapons material spread across the globe."[12] Roe based his judgment on the fact that DOE officials "quit trying to remove bomb fuel from eight reactors that proved to be difficult cases … and other potentially dangerous facilities have never been targeted."[13] One DOE official provided the prototypically bureaucratic defense, acknowledging that the program was "evolving."[14]

DOE's previously successful border monitoring work also suffered severe setbacks despite significant budget increases that by the middle of the decade took the program's funding level to over $100 million. After my departure subordinate managers who had made significant contributions to the program were treated as outcasts. Within the bureaucracy rarely are there "finger-prints" that prove the hostile intent of senior managers against junior manag-ers, but it was highly discouraging when the SLD managers felt compelled to take other jobs outside the department. In the wake of this real but unofficial purge, Baker brought in Bruce Pentola, a favorite of the laboratories, to run the Russian part of the border security work. It foundered. Work slowed and, once again, funding was diverted from critical work in Russia to a series of other projects. When questioned about the diversion of funds from the Russia work by a consultant to Congress, Pentola denied that this had happened, an assertion contradicted by program insiders.

DOE also has had significant personnel problems in the relatively new work it began outside Russia. Its megaports project, to install nuclear detec-tion monitors at overseas ports that ship goods and materials directly to U.S. ports, is a useful addition to previously established work. In early 2007, the two women running the program were so frustrated with the managerial meddling of Baker and Huizenga that they and several other program officers were submitting mass resignations. DOE senior management then proceeded to take its normal approach of keeping that information from circulating in Washington.

The havoc roiling the DOE programs stands in direct contrast to the pro-gress made by DOD's Cooperative Threat Reduction Program (see Table 2.1). Because of its more robust managerial practices and auditing mechanisms, DOD continued to press forward in its nuclear work as well as its parallel work addressing chemical and biological weapons proliferation problems.

Within DOD's Cooperative Threat Reduction Program progress also was being made in the critical areas of securing warheads at warhead storage

TABLE 2.1 A Record of Success

Since its inception, the work carried out in the former Soviet Union by the Depart-ment of Defense has deactivated or destroyed:

- 6,564 nuclear warheads
- 568 intercontinental ballistic missiles (ICBMs)
- 477 ICBM silos
- 17 ICBM missile launchers
- 142 bombers
- 761 nuclear surface-to-air missiles
- 420 submarine missile launchers
- 543 submarine-launched missiles
- 28 nuclear submarines
- 194 nuclear test tunnels

Source: www.ctr.osd.mil

bunkers and enhancing the security of warheads in transit, an area of well-recognized vulnerability. DOD has invested considerable effort in working productively with Russian experts from the twelfth main directorate of the Russian Ministry of Defense, also known as the twelfth GUMO. The relationship has had its high and low points but there has been overall agreement of the priorities and direction for the program's resources. For example, both sides agree that DOD's plans to enhance the security at more than 120 national-level storage bunkers are appropriate and that work was well underway. The importance of these and related efforts is reflected in an FY 2008 budget request from the Bush administration of over $530 million.

As the DOE and DOD threat reduction programs were moving in opposite directions, other parts of the Bush administration were taking aggressive measures to develop new policies to stop or slow the spread of weapons of mass destruction. From its first days in office the administration held deep concerns about the problems posed by countries such as North Korea. Those concerns were reinforced when North Korea conducted a nuclear test in 2003 to go along with a frequently demonstrated and documented policy of willingness to assist the WMD ambitions of other nations. The administration equally was concerned about the ongoing nuclear black market operations established by Pakistani scientist A. Q. Khan and a far-flung network of accomplices. Khan had worked hard to establish himself as a one-stop shopping service for those willing to pay for his expertise and access to nuclear-related equipment. The linkage between these nations, and other nations such as Iran, with its own growing nuclear and missile ambitions, was troubling. Added to this mix after the September 11 attacks was the possibility that nuclear-capable nations might transfer expertise or technology to Islamic fundamentalist groups.

The administration's most visible and tangible response to this evolving threat was the development of a Proliferation Security Initiative (PSI), led by John Bolton, then Undersecretary of State for Arms Control and International Security Affairs. Known for uncompromising assessments of the threats to U.S. national security and ways to respond to them, Bolton can be considered the architect of one of the Bush administration's most creative and successful nonproliferation initiatives.

In one respect the PSI was a multilateral extension of the Clinton administration's focus on stopping the flow of dangerous materials with bilateral assistance programs designed to secure dangerous materials in situ and other programs whose mission was to interdict at border crossings materials that might be smuggled from those facilities. As described by Bolton in remarks in Paris on September 4, 2003, the PSI was designed as a set of activities, not an organization. Reflecting the importance the administration attached to this initiative, President Bush personally announced the plans for multilateral cooperation in interdicting shipments of WMD and related materials in May 2003 in Krakow, Poland. The PSI was seen by the administration as a clear manifestation of the goal of United Nations Security Council Resolution 1540

PROLIFERATION SECURITY INITIATIVE: PRINCIPLES OF INTERDICTION

At the September 2003 meeting of the founding PSI participants in Paris, agreement was reached on a set of principles of interdiction that remain in effect today:[15]

- Nations will undertake effective measures, either alone or in concert with others, for interdicting the transfer or transport of WMD, their delivery systems, and related materials to and from states and non-state actors of proliferation concern.
- Nations will adopt streamlined procedures for rapid exchange of relevant information concerning suspected proliferation activity and protect the confidential character of classified information provided by other nations.
- Nations would review and work to strengthen their relevant national legal authorities where necessary to accomplish these objectives, and work to strengthen when necessary relevant information, international law, and frameworks in appropriate ways to support these commitments.
- Nations would take specific actions in support of interdiction efforts regarding cargoes of WMD, their delivery systems or related materials, to the extent their legal authorities permit and consistent with their obligations under international laws and frameworks.

---

which called for international cooperation against nuclear trafficking. Central to the workings of the PSI was a negotiated set of interdiction principles agreed to by the founding group of cooperating nations that, in addition to the United States, included Australia, France, Germany, Italy, Japan, the Netherlands, Poland, Portugal, Spain, and the United Kingdom. The PSI, as conceived, was about the trafficking of weapons and materials between nations, not within nations. Over time the PSI would be accepted by over seventy nations, a remarkable achievement given that this level of cooperation was reached without any formal treaty or other newly negotiated legal instrument.[16]

It didn't take long for an attempted smuggling case to demonstrate the PSI's practical value and importance. In October 2003, a German-owned ship named the "BBC China" was stopped in the Mediterranean Sea as it sailed from the port of Dubai to Libya.[17] The U.S. intelligence community had received a tip several months earlier and had been trying to track the ship's movement from its point of origin in Malaysia. Convinced that illicit cargo was aboard the ship, and working in cooperation with British intelligence, the ship's whereabouts and suspected cargo were conveyed to German and Italian intelligence authorities. They agreed to divert the ship to Taranto, Italy, where a series of containers was found marked as holding "used machinery."

Refusing to accept the labeling at face value, the Italian authorities discovered quickly that the contents in fact were centrifuge parts whose only purpose would be for enriching uranium. The shipper and intended recipient also fueled the concerns of the intervening authorities and their U.S. counterparts. There was no doubt that the centrifuge parts were provided by Pakistani nuclear arms merchant A. Q. Khan and his coterie of nuclear entrepreneurs. On the receiving end, Libyan President Momar Qaddafi and those responsible for his covert nuclear program had been prepared to receive the shipment, another element in their continuing effort to join the nuclear club.[18]

What happened next proved conclusively what could be achieved with international cooperation against suspected smuggling operations. For many years the U.S. government had been cognizant of some parts of Khan's activities but for various reasons, described later in this book, had often turned a blind eye to them. The realization now was so clear that Khan and his network were an international danger that Pakistan President Musharraf took the first concrete actions to shut down Khan and his network. Recognizing that their nuclear ambitions not only had been exposed but could lead to further and perhaps more drastic actions by the United States (which had recently invaded Iraq) against his regime, Libyan President Qaddafi announced the strategic decision to abandon his nuclear program and chemical weapons programs on December 19, 2003. Qaddafi's pledge included:[19]

- Elimination of all elements of Libya's nuclear and chemical weapons programs
- Disclosure of all nuclear activities to the IAEA
- Allowing international inspections for the purpose of ensuring Libya's complete adherence to the NPT and the Additional Protocol, which gives the IAEA additional access to information and sites within a country for nuclear safeguards purposes.

It is instructive to assess Qaddafi's motives for the strategic decision he took to forgo the development of nuclear weapons. That decision came not long after the U.S. military had defeated the Iraqi army quickly and convincingly. Qaddafi may have been intimidated by American military presence in the region, but he doubtless also was aware of the heavy toll exacted on the Libyan economy, including its greatly reduced oil sales, by two decades of U.S. and U.N. sanctions. His stature in the Arab world was falling as fast as his economy, a rather undesirable outcome for such a pretentious leader. There also are reasons to believe that a range of political and economic incentives, or "carrots" in bureaucratic jargon, may have been proffered the Libyan leader. Whatever Qaddafi's reasoning or motives, the BBC China case provided incontrovertible proof that international cooperation could stop the world's most dangerous weapons from reaching the hands of unstable regimes. But more challenges were on the horizon.

Well into its second term, the Bush administration continued efforts, begun early in its first term, to enhance international cooperation against nuclear proliferation. From 2003 to 2005, DOE's nuclear material security work U.S.-Russia relations had taken some unexpected, and from the administration's perspective negative, turns since George W. Bush came into office, but in July 2006 in St. Petersburg, Russia, Presidents Bush and Putin jointly announced the creation of The Global Initiative to Combat Nuclear Terrorism.[20] The stated purpose of the Global Initiative is to enhance cooperation between and build on the capacity of all willing partner nations to combat nuclear terrorism. Agreed-on elements of that cooperation included efforts to:

- Improve accounting, control, and physical protection of nuclear material and radioactive substances, as well as security of nuclear facilities.
- Detect and suppress illicit trafficking or other illicit activities involving such materials, especially measures to prevent their acquisition and use by terrorists.
- Respond to and mitigate the consequences of acts of nuclear terrorism.
- Ensure cooperation in the development of technical means to combat nuclear terrorism.
- Ensure that law enforcement takes all possible measures to deny safe haven to terrorists seeking to acquire or use nuclear materials.
- Strengthen our respective national legal frameworks to ensure the effective prosecution of, and the certainty of punishment for, terrorists and those who facilitate such acts.

Few could argue with the intent or importance of the announcement. The administration received deservedly high marks for highlighting the importance of the risks of nuclear proliferation and its willingness to work cooperatively with Russia in reducing these dangers. The Global Initiative is intended to build on the activities of the existing threat reduction programs at DOD, DOE, and State. It also underscored the important role the private sector such as university research centers, commercial laboratories, and public utilities can play in protecting the nuclear infrastructure under their direct control. The only problem with the administration's approach, albeit soundly reasoned, was that key elements of the foundation on which it was based were crumbling. DOE's nuclear material security program was badly lagging, the border security program at DOE had largely turned away from its most critical work, and, as we will see in the next chapter, previously successful work on securing radioactive sources had taken a negative turn. This would constitute a continuation of the disturbing pattern of bureaucratic activities (or lack thereof) that was disconnected from presidential priorities and leadership.

Securing Radiological Sources

POORLY SECURED AND widely available radiological sources pose a unique threat to the United States and its allies. Unlike nuclear weapons which inflict mass casualties and destruction through blast, searing heat, and the release of massive amounts of radiation, a radiological dispersal device (RDD) or "dirty bomb" in common parlance doesn't trigger a nuclear explosion but uses conventional explosives to disperse small, perhaps vial-size amounts of radioactive material that are attached or placed next to the explosive. Relying on wind patterns to spread the radioactivity, an RDD would be used by terrorists to sow panic in the populace where it was detonated while also inflicting substantial economic costs. For these reasons an RDD is often referred to as a weapon of mass disruption (WMD) but that appellation does not adequately reflect the magnitude of the threat.

An accident in Goiania, Brazil, in 1987 provided a glimpse of the disruptive effects of the inadvertent spread of even small amounts of radiation. A group of Brazilian metal scavengers sold remnants of some scrap materials containing cesium-137 to relatives and friends. This act of "friendship" resulted in four deaths and the hospitalization of twenty Brazilians. The consequences of this seemingly inconsequential act didn't stop there but rather triggered far greater consequences. About 112,000 people had to be monitored for exposure to radiation and the extensive cleanup took six months to complete.[1]

The first and only documented, threatened use of a radiological weapon came in November 1995 in Moscow when a group of Chechen rebels, part of the movement within Chechnya seeking independence from Russia, hid a crude dirty bomb containing cesium as the radioactive source in a Moscow park. The group deliberately didn't explode the weapon but contacted a Russian national television station, detailing what they had done, presumably as a demonstration of their capabilities.[2]

Islamic fundamentalists also were expressing interest in dirty bombs. Osama bin Laden in late 2001 spoke of his desire to impose economic hardship on America, saying that "America is in retreat by the grace of God Almighty and economic attrition is continuing up to today. But it needs further blows. The young men need to seek out nodes of the American economy and strike the enemy's nodes." Was bin Laden thinking of dirty bombs as one means of achieving his objective?[3]

Al Qaeda operatives long have appreciated the utility of radioactive sources as a means of attacking Western targets. Abu Khabad, the al Qaeda chief responsible for developing or acquiring WMD, addressed this issue in a letter recovered in Afghanistan in late 2001 after the fall of the Taliban. "As you instructed, you will find a summary of the discharges from a nuclear reactor, amongst which are radioactive elements that could be used for military ends. One could use them to contaminate an area."[4]

Unlike highly enriched uranium and plutonium that, although poorly secured in some countries, are under the control of dedicated governmental facilities and laboratories, radiological sources are used for myriad and common industrial, agricultural, and medical applications in almost every country. There also are thousands of radiological sources of various types. For example, in radiotherapy,

> radioactive sources containing large amounts of radioactive materials are commonly used. Radioactive sources are even more abundant in industry … used worldwide for purposes of industrial radiography, particularly in countries with large oil and gas piping installations.... Often unneeded radioactive sources are simply discarded and thus they became abandoned and orphaned of any control.[5]

The good news, if it can be so described, is that every radioactive source is not suitable for use as a dirty bomb. There is a small subset of perhaps forty radioactive sources identified by scientists as having the requisite and most desirable properties and characteristics for weaponization or utility in making a dirty bomb. As described in various publications, the sources at the top of that list are:[6]

- Americium-241
- Californium-252
- Cesium-137
- Cobalt-60
- Iridium-192
- Plutonium-238
- Polonium-210
- Radium-226
- Strontium-90

In the wake of the September 11, 2001, attacks, Congress appropriated $20 million through the Emergency Wartime Supplemental Appropriations Act. Supplemental funding is provided outside the annual budget cycle and has been used frequently to support, inter alia, the war in Iraq and counterterrorist initiatives. Congress authorized DOE to develop a new program, placed under my authority, to "protect, control and account for radiological dispersal device materials."[7] Congressional staffers informed me that this first international radiological security program set up by the U.S. government reflected recognition of the progress being made by my program's ongoing efforts to secure nuclear materials. I viewed this unexpected funding (no DOE or administration official had requested the funding) as an opportunity to establish from the start a program whose inner workings perhaps wouldn't be so heavily burdened with the usual DOE bureaucratic baggage that had slowed other threat reduction programs. Fortunately, the problems the Material Protection, Control, and Accounting (MPC&A) and Second Line of Defense (SLD) programs were having with Baker did not spill over into the new radiological security work, possibly because he understood that Congress wanted the new initiative to get off to a fast start.

Creating a new federal program is time-consuming, both in terms of identifying and assembling the best personnel for the job as well as establishing a set of managerial guidelines to ensure the money would be well spent and properly managed. These requirements at first blush might appear at odds with the sense of urgency inherent in the new mission, but in my judgment there was no alternative but to infuse this effort from the start not only with the priority it merited but also the proper managerial oversight. I was fortunate in at least one respect. The managerial practices I had inherited on my arrival at DOE had been revamped considerably with the extensive assistance of my talented deputy, Ken Sheely. We had already begun using these revamped practices, which focused on accountability and metrics or measures of success, widely in the MPC&A program, and were confident they could be suitably applied to the new radiological security program as well.

I turned to Pat Cahalane, one of the program's most technically competent as well as most trusted managers, to assume direct responsibility for establishing the program and moving it forward quickly. Cahalane's recognized scientific skills along with his no-nonsense style already were well respected by his Russian counterparts at the Ministry of Atomic Energy whose cooperation we would need to set our plans in motion. Out of courtesy I then contacted senior State Department officials, including Undersecretary of State John Bolton, who offered the State Department's political support for the funding we had received. This was something that all DOE programs had learned they could not take for granted. Through the years there had been a series of incidents in which a few mid-level State Department officers had sought to impede (as some at DOE would describe it) the programmatic work of various DOE and Department of Defense (DOD) programs. Most of the bureaucratic problems arose when State Department officers didn't understand or agree with a particular program's priorities or approach. This was not a trivial matter if only because State Department officers could, and from time to time did, deny travel requests for some DOE and (less frequently) DOD personnel carrying out threat reduction program work in Russia. These delays cost the programs time and money and did little to build trust on the part of the Russian hosts. This caused an inevitable amount of friction within the U.S. interagency and some at DOE believed that State abused its prerogatives at times. No one at DOE was willing to take on the problem directly, another reflection of its weakened status in the interagency. Having seen past bureaucratic clashes play out at various times from my previous job at the NSC, I endeavored to work with State Department counterparts from the early days of the radiological security program to ensure they understood the program's activities and the purpose behind them. That approach almost always paid dividends for the program. In my experience the State Department was unstinting in its support for our programmatic efforts, as it was for the MPC&A and SLD work.

Prior to any approach we would make to our international partners, Cahalane, Sheely, and I agreed that it would be useful to have in place an unclassified assessment of the economic consequences of a dirty bomb attack. I believed it was essential to undertake this work in the most responsible and sober-minded way possible. In the wake of the September 11 attacks there had been an inevitable flood of media reports regarding various terrorist plots and potential attack scenarios that ranged from the possible and realistic to the fantastic. Because my program had been entrusted with a considerable amount of funding and was venturing into uncharted waters, I wanted to ensure we understood the problem before laying out a strategic approach to it.

To accomplish this objective I funded an unclassified study by a group of economists associated with one of the leading private consulting firms in the Washington, DC, area. I asked the economists to calculate the financial consequences of a radiological attack involving the explosion by conventional means of a vial-size amount of cesium, a powdery substance that is easily dispersed by the wind. The five attack scenarios were:

1. Washington, DC, near the Mall
2. New York City near Wall Street
3. The I-95 transportation corridor near Newark airport, a corridor that thousands of vehicles use daily
4. The port of Long Beach–Los Angeles, the West Coast hub for international transit and commerce
5. The San Joaquin Valley, one of America's most important agricultural areas.

To isolate the study from charges that the program was pursuing any type of political agenda or "hyping the threat," a small group of senior, highly accomplished consultants was assembled from both sides of the political spectrum to review the results with the economists and me. This group included former Chairman of the Joint Chiefs of Staff and Ambassador to the United Kingdom William Crowe; Susan Eisenhower, who directs the Eisenhower Institute, had been part of the Baker-Cutler study group, and had a great deal of experience working with the Russian government; and Leon Fuerth, former national security adviser to Vice President Al Gore.

The study results were sobering. In each of the scenarios presented to the economists, their estimate was that the financial loss resulting from these attacks would easily run into the low tens of billions of dollars. By way of comparison, the economists described how some of the major hurricanes that hit the United States East Coast in the 1990s had resulted in financial damage reaching that same level. Those figures reflected loss of tourism dollars in cities like Washington and New York as well as the widespread disruption to commerce and small businesses. However, the economists conceded that their estimates could not even begin to calculate the cost of cleanup for any of the study scenarios.

John Sudnik, Deputy Chief of the New York Fire Department, in 2006 completed his own assessment of the consequences of an RDD attack that contaminated forty city blocks in Manhattan. He reached many of the same conclusions as those of the DOE study, emphasizing the staggering economic impact in the "financial capital of the world" as major brokerage houses and investment banks likely would be forced to move elsewhere, taking with them thousands of jobs and inevitably collapsing real estate prices for an indefinite period of time. As one of New York City's leading "first responders," Sudnik also underscored the unpredictable consequences if widespread panic were to occur as well as the potential that contaminated buildings might have to be razed, adding to the enormous financial toll a possible requirement for a massive rebuilding program. For Sudnik, any description of an RDD event as simply mass "disruption" badly understates the consequences of such an event.[8]

Just as sobering was the recognition that the terrorist attacks assessed by the economists almost certainly could have been carried out at low cost, perhaps as low as a few tens of thousands of dollars. Those expenses are primarily related to the cost of procuring the conventional explosives, the small amount of source material, and the associated materials in which the weapon might be placed. From the hard experiences learned from various terrorist attacks carried out since September 2001, it is now well understood that imposing financial pain is an attractive and even priority objective for Islamic fundamentalists. The attack on New York's World Trade Center—one of America's most prominent business centers—made that point with unmistakable clarity. That attack cost al Qaeda, by U.S. government estimates, about $400,000 to $500,000, a paltry sum compared to the financial loss and psychological pain imposed on New York City and America.[9]

Similarly, the asymmetrical nature of the financial aspect of terrorism, whereby substantial political gains can be realized from the expenditure of limited funds, also has played out in Europe. The cost of the March 2004 Madrid train bombing is estimated by U.S. experts to have been about $50,000.[10] The July 2005 attacks on public transportation in London probably were carried out for about the same amount. Given this track record of gaining huge returns from modest investments, it is readily apparent how radiological attacks would hold special appeal to Islamic fundamentalists seeking to impose financial pain on the West.

With the U.S. programmatic elements in place, a strategy had to be devised to ensure that securing radiological sources would not encounter obstacles overseas. Given the congressional mandate which stipulated that our program should begin in Russia and other parts of the former Soviet Union, wholly appropriate guidance given the vast quantity of poorly protected sources there, the cooperation of Russian authorities was essential. Moreover, because my long-term plan was to use our bilateral cooperation as a model for anticipated future cooperation with other countries, I deemed it essential also to solicit the advice and support of the International Atomic Energy Agency (IAEA). I long had viewed the IAEA as a somewhat underappreciated organization by some U.S. government officials but under the steady leadership of Mohammed el Baradei it has assumed an important role in various nonproliferation issues, including its inspections of Iranian nuclear facilities. Some American officials have been frustrated through the years by el Baradei's approach which emphasizes the slow gathering of evidence and a refusal to rush to judgment. From my perspective the IAEA actually serves U.S. interests best when it is seen as taking an even-handed rather than pro-American approach to proliferation matters. The IAEA's receipt of the 2005 Nobel Peace Prize was richly deserved.

The IAEA had been a leader in calling attention to the problems posed by radioactive sources since the early 1990s when it published for its member states the not-so-eloquently titled "The International Basic Safety Standards for Protection Against Ionizing Radiation and for the Safety of Radiation Sources," or BSS.[11] The BSS, inter alia, requires that radioactive sources be kept secure as to prevent theft or damage. The IAEA also played a leading role in 1998 when it joined with the European Commission, the International Criminal Police Organization (Interpol) and the World Customs Organization (WCO) at a large international conference in Dijon, France. The result was the subsequent adoption of an International Action Plan to strengthen the global security of radioactive sources.[12] The Dijon conference was followed by another gathering in December 2000 in Buenos Aires, Argentina, that resulted in additional strengthening of the original International Action Plan. In these actions the role of international organizations has been put on display. For example, within Interpol heightened awareness of the RDD problem has resulted in greater cooperation with the IAEA and World Customs Organization in information sharing as well as improved in-house training in detecting the smuggling of radioactive materials. New patterns of international cooperation can be achieved by existing organizations and in doing so contribute to reducing America's vulnerabilities.

In Washington, DOE's efforts to secure radiological sources benefited enormously from the positive responses received from both the Russian

government and the IAEA. In Moscow, the Ministry of Atomic Energy officially accepted the proposed U.S. initiative and assigned two senior staff
members, Nikolai Agapov and Mikhail Ryzhov to represent their interests. I
had not met Agapov prior to this project but Ryzhov was very well known to
me as one of the senior Russians who met with the U.S. delegation, of which
I was the White House representative, on negotiations centered on Iran's nuclear and missile programs discussed in a future chapter. Ryzhov spoke
impeccable English, occasionally correcting mistakes or linguistic nuances
missed by the official Russian interpreter. As I had seen from our previous
encounters, he also could be a most relentless negotiator, seldom giving
ground on any point of contention. However, Ryzhov also had the seniority
and confidence to take action or make things happen in a system that by nature and habit often frowned on personal initiative. I knew that if Ryzhov
made a commitment to this work that the Russian side would honor those
commitments.

Within the IAEA, Dr. Abel Gonzalez was the senior official tracking radiological security problems and the leader of existing international efforts to
address the radioactive source problem. Gonzalez was not only highly dedicated but also one of the world's foremost experts on radioactive sources,
having spent years working on this problem long before it took on a new
prominence in an age of terrorist threats to the security of those sources. In
addition to his considerable substantive expertise, Gonzalez was a highly sophisticated international public servant adept at dealing with officials from the
IAEA's many member states. Given decades of nationalistic rivalry, and at
times enmity, it would hardly have been surprising if U.S.-Russian negotiations on a new and highly sensitive area would be protracted. I wanted to
avoid that at all costs and was very pleased to have Gonzalez as a potential
ally committed to forging an agreement.

As events unfolded, Gonzalez's formidable diplomatic skills were seldom
required. Over several days in Vienna in 2002 Gonzalez hosted a series of
meetings between me and my Russian counterparts. From the start it was
apparent that the Russian government was committed to moving quickly toward an agreement. Ryzhov and Agapov spoke passionately of the threat
posed by unsecured sources not only in Russia but in other parts of the former
Soviet Union such as Moldova and Georgia. For example, within Russia my
interlocutors acknowledged that there are about sixteen large regional storage
sites, called Radon sites, scattered around that vast nation serving as reposito-
ries for radioactive sources discarded or no longer in use. There are about
another 16 Radon sites in various countries on Russia's periphery that were
part of the former Soviet system. The Radon sites had never been deemed a
significant or even worrisome security concern during the Soviet era because
those sites were not used to store highly enriched uranium or plutonium, the
materials for making nuclear devices. Moreover, during Soviet rule, borders
were deemed secure and any external threat to the sites was rightly judged to

be highly remote. Consequently, physical security at Radon sites often was minimal or almost nonexistent. In addition, representatives of the Russian regulatory authority known as Rostekhnadzor, the counterpart to the U.S. Nuclear Regulatory Commission, told me that there were about 2,100 entities within Russia licensed to use various types of radioactive sources.[13] The regulators' concern was that many of these private entities had become lax in reporting to governmental authorities changes to their inventory of radiological sources.

The Russian negotiators were sufficiently astute to recognize that changing political conditions resulted in a changing threat environment. For them the conflict in Chechnya in which a small but fierce group of people in Southern Russia had struggled for years to break free of Moscow's control was particularly troubling. Politically, both the Clinton and Bush administrations had criticized what they assessed to be the Russian government's heavy-handed tactics to put down the unrest. For its part, the Russian government had rebuffed both administrations, reminding Washington that the Chechens were aided by various Islamic fundamentalist factions. Setting aside these political disputes, what agitated the Russian negotiators was that the Grozny, Chechnya Radon regional storage site had been looted in 2001 by Chechen rebel (something I was told by my counterparts).[14] The Russians never disclosed how much or what type of materials had been removed illicitly, but the materials apparently were never recovered. It also is unknown if those materials were sold or otherwise transferred to other terrorist groups.

After two days of negotiations, agreement was reached in late 2002 on a United States-Russia-IAEA Tripartite Agreement to begin a cooperative program of radiological security within Russia. The agreement called for the development of an inventory of sources of concern and their location as well as locating and taking appropriate steps to recover and provide for their physical security. In addition to the resources that I would commit to security upgrades there, the Russians and IAEA offered to use their good offices to encourage other countries in the region also to work cooperatively with us in securing other at-risk sources.

Buoyed by this success, I wanted to move as quickly as possible to demonstrate tangible results. Throughout the Clinton and Bush administrations, many cooperative programs had been undertaken with the Russian government. Some of those had badly failed to meet the expectations each side had established. In some cases Russian intransigence reflected in the setting of nearly impossible conditions for working there undermined U.S. programmatic efforts. In other cases, what can only be described as heavy-handed, condescending, or overly demanding U.S. approaches had soured the Russians on working with the United States. Recognizing these pitfalls, I directed Pat Cahalane, who was managing the program's initial phases under my guidance, to work closely with me to ensure that we avoided these all-too-common pitfalls and use the money given us by Congress to achieve demonstrable results.

In this respect, the program's most pressing challenge, along with managing the politics of the cooperative effort, was establishing the priorities for those efforts. Once we came to fully understand through our subsequent bilateral conversations with Russian officials the daunting scope of the problem, within and around that massive country, we realized that the initial resources provided us by Congress would make only a minimal down payment in addressing the extant radiological security challenges. We began with security upgrades at the very large Radon site outside Moscow, applying many of the same principles and approaches used in our MPC&A security upgrades work. As recounted in a 2006 report by the National Research Council, "DOE has made a very good start in working with Russian organizations to upgrade security of radioactive sources."[15]

In addition to work we planned to commence at Moscow and several other Radon sites, Russian officials confided their concerns regarding radiothermoelectric generators, or RTGs. Powered by strontium-90, which we knew was high on the list of desirable "candidate" material for a dirty bomb, RTGs were used as navigational beacons to guide aircraft flying in remote areas. During a preliminary visit to Moscow, Ryzhov informed Pat Cahalane, Sergei Tsivunin, the best interpreter I ever worked with, and me that in the Soviet era about 1,000 RTGs had been produced and deployed across Russia. Ryzhov acknowledged that many of them—perhaps several hundred—had not been located. In several instances other RTGs had been found but on examination there were clear indications they had been tampered with, probably by unsuspecting individuals unaware of the considerable danger in carelessly handling such lethal material. The program agreed to use funding to support efforts to secure those sources. By the time of my departure from program management in late 2002, the radiological security work was well underway, enjoying a high level of cooperation from our international partners.

In late 2006, a variant of the radiological threat may have surfaced in the wake of the poisoning and death of Alexander Litvinenko, a former Russian intelligence officer who left Russia for London and turned into one of Russian President Putin's most vocal critics. Notwithstanding the political turmoil caused by the death on British soil of a Russian national that may or may not have had the approval of Russian authorities, the nature of the assassination—polonium-210 apparently slipped into Litvinenko's tea—underscored that there is much Western experts don't fully appreciate about how radioactive sources can be used in terrorist scenarios. According to Dr. Peter Zimmerman, a highly respected and experienced scientist, much of the focus of experts such as those at DOE has been on gamma emitters such as the cobalt and strontium sources described above. Those threats have not abated. However, Zimmerman argues that in addition to those threats, alpha emitters such as polonium-210, a soft, silvery-gray metal that is produced in reactors by irradiating bismuth-209, is extraordinarily toxic if swallowed or ingested, could become effective weapons in the hands of dedicated terrorists. Zimmerman points out, as is the case with other radioactive sources, that polonium is commonly found in everyday use. He cites polonium as being "used by industry in devices that eliminate static electricity, in low-powered brushes used to ionize the air next to photographic film … in quite large machines in a textile mill … and to control dust in clean rooms where computer chips and hard drives are made."[16]

How might an attack be carried out using alpha emitters such as polonium? Zimmerman acknowledges that because alpha emitters only pose a significant health threat if they are inhaled or ingested—something Litvinenko did albeit inadvertently—the challenge for a terrorist group is to devise the means to burn, pulverize, or blow up the material so that the would-be victims were unaware of the dangers harbored in being exposed to and breathing such materials.[17] Its toxicity—one microgram or millionth of a gram—can be fatal. Nonetheless, under proper conditions, such as placing it in a sealed capsule of metal or glass, the material can be handled safely until put to use against an unsuspecting individual or group. Extensive media coverage of the poisoning fueled speculation that Russian authorities knew or condoned the assassination because of Litvinenko's outspoken criticism of Russian policies. As of early 2007 no substantive proof had been made available to the public to support that theory. It is well understood that the Russian nuclear weapons plant at Avangard produces more polonium than any other site in the world, but officials there maintain that security standards are rigid.[18] Moreover, the IAEA reports that prior to 2006 there had been some fifteen documented cases of polonium theft, most in the United States. Given the widespread use of polonium, it may be impossible for law enforcement authorities in the United Kingdom or Russia to identify definitively the source of the polonium.

One indication of the mounting concern about polonium came in January 2007 when British authorities acknowledged that they were working with officials in forty-eight nations, including the United States, to assess if those who had been in London around the time of Litvinenko's poisoning had suffered any exposure to polonium.[19] Traces of polonium had been found at seventeen locations and the Health Protection Agency in the United Kingdom stated that about 103 people had probable contact with polonium through such means as sitting near Litvinenko but that those exposed in that way were at low risk of suffering serious health effects. Nonetheless, it is illustrative of the nature of this problem that even minute traces of a radioactive substance can generate the expenditure of time and resources required to solicit the public health agencies of forty-eight nations.[20]

As is the case with other types of potential radioactive attacks, it is virtually impossible to handicap or estimate the chances of this material being used in a terrorist attack. What the evidence suggests is that the relative ease of carrying out such attacks assuming the material is handled properly, the availability of the materials to do so, and the frightening consequences of a successful attack underscore the importance of taking aggressive measures to reduce the risk. For Zimmerman the solution lies in tightening regulations such as those under the purview of the U.S. Nuclear Regulatory Commission. Although some loose controls existed on such materials, as of early 2007 the Commission was considering but had not passed a tighter set of regulations that would make it far more difficult for such materials to be diverted or stolen by the registering or licensing "of any person or company seeking to purchase alpha sources stronger than one millicurie, about a third of a lethal dose."[21] Zimmerman's assessment and diagnosis is persuasive and his long-term recommendation that concerted effort must be made to greatly reduce the common use of polonium deserves the strongest consideration.

According to the Government Accountability Office (GAO), the investigatory arm of Congress, DOE's efforts over the past several years to secure radiological sources has moved in the same negative direction as has its nuclear material security work in Russia.[22] In a blistering report drafted in January 2007 and released in March 2007, the GAO said that security has been improved on hundreds of sites containing radioactive material but that "many of the highest risk and most dangerous sources still remained unsecured."[23] The report went on to catalogue a number of significant shortfalls in DOE's recent programmatic efforts:

- DOE has failed to secure hundreds of large devices known as RTGs, which remain operational or abandoned in Russia. Each of these devices has activity levels ranging from 25,000 to 250,000 curies of strontium-90, similar to the amount of strontium-90 released from the explosion at the Chrernobyl reactor in 1986. I had committed to Ryzhov and Agapov in 2002 that DOE funds would be made available for securing RTGs.
- DOE has largely ignored sixteen of the twenty radiological waste sites (the regional Radon facilities) in its security upgrade work, the central focus of the program's initial efforts in 2002 to 2003.
- DOE has not developed a plan to ensure that countries receiving security upgrades will be able to sustain them over the long term.
- Every country receiving DOE assistance has identified transportation of high-risk radioactive sources as the most vulnerable part of the radiological supply chain and DOE has done little or nothing to address this. Parenthetically, transportation security has been a feature of DOE's nuclear material security work since at least 2000.
- Security manuals and procedures for newly installed equipment are provided in English, instead of the native language.
- There have been some improvements in DOE's cooperation with other agencies but it still does not provide information needed to the IAEA or State Department. It also refused to send to the Nuclear Regulatory Commission in fiscal year 2004 $5 million as directed by the Senate Appropriations Committee for NRC work on domestic radiological security issues.

As another example of DOE's recent failures to carry out its congressionally-mandated mission, the GAO report is troubling, highlighting again the risk to U.S. security arising from poor program management. How will Congress or the administration react to the GAO report? From another and perhaps broader perspective, the current failings of the radioactive security program represent another example of a broader pattern of DOE managers committing resources to the easiest parts of a problem, doubtless as a way to pad the numbers to make the case to Congress and the public that they are making more progress than actually is the case. The GAO report also underscores the galactic chasm between the presidential and congressional priorities in this area and the scope of the radiological security threat on the one hand and the lagging work being carried out by the part of the bureaucracy charged with reducing it on the other hand.

PART TWO

Proliferation Case Studies

Pakistan

THROUGH THE PRISM of past U.S. policymakers, Pakistan has been viewed as an important ally, both for its willingness to allow the Central Intelligence Agency (CIA) in the 1950s to deploy on its territory listening posts to monitor Soviet missile activities and because of its strategic location as a check against the Soviet Union's aspirations for direct access to the Arabian Sea. In more recent times, Pakistan has presented U.S. policymakers a vexing set of policy challenges. That strategic location, bordering India, Iran, and Afghanistan, places Pakistan in the center of one of the world's most politically fragile areas. Pakistan also is a Muslim nation in possession of an estimated fifty nuclear weapons. Its Western educated president, Pervez Musharraf, is a military officer who refuses to relinquish either his military status or political power while at the same time narrowly escaping at least two assassination attempts. Musharraf's security establishment, particularly the Inter-Services Intelligence Agency (ISI), harbors an unknown number of senior officials with barely concealed sympathies for al Qaeda and the Taliban has operated for years with near impunity on Pakistani soil.

Every U.S. president in the nuclear age has had a declaratory policy of portraying in stark terms the threat to U.S. national security posed by nuclear proliferation. President John Kennedy, for example, spoke in 1963 of the possibility that within a decade the world would have in its midst fifteen to twenty nuclear powers.[1] Pronouncements by subsequent presidents echoed similar themes although some held radically differing views in private. Available to them has been a wide array of policy options—bilateral and multilateral diplomacy, economic sanctions, and military action—that could be applied to slow or stop those seeking to acquire or develop nuclear capabilities. A close examination of the more than thirty-year record of U.S. engagement with Pakistan reveals that those policy options were seldom applied aggressively or consistently, despite convincing evidence of Pakistan's lengthy quest to become a nuclear power. The record shows that both Democratic and Republican presidents almost always chose other and often short-term policy objectives over its long-term nonproliferation goals in formulating its policies with Pakistan.

To assemble a clear picture of these dynamics it is necessary to turn back the clock to 1972 and the start of the Pakistani nuclear program under Zulfiqar Ali Bhutto, Minister for Fuel, Power, and Natural Resources who would later become president and prime minister. At a meeting of high level military and civilian bureaucrats in Multan on January 20, 1972, there was great acclaim from his audience when Bhutto disclosed his intention to launch a nuclear weapons program.[2] Pakistani relations with India, tense and contentious during the best of times, had ebbed following the 1971 loss of East Pakistan in the war with India. For Pakistan, the inescapable truth was that not only was India superior in conventional military capabilities but India's 1974 nuclear weapons test—which received only a mild rebuke from Washington when the Indian government claimed it was a peaceful demonstration—showed that India was developing strategic capabilities unmatched by Pakistan. For Pakistan, nuclear weapons would have to be the equalizer in a strategic balance tilting heavily in India's favor. From this perspective, Bhutto's decision in 1972 appeared unquestionably logical. Reflecting back on the period, no less an authority than President Pervez Musharraf in his 2006 memoirs described his feelings about that period. Musharraf writes of India's "grandiose ambitions of projecting its power regionally and even globally."[3] He proceeds to claim that "we needed to defend ourselves against the Indian threat. India's intentions were offensive; ours were defensive. The world relentlessly pressed us to desist without pressing India. I always considered it unjust."[4]

For Pakistan, the policy conundrum was how to quickly realize the ambitions reflected in the strategic decision to develop an adequate and recognized riposte to India's looming nuclear capability. A critical part of the answer would be supplied by Dr. Abdul Qadeer Khan, a metallurgist who was born in Bhopal, India in 1936. Khan fled to Pakistan in 1952, receiving an undergraduate degree in science in Karachi and proceeding soon thereafter to Europe to study in Germany, the Netherlands, and finally, Belgium where he completed his doctoral degree from the Catholic University of Louven in 1972.[5] There was nothing particularly remarkable about Khan's training or skills with one exception. Through the recommendation of one of his former professors, Khan secured a job at URENCO, an international consortium of British, German, and Dutch companies. Located in the Netherlands, URENCO at that time was "at the forefront of Europe's attempts to develop the latest, most advanced centrifuge technology for nuclear fuel."[6] Despite the sensitivity of the work on centrifuges, Khan learned quickly that URENCO's existing security procedures posed little obstacle to his gaining access to information to which he wasn't formally entitled, including direct access to the secret centrifuge plant.

Sloppy security procedures at such facilities are always a source of proliferation concern, but Khan's ambitions would demonstrate the extraordinary damage to the cause of nuclear nonproliferation caused by such laxness. There is no indication that Khan set out from the start of his employment at URENCO to divert the expansive nuclear expertise that surrounded him, which included classified designs, drawings, and specifications for the new centrifuge. Rather, he seems to have chosen a path of purloining sensitive technologies for Pakistan's fledging and covert nuclear program out of a sense of national patriotism borne of anger over Pakistan's humiliating 1971 military defeat at the hands of India. In September 1974 Khan wrote to Prime Minister Bhutto, offering his access to the sensitive technologies at URENCO as well as personal insights and recommendations regarding the most effective path for Pakistan to advance its nuclear ambitions.[7] What Khan might have believed began as a bold and patriotic effort to serve Pakistan over time would evolve into an unprecedented global black market for nuclear technologies.

Khan's offer was accepted without question and he went to work quickly; his spying on Pakistan's behalf continued unabated through most of 1975. Khan's boldness turned into arrogance and recklessness, but by the time suspicions about his activities grew into genuine alarm among some of his colleagues, much of Khan's initial work had been completed. As recounted by one assessment of the scope of Khan's efforts, "he stole the designs for almost every centrifuge on the drawing board."[8]

Sensing that his activities were about to be exposed, Khan fled to Pakistan in late 1975. His apparently genuine sense of patriotism, combined with a genuine hatred for the West, was accompanied by equally fierce personal ambition. Once back home he clashed with established Pakistani scientists but, through a mixture of craftiness and bluster—such as claiming that Pakistan's enrichment efforts needed to be accelerated and only he could do so— Khan persuaded Prime Minister Bhutto by mid-1976 to open the Engineering Research Laboratory at Kahuta, near Islamabad. The facility later was renamed the Khan Research Laboratory (KRL) as a testament to the contributions Khan and the lab were making to Pakistan's nuclear program. Of course, Khan was put in charge of the laboratory that almost from its inception operated independently of the Pakistan Atomic Energy Commission (PAEC), leading to recurring friction between the two organizations.[9]

Khan's considerable and mostly illegally acquired technical and scientific knowledge of uranium enrichment was not the only stimulus for Pakistan's nascent nuclear program. Substantial resources are required for the full scale research, development, and design of a nuclear weapons program. As a poor country, Prime Minister Bhutto knew that Pakistan would struggle under the financial weight of supporting such an effort. Bhutto seems to have harbored no illusions about the purpose of Pakistan's efforts; India's growing conventional capabilities and newly demonstrated nuclear capabilities were his immediate concerns. Nonetheless, Bhutto was not indifferent to the political and financial benefits accruing to Pakistan as others in the Muslim world clamored to support and share in the prestige of any Arab nation working to develop an "Islamic bomb." He exploited both the anger in the Arab world over Israel's victory in the

URANIUM, CENTRIFUGES, AND NUCLEAR WEAPONS

Enriched uranium is one path to making a nuclear weapon but doing so requires a multistep process as well as specialized knowledge and equally specialized equipment. The steps in the process include:[10]

- Mined uranium ore is bathed in sulfuric acid to leach out pure uranium.
- Dried uranium is filtered and becomes the powdery substance yellowcake.
- The yellowcake is exposed to fluorine gas and heated to 133 degrees F, converting it into a gas called uranium hexafluoride.
- The uranium hexafluoride is pumped into a centrifuge that spins at the speed of sound. As it does so the heavier uranium-238 moves toward the outside of the centrifuge while the lighter isotope uranium-235 collects closer to the center. This is the highly fissionable isotope.
- The slightly enriched uranium-235 is then fed into another centrifuge for additional enrichment. The process continues as each centrifuge adds only a small amount of enrichment to the uranium. At least 1,500 or more centrifuges would have to be involved in any effort to enrich the uranium to levels of proliferation concern. Uranium enriched to 20 percent is considered highly enriched and this level is much higher than the 3 percent to 5 percent enrichment level found in nuclear reactor fuel. At about 90 percent enrichment the uranium is considered weapons grade. Linking the requisite large numbers centrifuges together in "cascades" is probably the most technically demanding part of the entire process.
- The uranium still has to be fabricated into a nuclear weapon which requires the uranium to be converted into uranium oxide, a powdery substance which then can be molded into a weapon.

1973 war with Egypt and the growing wealth of the Arab states in the Persian Gulf stemming from the rising oil prices for Pakistan's financial interests. Saudi Arabia, the most prominent beneficiary of the new oil wealth, began a program of sustained financial support to Pakistan as did Libya's new leader, Colonel Qaddafi.[11]

On the technical front, Khan's theft of the URENCO uranium enrichment designs was not the only boost to Pakistan's program. Of equal or perhaps even greater importance was the considerable expertise provided by the People's Republic of China. Embracing the adage that "the enemy of my enemy is my friend," Chinese relations with Pakistan had blossomed over the past decade, doubtless in part because they served as a useful counterbalance to China's troubled relations with India. China had become a major supplier of conventional arms to Pakistan and, given the confluence of strategic interests, it wasn't surprising that China would become the most important external source of scientific and technical expertise to the Pakistani nuclear program.

It also wasn't surprising that Pakistan's nuclear aspirations and its willingness to turn to external assistance to develop them would pique the interest of the CIA. The U.S. intelligence community's growing curiosity coincided with a similar interest in nonproliferation from the Carter administration that took office in January 1977. India's successful nuclear test in 1974 had shown that mastering the awesome power of nuclear energy was not a capability reserved only for the rich or technically advanced nations. What had been at the end of the 1960s a rather exclusive club of nuclear states appeared to be on the verge of undergoing rapid and undesirable expansion not only because of the aspirations of India and Pakistan but also the growing availability of the expertise and materials needed to advance those programs.

What ensued over the next several years, and continues largely unabated to the present, was a deadly cat-and-mouse game in which nations such as Pakistan and later North Korea, Libya, and Iran would seek to acquire nuclear weapons. Concurrently, various nations, acting unilaterally as well as in concert with the international community through such mechanisms as the Nonproliferation Treaty (NPT) that was agreed to in 1968 and entered into force in 1970 obligating its nuclear signatories to refrain from transferring nuclear weapons or other nuclear devices to nonweapons states, worked to impede those programs. Pakistan and India have not become signatories to the NPT.[12]

Unlike the Nixon administration's (at best) ambivalence to the dangers of nuclear proliferation, Presidents Gerald Ford and Jimmy Carter evinced considerable unease with Pakistan's nuclear aspirations. A January 30, 1976, State Department Memorandum, for example, assessed that Pakistan had "undertaken a crash program to develop nuclear weapons."[13] Carter applied his

---

ONE U.S. ADMINISTRATION'S DISDAIN FOR THE NONPROLIFERATION TREATY

Like all U.S. presidents in the nuclear age, President Richard Nixon's declaratory policy was to highlight the dangers of the spread of nuclear weapons. The NPT, despite its limitations, was a significant step in that direction. In February 1969 Nixon formally asked the Senate to take up the NPT for ratification and at a news conference stated that he would "make it clear that I believe that ratification of the treaty by all governments, nuclear and nonnuclear, is in the interest of peace and in the interest of reducing the possibility of nuclear proliferation." However, the Nixon administration in its internal discussions apparently judged that other foreign policy objectives with nations of proliferation concern took a higher priority than nonproliferation. The result was the simultaneous issuing of the classified National Security Decision Memorandum 6 which stated, "there should be no efforts by the United States government to pressure other nations to follow suit. The government, in its public posture, should reflect a tone of optimism ... while clearly disassociating itself from any plan to bring pressure on these countries...."[14]

moralistic vision to this issue shortly after settling into the White House. One of the first manifestations of the revised U.S. policy occurred when its suspicions regarding Pakistan's intentions stirred the Carter administration into a series of actions. Joseph Nye, an academic who had joined the Carter administration as a nonproliferation expert serving in the State Department, was dispatched to discuss with French counterparts its growing interest in becoming a major supplier of nuclear technologies in the wake of the Carter administration's desire to reduce the activities of U.S. firms in this area. Nye claims to have received French willingness to close off the nuclear tap at least to Pakistan.[15] Some economic sanctions, especially the April 1979 decision to cut off U.S. assistance to Pakistan under Section 669 of the Foreign Assistance Act of 1961, also were imposed, but the effect on Islamabad was minimal. Of potentially greater consequence for U.S. policy occurred when Secretary of State Warren Christopher directed Nye to prepare a secret memorandum exploring the pros and cons of using military force to destroy a country's military programs.[16]

Christopher's willingness to even ponder hypothetically such an option was at complete variance with the Nixon administration's general refusal to take tangible steps against nations seeking nuclear weapons as well as its private support for Israel's nuclear program. (Ironically, it was Israel in 1981 that would choose the military option contemplated by Warren Christopher when it carried out a successful air attack on the Iraqi nuclear reactor at Osirak. Using purchased U.S. F-16 aircraft, within ninety seconds Israeli pilots scored hits with fourteen of sixteen bombs, obliterating the facility.) The Carter administration also supported the development of what was originally called the London Club and later the Nuclear Suppliers Group, a multilateral commitment of nations such as Japan, the Soviet Union, and Germany whose purpose was to ensure that nuclear cooperation didn't inadvertently aid the proliferation goals of nations by curbing the export of enrichment and reprocessing facilities, something the NPT had not required. Some limited financial sanctions also were imposed by Washington on Pakistan because of Islamabad's continuing nuclear activities.

It wasn't long before other foreign policy priorities washed over the Carter administration's proliferation concerns, particularly as they pertained to Pakistan's fledgling efforts. The December 1979 Soviet invasion of Afghanistan, as brazen as it would ultimately prove to be foolhardy, had a chilling effect on U.S.-Soviet relations. That same year the U.S. relationship with Iran moved into an entirely new orbit when the Shah of Iran, America's erstwhile ally in the region, was overthrown by a theocratic regime led by Ayatollah Khomeini and openly hostile to the United States.

The near simultaneous blows to U.S. interests in the region required both a new diplomatic focus and concrete action. The diplomatic track was reflected in the administration's recognition of Pakistan's deep concerns about the Soviet invasion. Pakistani-Afghan relations had been troubled for some time, the product in part of a dispute over the status of ethnic Pashtuns in Pakistan's border regions. This festering sore, combined with Pakistan's strong anti-communist sentiments and growing alarm about how to manage the 300,000 refugees who fled into Pakistan at the start of the war (a figure that would grow ten-fold by war's end), coalesced into a shared view with Washington that the invasion required a concerted response. This view coincided with the judgment reached earlier by Zbigniew Brzezinski, President Carter's national security adviser. Writing a memorandum for Carter on December 26, 1979, Brzezinski concluded that "if the Soviets succeed in Afghanistan ... the age-long dream of Moscow to have direct access to the Indian Ocean will have been fulfilled."[17]

With few policy options available to it in Iran, the Carter administration concluded that it could and indeed must attempt to restore some of its lost credibility in the region by sowing havoc for the Soviet occupying force in Afghanistan. Open confrontation was out of the question, leaving covert action against the Soviet military the preferred policy action. As events would show conclusively in more contemporary times, there was no better place than Pakistan from which to launch incursions into Afghanistan.

What began under Jimmy Carter's presidency as Operation Cyclone and accelerated during Ronald Reagan's presidency was an aggressive campaign of sabotage, propaganda, and rocket attacks against the Soviet military. U.S. funding, along with considerable assistance from Saudi Arabia and China, provided the financial lubrication for the program. The daily management of the covert program, however, was in the hands of the Pakistan military and the security service, the Inter-Services Intelligence Agency (ISI). Under this arrangement it became clear to Islamabad's ruling clique that neither a liberal Democratic president nor his successor, a conservative Republican, would expend much energy criticizing its new strategic partner, Pakistan, particularly Pakistan's nuclear development efforts that continued unabated through the 1980s. Ironically, aside from the negative consequences that choice would have on nonproliferation grounds, the rise of the mujahadeen, including the participation of a tall, rich Saudi who traveled to Afghanistan named Osama bin Laden, laid much of the groundwork for the subsequent rise of radical Islamic activity. Furthermore, the vast flow of foreign assistance for the covert program being run through Pakistan almost certainly had the unintended consequence of enhancing the bureaucratic influence of the ISI within the Pakistan government, another development that viewed through the lens of history seems inimical to U.S. interests.

With U.S. policy in the region focused on Afghanistan, Khan was able to pursue in Pakistan a range of programmatic activities, although not completely unfettered. He suffered a temporary embarrassment in 1983 when a Dutch court convicted him in absentia for attempted espionage; in 1985 the conviction was overturned on appeal based on the technicality that Khan had not received a proper summons. The Dutch prosecutor dropped the case soon thereafter, apparently convinced that Khan would be shielded from further legal exposure by the Pakistani government. Khan also sparred with domestic rivals such as Munir Khan, Director of the PAEC, which carried out its own nuclear research, but once again A. Q. Khan emerged victorious. These distractions did not prevent Khan and KRL from branching out from their previous and exclusive focus on nuclear-related issues into the development of various conventional weapons, including short-range missiles and laser range finders. But nuclear development work remained the raison d'etre of the facility and Khan's personal attention remained focused primarily on those activities.[18]

Political and bureaucratic problems were not Khan's only worries during this period. The URENCO design information was extraordinarily useful for a developing program such as Pakistan's but it could not forestall several technical problems in the late 1970s and early 1980s. "Many of his (Khan's) early designs didn't work properly and there were immense technical problems," was the assessment of one commentator.[19] Khan also was in the process of changing the centrifuge types he was using, converting KRL's focus from the aluminum rotors of the P-1 early design to the more robust P-2 rotors that used the more reliable maraging steel.[20] Fortune smiled once again on Khan. In this case it was from an unlikely source; U.S. success in convincing France not to conclude a deal to provide Pakistan a reprocessing plant, the type of assistance that could directly support the production of plutonium, the other path and material for making a nuclear device. For Pakistan, the loss of this option—which later would be pursued through other sources—left Khan and his path to the bomb through the uranium enrichment route as the government's seemingly only viable option. He didn't disappoint his political masters. It is now almost certain that by the mid-1980s Pakistan had produced enough HEU for at least one nuclear weapon.[21]

Ronald Reagan came to office in 1981 firmly convinced of the moral bankruptcy of communism and just as firmly committed to confronting it. The Soviet invasion of Afghanistan, into its second year when Reagan assumed the presidency, was a primary battleground to do so. Reagan's friend and trusted confidant, CIA Director Bill Casey, would make a number of visits to Pakistan, the key partner and the front-line nation in the war against the Soviet invasion. Casey, another rabid anti-communist, made a number of visits to Islamabad that had little to do with Pakistan's nuclear program but everything to do with Afghanistan where the CIA's covert action program was expanding rapidly. Casey would fight some bureaucratic battles in Washington, particularly with the Department of Defense (DOD), trying to secure rapid funding for the CIA's operations. His initial attempts were rebuffed but an unlikely supporter emerged in 1984 in the form of Congressman Charlie Wilson, a conservative Texas Democrat who, according to former CIA director Robert Gates "wanted to kill Soviets."[22] Wilson, through his powerful position on the House Appropriations Committee, would be instrumental in securing for Casey funds that expanded the Agency's purchase of such items as the shoulder-fired Stinger anti-aircraft missile that had a devastating effect on Soviet aircraft and troop morale.[23]

Backed by Casey and Secretary of State Al Haig, Reagan made his priorities clear regarding U.S. policy to Pakistan with the approval of a five-year $3.2 billion assistance package, a significant increase from anything previously offered by any U.S. administration. Later, in a separate deal the Reagan and George H. W. Bush administrations agreed to the sale of forty advanced F-16 aircraft to the Pakistan military. In so doing the Reagan administration received some challenges from a Congress growing increasingly restive over Pakistan's nuclear activities. In 1985, the Pressler Amendment was passed, calling for the imposition of economic and military sanctions unless the president certified that Pakistan did not have or was not attempting to acquire nuclear weapons. As is often the case with such legislation, the president was given the authority to waive the sanctions if he certified that Pakistan was not pursuing those capabilities. Reagan promptly did so, preserving the economic flow and the political relationship throughout the balance of his term in office.

It was also in the mid-1980s that Khan's entrepreneurial spirit took a new and dangerous turn. No longer content to carry out illicit activities only for Pakistan's direct benefit, Khan set out to develop a new set of international customers. What would follow over about a fifteen-year period was the creation of a nuclear black market of unprecedented daring, scope, and danger. In the mid-1980s some murky reports surfaced that an Arab country may have contacted Khan about supplying nuclear technologies and expertise but this has never been confirmed. What is fully documented is Khan's deep relationship with Iran, beginning around 1987, and those supporting Tehran's nuclear development program.

Iran's earliest interest in nuclear technology dates to its 1957 nuclear agreement with the United States as part of the Atoms for Peace Program. In 1976, the Shah of Iran signed a $4 billion to $6 billion deal with German companies Siemens AG and Telefunken to build two nuclear power plants near the city of Bushehr and two small fishing villages in southeastern Iran.[24] During this period, training for a number of Iranian scientists also was underway at such prestigious American universities as MIT and the California Institute of Technology. The Bushehr deal ostensibly was benign—commercial nuclear power plants were operating in many countries—but alarm bells went off in some areas of the Washington national security establishment over the Shah's long-term intentions. The Shah's overthrow in 1979 would silence his nuclear plans, whatever their ultimate goal. By the fall of 1980 what had become Khomeini's Iran was embroiled in the initial stages of a long and bloody war with Iraq which, by 1984, had degenerated into Iraqi use of chemical weapons.

How much these events, if at all, propelled the new Iranian regime to consider a military option for its nuclear technology program is unclear. There likely are other reasons as well but they are shrouded in mystery. For example, since Iran has never officially acknowledged interest in developing or acquiring nuclear weapons Western analysts can only speculate on the extent to which in the early years of Khomeini's rule that Iran, a Shiite nation, viewed the "Muslim bomb" developed by Pakistan and financially backed by Saudi Arabia, both

Sunni-dominated nations, as inherently threatening. Moreover, U.S. nuclear capabilities were well understood by Khomeini as was Israel's growing nuclear prowess. At least for A. Q. Khan in Pakistan, such religious or political considerations were secondary to the prospect of financial gain. By 1986 to 1987, Pakistan and Iran are suspected of "signing a secret agreement on peaceful nuclear cooperation. Allegedly, the deal includes the provision for at least six Iranians to be trained in Pakistan.... Iranian scientists also might receive centrifuge training at KRL."[25] As with Khan's subsequent business arrangements with other nations, in dealing with Iran he relied considerably on a complex and elaborate network of suppliers and middlemen who assisted in various procurement activities and the issuance of false end-user certificates to confuse those carrying out customs or border inspections. Khan and his associates apparently also went to considerable lengths to share with Iranian agents the "tricks of the trade" on how to set up international procurement and smuggling operations. Iran learned its lessons well and over time its own efforts in this area would dwarf what had been done by Khan's organization. Such efforts were not the path nations took when interested in developing only civil nuclear programs.[26]

In a word, the scope of Khan's assistance to the Iranians was extensive. Blueprints, specifications, technical design data, various components, and enrichment equipment all found their way into Iran's program because of his assistance. Perhaps more than anything Khan saved the Iranians time— probably years—if forced to solve for themselves the myriad problems attending various aspects of nuclear research and development. Iran, which been incapable of solving a few enrichment technology problems during the war with Iraq, was able to solve more of those problems with Pakistani design assistance. Khan's brazen activities outside Pakistan made him rich but his value to Iran was incalculable.

There are differing perspectives, doubtless with self-serving elements that must be read with some scrutiny, regarding the complicity of various Pakistan officials in Khan's dealings with Iran. President Musharraf has tried, in retrospect, to distance his government from these activities as did Prime Minister Navaz Sharif in a 1992 denial of Pakistani cooperation with Iran in developing a research reactor.[27] For his part, Khan, when finally forced to account for his actions some fifteen years later, would claim that several prominent officials from that period in Pakistani politics, including Army Chief of Staff Mirza Beg, had approved the transactions. There may be some truth in this contention as in 1991 General Beg told U.S. Ambassador to Pakistan Robert Oakley that during that period he (Beg) had discussed various forms of military cooperation with Iran. Overall, it is highly likely that during this period, at a minimum, there was tacit acceptance by some senior Pakistani officials of Khan's global adventures.

It fell to the new U.S. president, George H. W. Bush, to undertake a fresh approach to U.S. policy on Pakistan. After a decade of futility and failure, the Soviet invasion of Afghanistan was brought to an end by Soviet President Mikhail Gorbachev who refused to preside over both the ongoing hemorrhaging of badly needed resources and his nation's battered prestige. In the eyes of Washington officials, Pakistan would no longer be needed to play a critical role in the U.S. government's covert action against the invading Soviet forces, clearing the way for a reassessment of Pakistan's nuclear activities.

The new administration coincided with a change in political leadership in Pakistan. Pakistani President Zia was killed in a mysterious plane crash in August 1988 which also killed the U.S. Ambassador to Pakistan. Pakistan also endeavored to mollify Washington's growing concerns about its nuclear intentions. Benazir Bhutto was elected president of Pakistan and in April 1989 the Pakistan government proclaimed the Benazir Doctrine which stated that Pakistan would not assemble a nuclear device unless its security was threatened and would not export nuclear technology to other countries.[28]

Bhutto visited Washington in 1989 and received a warning from President Bush that for his administration to certify after 1989 that Pakistan did not have a nuclear weapon—certification was essential for preserving Washington's assistance programs to Pakistan—Bhutto would have to commit to not enriching uranium above 5 percent. Her commitment was largely of symbolic rather than substantive importance because any nation able to enrich uranium to 5 percent would have little difficulty continuing the enrichment process to the higher levels required to make a nuclear device. Nonetheless, the meeting was a political success in papering over the existing problem temporarily but that respite didn't last long.

In August 1990, Bhutto was forced from power in a classic military coup, the victim of savage opposition from the Pakistan military and the ISI. Within two months President Bush invoked the Pressler Amendment which cut off U.S. funding. Bush's actions set U.S.-Pakistani relations on a collision course that would last through much of the decade. The bitterness within Pakistani ruling circles at the loss of U.S. assistance was reflected in the following remarks by Pakistani Senator Sartaj Aziz in a speech in New York City. "Pakistan's need for security," he asserted, "accentuated by the dispute over Kashmir, obliged Pakistan to rely on the global alliance system to bolster its defense." He claimed that alliance did not help Pakistan, noting that

> Our appraisal of the history of those [U.S.-Pakistan] relations is marked by a feeling of a letdown. The sense of let down was especially acute when Pressler was imposed in 1990. Pakistan had suffered the consequences of the Afghan War and expected the U.S. to be sympathetic to its economic needs.... Instead, Pakistan faced economic sanctions and it was obvious that the end of the Cold War had changed priorities for the United States in which the needs of an erstwhile ally did not figure.[29]

In hindsight it seems unlikely that a continuing flow of U.S. assistance would have served to brake Pakistan's indigenous nuclear program efforts or the nuclear black market Khan was establishing in Iran or elsewhere.

Pakistan's internal politics were in a state of disarray during much of the period as four different leaders were brought to power in elections. However, one constant was the predominant position of the military and ISI in Pakistan's domestic politics. The other constant was Pakistan's crushing poverty which was corroding the loyalty of its scientists. According to one Web-based Pakistani exile newspaper, dating to the mid-1990s at least nine nuclear scientists had emigrated from Pakistan. Their whereabouts were unknown but the assumption was that they left for better pay.[30] Apparently, not every member of Pakistan's nuclear establishment was living as well as A. Q. Khan.

Pakistan's support to Iran would continue unabated through the 1990s, largely escaping the attention of U.S. policymakers and the intelligence community. Robert Einhorn, one of the Clinton administration's most senior and highly regarded nonproliferation experts, spoke to this issue as follows. "it was our assumption through the 1990s that didn't see this (centrifuge equipment from Khan) as a promising basis for a program.... It was our assumption that Iran considered the equipment to be out of date and not very effective.... Pakistan was not on our radar screen."[31] That oversight would not be the last to plague U.S. nonproliferation policies to Pakistan.

Recognizing that there would be little or no domestic opposition to his international activities and almost as limited likelihood of effective U.S. pressures on the few Pakistan officials who oversaw his work, Khan continued developing international clients for his now wide-open nuclear supermarket. The Democratic People's Republic of Korea (DPRK), commonly called North Korea, was another favored client. Although the relationship focused initially on missile rather than nuclear technology, many of the same characteristics of Pakistan's assistance to Iran later resurfaced in the Pakistan-North Korea relationship. Once again Pakistani experts shared the secrets of uranium enrichment with North Korea. Once again Pakistani smugglers associated with Khan schooled their North Korean counterparts on ways to subvert and go around various export control laws, touting Dubai as a particularly useful location to carry out such commercial dealings. Khan, an inveterate traveler, also journeyed to North Korea frequently, much as he did in his work with Iran. Finally, as with Iran, the Pakistani assistance saved the North Koreans probably years of developmental effort.[32]

The Pakistani-North Korea relationship also highlights the exceptional difficulties of stemming the proliferation of weapons of mass destruction (WMD) when there is a confluence of equally strong if sometimes differing interests between two nations determined to carry out such transactions. Such was the case between the ruling factions in Islamabad and Pyongyang. By any standard, North Korea is one of the most isolated and poorest nations on earth, the tragic consequence of the paranoid megalomania of Kim Il Sung and after his death in 1994, his equally paranoid son, Kim Jong Il.

Under most circumstances North Korea would have few technically sophisticated products to offer any nation, but it had something of enormous appeal to Pakistan, missile technology. As U.S. support for Pakistan ebbed and Islamabad's relations with India continued on a rocky path—another conflict between the nations erupted in spring 1990 over Kashmir—Pakistan had reached a crossroads in its internal debates over how best to protect the country. There seems little doubt that Pakistan by that time had produced enough fissile material to make at least one nuclear device, although uncertainty still surrounds whether the lion's share of credit for that accomplishment belongs with Khan, his rivals at the PAEC, or their "silent partners," the Chinese.

For Pakistan, as any nation, possession of nuclear devices, to have military utility, must be accompanied by the capability to deliver the weapon to target by at least one of a number of various platforms. For developing countries, the means of delivery usually center on land-based missiles of various ranges or aircraft. U.S., Russian, and British naval capabilities to deliver long-range missiles to distant targets from submerged platforms, for example, require resources and the mastery of myriad sophisticated technologies beyond those available at present to North Korea and Pakistan. For Pakistan, desperately trying to balance the military scale with an Indian military that was larger and more advanced, the pressing strategic requirement was to develop the means to hold at risk with nuclear weapons at least portions of India with a survivable nuclear deterrent.

Chinese cooperation, so critical to Pakistan's progress in nuclear technologies, also played some role in Pakistan's missile development but it was North Korean assistance that changed the dynamics of Pakistan's military posture. It is likely that the relationship was forged during the Pakistani Prime Minister's December 1993 visit to Pyongyang, although there are indications that a year earlier Pakistani engineers and scientists may have been inspecting the North Korean Nodong missile, a liquid-fueled missile derived from the Russian Scud missile, with a range of about 1,000 to 1,200 kilometers.[33]

In its earliest incarnation, North Korea's missile assistance, which ultimately included the 300 kilometer M-11 missile, was almost certainly a cash transaction. Khan and his KRL colleagues still benefited from this cooperation because KRL, which had been working to develop short-range missiles for the Pakistan military, would become the home for the Nodong, which KRL and Khan later would claim as their own. Khan also would give the missile a new name, the Ghauri, after an ancient Muslim warrior.

That arrangement, albeit satisfactory to both parties initially, gave way to new realities on both sides. For Pakistan, its financial resources in the 1990s continued to dwindle as a result of the cut off in U.S. assistance and poor internal management of the economy. For North Korea, its nuclear program, now far removed from initial nuclear training received by its first nuclear scientists from the Soviet Union in the 1950s and 1960s, had reached a critical point. North Korea had joined the NPT in 1985 but its nuclear-related activities soon raised suspicions in the West. In 1987, construction had been completed on a research reactor at Yongbyon, the type of facility that would allow North Korean scientists to begin reprocessing the fuel rods which would lead to the production of plutonium.

It wasn't until 1992 that IAEA safeguards inspections of North Korea began but those inspections almost immediately raised suspicions about possible covert nuclear activities involving plutonium, a direct violation of Pyongyang's NPT obligations. Troubled by its initial findings, the IAEA in February 1993 proposed a "special inspection" for two waste facilities near Yongbyon only to be rebuffed by North Korea, triggering heightened suspicions. For Washington and the new Clinton administration, a crisis was in the making. Secretary of Defense William Perry presented to senior U.S. officials the possibility of carrying out military action against the North Korean facilities, not unlike actions contemplated by Secretary of State Christopher more than fifteen years earlier.[34]

The impetus for such a drastic policy choice was blunted by two sets of diplomatic engagements. The first, carried out by former President Jimmy Carter, was the product of a wholly unauthorized visit to North Korea that infuriated Clinton administration officials but yielded the prospect of Pyongyang's first signs of willingness to negotiate a compromise. This was followed by the 1994 Agreed Framework by which North Korea agreed to freeze its plutonium production in return for the annual provision at no cost to North Korea of 500,000 tons of heavy fuel oil and the construction of two lightwater nuclear power reactors, generally viewed as a much reduced proliferation threat compared to North Korea's graphite-moderated reactors. Republicans in Congress, having just ascended into the majority, took a dim view of the agreement but were powerless to overturn it. U.S. negotiator Robert Gallucci had not signed a treaty but rather a type of memorandum of agreement which was not subject to ratification or formal debate in the Senate.

The Agreed Framework cooled political tensions between Washington and Pyongyang temporarily but it did not temper for long North Korea's desire to develop nuclear weapons. As Gallucci and others surely knew, the enrichment path to nuclear weapons was much easier to conceal than the plutonium production path the North Koreans had been pursuing. China, a natural and potential source for North Korea to turn to for nuclear assistance, was under close scrutiny by the United States and not inclined to antagonize the U.S. government, at least on Pyongyang's behalf. Under these circumstances it is hardly surprising that the North Koreans also would find additional and compelling reason in the mid- to late 1990s to reinvigorate its relationship with Pakistan. What had begun as a cash for missiles deal changed dramatically.

What transformed the most troubling part of that relationship was agreement, probably reached in 1996 or 1997, by which Pakistan, desperate to advance its missile program but with limited funds to do so, agreed to start supplying North Korea with nuclear assistance. According to U.S. experts, "in 1997 Pakistani nuclear scientists made secret trips to North Korea, providing technical support for that country's nuclear weapons program in exchange for Pyongyang's help in developing long-range missiles."[35]

The scope of the enhanced cooperation was impressive as it was worrisome. Pakistan received between twelve to twenty-five long-range missiles, shorter-range missiles, and associated technical support. In return, North Korea received at least a dozen centrifuges, as well as blueprints and designs, and, albeit unconfirmed, a Chinese weapons design.[36] This assistance did not prove to be the panacea for their program hoped for by the North Koreans. Press reporting in early 2007 indicates that after the Agreed Framework collapsed, the North Koreans returned at least some of their focus to the production of plutonium—which was the material used for their first nuclear test on October 9, 2006—although large quantities of uranium were being produced by 2001 in North Korea.[37] In any event, barter, the oldest form of commercial transaction, had proven to be the perfect mechanism for two nations to acquire some of mankind's most modern and deadly weapons.

Much of this activity, as noted, passed without direct challenge from Washington until spring 1998. In April of that year the Pakistan military carried out a successful test of the Ghauri medium-range ballistic missile, signaling the Indian government that its cities could be attacked directly for the first time. India responded almost immediately, conducting five nuclear tests between May 11 and May 13, 1998. Not to be intimidated, Pakistan joined the nuclear club with six of its own nuclear tests between May 28 and May 30. Some Western experts claim several of those tests may not have been completely successful or were possibly less powerful than claimed by Pakistani officials, but there could be no doubt about the fundamental nuclear capability demonstrated by Pakistan for the first time. Khan became a national hero and was greeted with acclaim everywhere he went in the country. He received from President Tarar a gold medal in recognition of his contributions to Pakistan's nuclear program. He also had become wealthy; one estimate claimed Khan was worth about $400 million.[38]

This combination of events provided a significant challenge to the Clinton administration's relations with Pakistan as well as India for several reasons. Did the nuclear brinksmanship displayed by both sides portend the start of another round of even more deadly hostilities? There also were a set of broader concerns. Experts in Washington also understood that the Pakistani missile test's flight profile showed the direct lineage between the North Korean Nodong and the Ghauri. Closely related to these considerations was a third and inescapable question: If North Korea was giving so much of value to Pakistan, what was it getting in return?

For U.S. policymakers there was a consistent willingness to engage Pakistan in discussions over Islamabad's emerging relationship with Pyongyang. At the highest levels, including President Clinton; at least one cabinet member, Energy Secretary Bill Richardson; and Assistant Secretary of State Robert Einhorn, the administration spoke often but achieved little with Sharif and then Musharraf. At least part of the reason for the diplomatic dead end was that the administration had few options either in the form of the so-called carrots or sticks with which to induce or compel change in Pakistan's relationship with North Korea. After the 1998 nuclear tests, sweeping U.S. economic sanctions as required by the Arms Export Control Act and the Export-Import Bank Act were placed alongside those imposed in 1990.[39]

The United States also tried to use international leverage on Pakistan through the United Nations. The United Nations Security Council weighed in on June 5, 1998, calling unanimously for both sides to refrain from future nuclear testing. Perhaps as a harbinger of their more recent attitudes of reluctance to support the imposition of strong sanctions against Iran, France and Russia did not impose any sanctions on either country after the 1998 tests. The Security Council action, moreover, stood silent on the evolving Pakistan-North Korea relationship.

Predictably, the effect of the limited U.N. response intended to signal concerns about Pakistan's and India's behavior was fleeting. In addition, U.S. domestic politics almost immediately would begin corroding the impact of the international sanctions required by law. According to one authoritative report,

> Congress intervened on behalf of U.S. wheat growers by passing the Agriculture Export Relief Act.... This freed up U.S. wheat farmers to participate in auctions in which Pakistan was a substantial buyer.... Congress later passed the India-Pakistan Relief Act of 1998 ... that authorized the President to waive, for a period of one year, the application of sanctions....

Congress provided permanent authority to waive all the economic sanctions imposed against India and Pakistan for their nuclear tests via the Department of Defense's Appropriations Act, signed by the president on October 25, 1999.[40] Other U.S. sanctions would remain in place against Pakistan as a result of the military coup against Prime Minister Nawaz Sharif staged by Pervez Musharraf in another example of the decade's long struggle for ultimate political authority between civilian and military figures.

Washington's concerns about Pakistan's internal and international security policies may not have resulted in any immediate tangible policy success, but its pressure was starting to take a toll on Khan's credibility. In the late 1990s, Prime Minister Sharif approved an ISI investigation into Khan's finances. This was followed in 2000 by now President Musharraf's decision, immediately following President Clinton's visit to Pakistan in March 2000, to launch another investigation into Khan and his shadowy world. The results showed that Khan had about $8 million in various bank accounts. Khan's wide-ranging travels throughout Europe, Asia, Africa, and the Middle East also raised alarms to the investigators, albeit years after such scrutiny should have occurred.[41] Musharraf claims to have realized over time that Khan was "the problem."[42] The new Pakistani president did not enjoy unlimited popularity and Khan, branded a hero in his country and widely credited as being the "father of Pakistan's bomb" had reached near iconic status. Musharraf moved cautiously but still managed to arrange for Khan to accept a forced retirement in March 2001 while offering Khan a largely ceremonial posting as a science adviser. Khan's access to his beloved Kahuta facilities was severed but he had not been cut off from an international network of suppliers, mainly Europeans, and deal makers. The sigh of relief breathed in Washington did not last long.

The attacks against New York and Washington by Islamic fundamentalists on September 11, 2001, required immediate decisions from a still new Bush administration. Prior to the September attacks part of the evidentiary record shows that administration officials such as Deputy Defense Secretary Paul Wolfowitz were skeptical of the April 2001 recommendations of White House counterterrorism chief Richard Clarke that the Taliban as well as Osama bin Laden and his al Qaeda network should be the targets of increased U.S. military pressure.

The Bush administration's perspectives changed dramatically in the wake of the attacks. What emerged was a policy lumping nations into two categories; those who would support America's war on terrorism and those who wouldn't support those efforts. The administration also touted the risk posed by nations that might harbor or support terrorist organizations and declared the right to take preemptive military action against them. Was Pakistan in the crosshairs of U.S. rage? Deputy Secretary of State Richard Armitage, in the days immediately following the September 11 attacks, was alleged to have threatened General Mahmood Ahmed, the Director of Pakistan's Intelligence Service, the ISI, with a warning that the United States would bomb Pakistan "into the stone age" if it did not cooperate with the United States, a charge Armitage has denied vehemently.[43] Armitage has confirmed that he handed his Pakistani interlocutor a list of "arduous and onerous" demands.[44] Those demands were:

1. Stopping al Qaeda operations on the Pakistani border, intercepting arms shipments through Pakistan, and stopping all logistical support for bin Laden
2. Blanket overflight and landing rights for U.S. planes
3. Access to Pakistan's naval bases, airbases, and borders
4. Curbing all domestic expression of support for terrorism against the United States, its friends, and allies
5. Cutting off fuel supply to the Taliban and stopping Pakistani volunteers going into Afghanistan to join the Taliban
6. Pakistan's breaking diplomatic relations with the Taliban and assisting the United States in destroying bin Laden and his al Qaeda network.

In any event, Washington also was prepared to offer more positive incentives to Pakistan for its support as President Bush did on September 22, 2001, just weeks after the terrorist attacks in America, when he lifted all nuclear test-related economic sanctions against Pakistan as well as India. However, sanctions put in place under Section 508 of the Foreign Assistance Act prohibits many forms of U.S. assistance to any country whose elected head of government is deposed by a military coup remained in place for Pakistan. In the following years the 9/11 Commission, in one of its many formal recommendations, struck another positive note in stating that "the United States

DID PAKISTAN OFFER TO ASSIST IRAQ IN DEVELOPING NUCLEAR WEAPONS?

Much of the extraordinarily bitter debate over the U.S. military presence in Iraq began as a dispute regarding the original reasons for the Bush administration's decision to invade the country in March 2003. In the lead up to the invasion and for a protracted period thereafter, senior administration officials touted a primary justification for the invasion to be its conviction that Iraq was pursuing the development of various types of WMD, including possibly nuclear weapons. While the evidence for the nuclear case proved to be unsustainable, it is likely that Iraq had been approached by A. Q. Khan some years earlier with an offer of assistance. Such an offer would have been totally in keeping with his indiscriminate offers of assistance elsewhere. As early as October 6, 1990, the operational arm of the Iraqi intelligence service (Section B-15) sent to its counterpart nuclear weapons directorate (Section S-16) a memorandum concerning an alleged offer by Khan to help Iraq produce nuclear weapons. The offer of assistance could have included the production of gas centrifuges and the design for nuclear weapons. The offer was confirmed several years later in documents uncovered by IAEA inspectors. There is no evidence that any formal arrangement between Khan and Iraqi experts for cooperation was consummated.[45]

should be willing to make a long-term commitment to the future of Pakistan, if Musharraf stands for enlightened moderation."[46]

The Bush administration's expectations placed Pakistan and President Musharraf, in a most uncomfortable position. Once again, because of its strategic location bordering Afghanistan where the Taliban and al Qaeda clearly were operating, Pakistan had been thrust into the front line of another American war. For the new Pakistani president there were multiple considerations to ponder. On the one hand the U.S. government was expecting Musharraf to take all reasonable steps to assist in disrupting and, ideally, disbanding, Taliban and al Qaeda operations, no small request given the ease with which those groups for years had crossed between Afghanistan and vast expanses of Pakistan's unprotected and lawless borders. Sentiment against the United States also ran very high within the country, including within the military and ISI. There was little doubt but that ISI elements had supported the Taliban for at least a decade. Within the general populace in impoverished major cities such as Karachi there were hotbeds of radicalism stoked by the influence of the madrassas, religious schools that often taught the most virulent interpretation of the Koran while blaming Western nations for many of the woes within the Arab world. One estimate put the number of these schools at 10,000 in Pakistan.[47]

As if this wasn't enough, Musharraf has admitted feeling "immense pressure" from the U.S. government for two other reasons.[48] The first was Washington's concern about Musharraf's personal safety and ability to remain in power, an entirely reasonable focus given that several assassination attempts against him had failed. The second was the worry held in various Washington policy circles regarding the safety and security of Pakistan's nuclear assets.

During that period I managed the Energy Department's international threat reduction program that secured nuclear materials in Russia. Judging that the program's experience and expertise might be of assistance in Pakistan, I proposed working with experts from the domestic side of the Department of Energy (DOE) with their considerable experience in protecting U.S. nuclear assets, in formulating a plan by which Islamabad would be offered options both for training nuclear personnel and, in an emergency, securing its nuclear stockpile. The White House and State Department fully supported this initiative. Cooperation throughout DOE on this project was exceptional. Unstinting support was provided by Kathy Carlson, a senior federal official from Nevada who was in Washington on temporary assignment. In short order a set of options was developed to present to Pakistani officials. Recognizing the inevitable sensitivities of the Pakistani security establishment to any proposed U.S. involvement in their most closely held programs, the proposal was designed in every way possible to minimize direct U.S. presence for those options that would have required direct or indirect U.S. presence. Other parts of the proposal offered various types of technical equipment. Our efforts weren't enough. DOE's offer of assistance was rebuffed by Islamabad, almost certainly out of a mixture of Pakistani hubris regarding its own security procedures as well as fear that U.S. experts would somehow compromise its military's control of those weapons and materials.

For his part, Musharraf made some other strategic decisions that went in a more positive direction and won the administration's approval. Perhaps the most important was his January 2002 broadcast to his nation in which Musharraf condemned the "violence and terrorism that has been going on for years," adding that Pakistan was "weary and sick of the Kalashnikov culture."[49] In the ensuing years questions would remain, mostly out of public view, regarding whether Musharraf was doing all he could to assist U.S. counterterrorism efforts, concerns reinforced by the Pakistan leader's signing a fall 2006 peace deal with pro-Taliban militants. Under the agreement tribal leaders in North Waziristan region of Pakistan would cease terrorist activities in exchange for the pullback of Pakistani military units operating in the region. In addition, the Pakistani government stipulated that foreigners would be allowed to stay in Pakistan if they obeyed the law. Was this a concession that bin Laden, a Saudi by birth, could remain in Pakistan with the impunity derived from Pakistan's concession?

For obvious and compelling reasons the administration's primary focus was fixed on Pakistan's role in combating al Qaeda and the Taliban, but Khan and his network of proliferators was not forgotten in policy circles. Unlike past administrations that viewed through the policy lens a dichotomy between proliferation concerns and broader U.S. strategic interests, for the Bush administration the two were very much intertwined. In addition to his extensive relationships with Iran and North Korea, Khan had begun meeting with Libyan nuclear experts in 1995, resulting in another series of complex and protracted supply arrangements that included the provision of nuclear weapons designs and centrifuges over a lengthy period. To help meet its parts commitments to Libya, in December 2001, months after his removal from KRL, Khan, with considerable assistance from his international collaborators, set up a manufacturing plant in Malaysia under the nondescript name of SCOMI Precision Engineering, known as SCOPE.[50]

Khan's brazenness finally was catching up with him. The Bush administration and its allies, beginning with the Blair government, refused to ignore the many warning signs emanating from Khan's activities. On January 31, 2004, President Musharraf fired Khan from the largely ceremonial advisory position he had been given in 2001. In short order Khan made a public confession, was placed under house arrest, but granted an immediate presidential pardon. Within the Bush administration there was a level of frustration both over the fact that Khan would escape legal prosecution as well as the refusal of the Pakistani government to allow U.S. officials to interrogate him. It was well understood in official Washington circles that there was little point in antagonizing Pakistan, again its critical ally, over activities that had been stopped.

A. Q. KHAN CONFESSES

On February 4, 2004, Dr. A. Q. Khan finally acknowledged, albeit somewhat obliquely, his central role in the development of Pakistan's nuclear program as well as ongoing support to nuclear activities in Iran, North Korea, and Libya. His confession, in part, stated:

> The recent investigation was ordered by the government of Pakistan, consequent to the disturbing disclosures and evidence by some countries to international agencies, relating to alleged proliferation activities by certain Pakistanis and foreigners over the last two decades. The investigation has established that many of the reported activities did occur, and that these were invariably at my behest. In my interviews with the concerned government officials, I was confronted with the evidence and the findings, and I have voluntarily admitted that much of it is true and accurate ... I also wish to clarify that there was never any kind of authorization for these activities by a government official.[51]

TABLE 4.1 Nuclear Club and Its Dropouts

Nuclear Weapons States

- United States
- Russia
- United Kingdom
- France
- China
- Israel
- India
- Pakistan
- North Korea

States That Inherited Nuclear Weapons But Are Now Nonnuclear Weapons States

- Belarus
- Kazakhstan
- Ukraine

States That Ended Nuclear Weapons Programs Before the 1970 Entry into Force of the Nonproliferation Treaty

- Sweden
- Canada
- Australia
- Egypt

States That Ended Nuclear Weapons Programs After 1970

- Argentina
- Romania
- Spain
- Taiwan
- Brazil
- South Africa
- South Korea
- Switzerland
- Libya
- Yugoslavia

On the Brink?

- Iran

Iran

THE PREVIOUS CHAPTER assessed Pakistan's nuclear weapons program, Pakistani scientist A. Q. Khan and his international network's contributions to that program, their concurrent and extensive assistance to developing programs in Iran, North Korea, and Libya as well as the policy responses of different U.S. administrations to those developments.

A review of Iran's nuclear and missile programs shows another set of vexing security challenges for the United States. The theocratic government in Tehran has made repeated claims that it seeks only to develop civilian nuclear power. There is no evidence that Iran, unlike Pakistan, has yet crossed the nuclear threshold. One of the most critical ambiguities of the Nonproliferation Treaty (NPT) is that under Article IV any NPT member is ensured access to peaceful uses of nuclear technology. Iran is an NPT member and its leaders never tire of pointing out their right to exercise that option. However, because the technology used to enrich uranium to 3 percent to 5 percent in the isotope 235, the enrichment level used for nuclear power reactors, is the same technology as that required to enrich uranium to higher levels suitable for a nuclear device, nations such as Iran could, if they chose, develop enrichment technology to a certain level under a "peaceful nuclear energy program" while reserving the option of "breaking out" at a future date with a program of higher-level enrichment. Moreover, and in conjunction with its legal pursuits of nuclear technology, a compelling case can be made that so many clandestine activities for so long have been carried out with Iranian governmental approval that it is pursuing the option of crossing that threshold as quickly as possible. It is highly difficult to predict when that threshold might be reached; such a step is not even inevitable. Whether Iran succeeds—whether its capabilities match its apparent ambitions—will depend on multiple political calculations and technical factors which will be discussed shortly.

As presented in Chapter 4, U.S. interest in Iran's nuclear development can be traced back to the 1950s when under the aegis of the Atoms for Peace

Program the United States signed a nuclear cooperation agreement with Iran. Until the fall of the Shah in 1979, throughout this period the United States provided various types of training and technical assistance to Iran. President Gerald Ford, for example, in 1976 was interested in providing Iran reprocessing equipment. Iran also would pursue various types of nuclear cooperation with other nations, including South Africa and China. Much of these cooperative endeavors were not of direct or immediate proliferation concern, but one of the inherent problems of nuclear technology is that they are dual use, by which advances in a civilian program can support weapons-related research. The Shah clearly understood this reality and may well have harbored his own plans, based on his seemingly benign cooperative relationships with the United States as well as other nations, to develop at least a nuclear weapons option.

After the Shah was overthrown in 1979, U.S. suspicions about Iran's real nuclear ambitions understandably increased when Ayatollah Khomeini and his anti-U.S. regime came to power and soon thereafter created the hostage crisis that severed diplomatic relations between the two countries. Once again ambition did not match capability and until Iran turned to Pakistan for assistance its nuclear programs lagged. For the U.S. government, albeit with a few notable exceptions, it wasn't until Bill Clinton's second term that a concerted U.S. diplomatic strategy was designed with the purpose of ending or slowing Iran's path toward a nuclear weapon, although later in Clinton's first term—March and May 1995—he signed executive orders banning U.S. companies from doing business with Iranian firms.

Albeit employing a different diplomatic strategy, the Bush administration also has expended considerable effort on the Iranian problem. Before tracing the intertwined history of Iran's programmatic efforts and the diplomatic maneuverings of the past and present administrations, the International Atomic Energy Agency (IAEA) and the United Nations, it's appropriate to pose a series of questions that illustrate the profound consequences of Iranian acquisition of a nuclear weapons capability:

- In an already badly troubled region, what changes likely would occur in U.S. relations with various Middle East nations that would be within range of Iranian missiles that would be nuclear-armed? Would those nations seek closer political or security ties to Washington or, alternatively, seek more independent policies?
- How would Tehran assess its new-found capabilities? Would it pursue regional policies that eschew brandishing its weapons or pursue more overtly aggressive policies by using its nuclear might as a political weapon or to support other policy options such as even more expanded support to terrorist organizations in the region such as Hezbollah? Little is known about Iran's thinking on the linkage between nuclear capabilities and political objectives.
- Even if Iran did not seek to provide nuclear materials or weapons to other states or terrorist groups, would it develop an appropriate level of security measures to protect those assets from theft or diversion?

- Would Arab states such as Egypt or Saudi Arabia come under severe domestic pressure to undertake efforts to match Iranian nuclear capabilities, further undermining the already shaky NPT? Gamal Mubarak, Egyptian President Mubarak's son and presumptive heir to the presidency, already has implied Egypt should consider such a response if Iran becomes a nuclear power. In early 2004, senior Saudi officials announced they were reviewing their options regarding possible "leasing" of nuclear weapons from China or Pakistan, an option that would be permitted under the NPT if China or Pakistan retained control of the weapons.[1]
- What are the implications for the region if Iran, a Shi'a-dominated society, becomes a nuclear power in a Muslim world where Sunni domination, both in terms of population and political influence, long has been predominant?
- How would Israel respond to or confront a threat described by former Israeli Prime Minister Benjamin Netanyahu in 1997, and other Israeli prime ministers who came to power, as "existential?" That threat could arise not only from direct military action but from Tehran's possible willingness to provide nuclear materials or weapons to terrorist groups.
- How would other regional actors such as Russia and Pakistan react if Iran crossed the nuclear threshold?

As with Pakistan and North Korea, Iran has traveled a long road in its apparent quest to develop nuclear technology and probably nuclear weapons. As discussed previously, Pakistani technical assistance in the mid-1980s was shown to be a major contributor to the initial interest of Iran's post-Shah interest in developing nuclear technology. What continues this assessment is that the 1989 death of Iran's Supreme Leader, Ayatollah Khomeini, resulted in a heightened rather than reduced interest in nuclear weapons among his successor, Ayatollah Khamenei, and Iranian President Rafsanjani.[2] Armed with this political top cover, Iranian procurement activities increased dramatically, searching for badly needed specialized equipment throughout Europe and meeting with partial successes. Recognizing that other unmet requirements might not be satisfied through their own procurement efforts, the Iranians also continued to use Khan's extensive networks. By 1994, bilateral agreement was reached in which Pakistan would supply older P-1 centrifuge designs, components, and drawings for the more advanced and robust P-2 centrifuge.[3]

In 1995 Iran's program began moving in new directions. What became recognized as a clandestine enrichment program moved from the Tehran Nuclear Technology Center to the more opaque cover of the Kalaye Electric Company.[4] That same year Russia signed an $800 million contract to build for Iran two light-water reactors at Bushehr. On the surface, the proliferation concerns inherent in the Bushehr design are much less than those arising from a heavy-water research reactor, although the spent fuel waste from a light-water reactor contains some plutonium that could make a bomb if certain chemical processes were carried out. Of more direct concern to the Clinton administration and Israeli government was the arrival in Iran, over time, of hundreds of skilled Russian technicians to work on various aspects of the Bushehr project.

It was feared, but could never be proved, that this expertise would be used to covertly support other Iranian projects of more direct proliferation concern.

In late 1995, the Iranians turned to Russia again for specialized assistance. Apparently frustrated with the quality of the parts being shipped over the past year by A. Q. Khan's clandestine network, Iranian authorities made a formal offer to the Russian government to buy an entire plant of centrifuges. If consummated, the deal would have provided Tehran at least 10,000 of the coveted pieces of specialized equipment, more than enough for an accelerated enrichment program. Quiet diplomacy by Clinton administration officials was successful in convincing the Russian government to stop the deal, a significant diplomatic success.[5]

Iran still had not come close to developing a nuclear weapon in 1997, but the scope and pace of its clandestine activities had reached such a level that President Clinton personally approved the commencement of a concerted diplomatic initiative. This initiative had two unusual features. The first was that it was not the product or result of U.S. intelligence assessments. Prior to joining the National Security Council (NSC) Staff in 1996, I had been directly involved for several years in the production of a series of intelligence reports on various aspects of Iran's nuclear program and Russian assistance to it. Those reports had clearly caught the attention of the administration's policymakers, particularly information provided on the breadth of assistance Iranian nuclear as well as missile experts were receiving from Russian scientists and technicians. These reports came at an awkward time for an administration committed to supporting the still-struggling Russian government led by Boris Yeltsin that had emerged from the breakup of the Soviet Union. During that period the reports were of sufficient credibility that the administration consistently raised the topic of Iran with senior Russian officials, including through the Gore-Chrenomyrdin Commission meetings. Over the past several years considerable effort has been expended by intelligence officials, including former Central Intelligence Agency (CIA) Director George Tenet as well as various Bush administration policymakers seeking to explain their version of how intelligence information did or did not support the administration's decision to invade Iraq. The level of mistrust between the intelligence and policy officials continues unabated. In light of the bitterness infusing these debates, I should consider myself fortunate that during this part of my CIA career I was never pressured by either Agency officials to slant any judgments about the Russia-Iran nexus or Clinton administration officials to dilute or withhold any information that would have reflected poorly on the Russian government.

Nonetheless, what galvanized the administration into action was not the work of the U.S. intelligence community. Rather, in February 1997 a team of Israeli military and intelligence officers briefed their overall assessment of Iran's nuclear activities to a group of senior administration officials in the office of Leon Fuerth, Vice President Gore's foreign policy adviser. Since Gore's earliest days in Congress, Fuerth had worked for him and the trust between the two was unshakable. In addition, Fuerth was an avid and sophisti-cated consumer of intelligence as I had observed during my tenure as an intel-ligence officer. We were joined in the briefing by Mike Hamel, an Air force officer of the highest caliber and Fuerth's assistant on the issue, as well as several other members of the NSC Staff. For at least an hour we sat silently as the Israeli briefers made a case that was powerful and comprehensive.

After the briefing concluded, Fuerth asked my impression of the Israeli pre-sentation before he briefed the vice president. Past experience in assessing those issues had instilled in me an inherent caution when trying to answer questions such as when Iran might acquire a nuclear weapon. There were an almost infinite number of uncertainties, not the least of which were the many gaps in both the U.S. and Israeli intelligence community's understanding of key elements of Iran's programs. Nonetheless, the overall impression I took from the briefing was that the Israelis had been thorough and convincing with-out any particular over-dramatization or blatant attempt to hype the threat. "Leon," I said, "they seem to have it right." That was all he wanted to hear and he left to brief the vice president.

Within a few months the administration had formulated the broad outline of its new diplomatic approach. The second novel aspect was that we would not be carrying our concerns to Iran, whose actions were the direct cause of mounting tensions in Washington. The 1980 severing of diplomatic ties between Washington and Tehran still was in effect, making it impossible to begin an official and protracted dialogue with the Iranian government. The administration chose to focus its diplomacy on Russia, one, but not the only, nation whose nuclear and missile experts were assisting Iran. The other major external source of assistance to Iran was North Korea, which was judged to be wholly unwilling to moderate that behavior at Washington's behest.

I was asked to represent the White House on the negotiations that were set in motion by a mid-1997 telephone exchange between Presidents Clinton and Yeltsin. Clinton was not about to hurl charges at his Russian counterpart but, at the same time, he also appreciated the consequences of unchecked Russian assistance to Iran. For his part, Yeltsin was not prepared to concede any offi-cial Russian culpability in such foreign adventures but acknowledged that some individuals could be engaged in illegal activities that were not, he emphasized, in Russia's interests or consistent with its policies or, as a nuclear state, its export control obligations. It was agreed that the negotiations would include an open-ended number of meetings between the two sides to exchange views on Iran's nuclear and missile programs. The U.S. goal was to convince the Russians to halt the technical assistance being provided to Iran, doubtless for a price. This goal was appropriate given that the consensus of U.S. experts at the time was that Iran had not reached a point in either its nuclear or mis-sile program where it could go it alone. If it was still reliant on external assis-tance, the logic was that in slowing or, ideally, ending that assistance, Iran's programs would be severely disrupted. Yeltsin chose Minatom Minister

Yevgeny Adamov to lead a delegation that would discuss all nuclear-related issues while Yuri Koptev, Director of the Russian Space Agency, would be our interlocutor for parallel talks on the missile proliferation problem.

The United States opted to have one team handle both negotiations. Chosen to lead the U.S. delegation was Ambassador Frank Wisner, one of America's most experienced diplomats who had served as U.S. ambassador in Egypt and India. Wisner made a personal sacrifice to take on this task as he was in the process of leaving public service for a lucrative private sector position. I thought the choice was excellent as Wisner, although not a nonproliferation expert, was a seasoned professional who possessed the experience and gravitas to represent U.S. interests well. Wisner and I were joined by Jim Timbie, a senior and highly respected State Department career officer, to form a core group that was augmented at times with representatives from various parts of the U.S. interagency.

Prior to holding any discussions with Russian officials, Wisner's team had to formulate a negotiating strategy whose goal would be to have Russian officials first acknowledge that problems existed, investigate them, and take measures to end the cooperation. Ideally, the delegation sought some public display of Russia's willingness to get tough on its experts who might be assisting Iran, but we would have settled for measures that quietly ended that cooperation. Underlying much of the discussions on strategy was the extent and ways in which the products from the U.S. government's extensive intelligence collection assets could be used. As noted, the Iranians were not claiming to seek a nuclear weapons capability—just the opposite was their stated case—and there was little prospect that answers to the questions the U.S. government had about Iranian intentions would be forthcoming through unclassified sources. The result was that the negotiating team was left to use whatever information collected by the intelligence community could be sanitized or "dubbed down" for use with the Russian side to make the case, first that the Iranian programs had a military purpose (in the case of the nuclear talks) and second, that Russian assistance was making a material contribution to both the Iranian nuclear and missile programs and, therefore, had to be stopped. Even if wildly successful in achieving those objectives, something Wisner, Timbie, and I never expected, we understood that we could at best considerably delay, but probably never stop, Russian assistance to Iran's nuclear and missile development. Simply put, it was our judgment that various entrenched individuals and organizations in Russia with vested interests in this cooperation were not prepared to bring it to a halt.

The questions of what and how much intelligence can be used in support of diplomatic initiatives is a long-running and recurring debate between various elements of the policy and intelligence communities. For the intelligence community the safety and preservation of its sources and methods—they way it collects information that feeds into the intelligence product sent to the policy community—are paramount. Albeit seldom expressed bluntly to policy officials, from my years at the CIA I understood that there were intelligence officers there who harbored deep reservations about the overall commitment of the policy community to safeguarding those sources. Conversely, the policy community at times viewed the intelligence community with suspicion and often described it as being reluctant to use even portions of its intelligence data to support their diplomatic efforts. Wisner, Timbie, and I understood this dichotomy and were concerned that without approval to use some specific information that our chance of convincing Russian authorities to investigate and close down any ongoing assistance to Iran would be dismissed immediately. For this reason we went to considerable lengths to fashion a compromise with the intelligence community. Nonetheless, there still ensued some intense conversations between the delegation and the intelligence community regarding the information we could present to our Russian counterparts. However, in this case there was sufficient good will on both sides so that we ultimately received approval for the use of a set of talking points approved by the CIA for presentation to our interlocutors. The approved talking points focused on broad examples or "cases" of alleged Russian cooperation.

By late August 1997, the two delegations were set to meet in Moscow. Before doing so, the U.S. delegation flew to Israel to confer with then Prime Minister Benjamin Netanyahu. In the sweltering Mediterranean summer heat Wisner, Timbie, and I, attired in Western business suits, visited Netanyahu at his vacation home where we sat informally under an umbrella-covered table. Accompanied by only one or two staff assistants, Netanyahu greeted us wearing white pants, a black tee shirt and brandishing his trademark cigar. His reputation as an articulate, intelligent, and highly opinionated leader was on display immediately. Netanyahu had an excellent grasp of the available data as well as a willingness to convey both his personal and his government's deepest suspicions about the pace and scope of Iran's nuclear and missile programs. In the most direct terms—and speaking impeccable English honed from many years spent in the United States—Netanyahu said that the Palestinian problem was a very troubling political problem for Israel but it was only a nuclear-armed Iran that could destroy Israel. Iran's nuclear and missile programs, he added, represented nothing less than an "existential" threat to Israel's existence. Netanyahu also agreed that his government would support the United States in any way possible, stay patient, and give diplomacy a chance to work.

On reaching Moscow the team conferred with U.S. Ambassador to Russia James Collins, another highly experienced diplomat with excellent insights into Russian policy. Collins's advice to us was simple and typically direct; don't expect too much was the crux of his advice. Consistent with the views of close observers in Washington, Collins emphasized that Russia very much wanted to preserve its relationship with Iran and that would be the overriding consideration driving the Russian approach to the negotiations.

From the delegation's initial meetings with Koptev and Adamov and throughout the first year there emerged an easily recognizable pattern to the negotiations. Drawing on the approved intelligence, Wisner would make extended presentations on what the U.S. government believed to be examples of Russian experts cooperating with Iran, occasionally asking Timbie or me to elaborate or clarify certain points. The response from Adamov and Koptev became predictable. Both officials refused to acknowledge such Russian involvement beyond anything that might best be described as fleeting and superficial. In the course of their denials they often would ask for more information, knowing that there were limits on the information we could bring to bear. Our standard response was that the Russians were well placed to investigate the information we were providing. Many sessions had a marathon quality, particularly with Koptev, where our discussions on missile issues would last for ten to twelve hours.

It was in those exchanges that the limits of the intelligence authorized for the delegation's use became most apparent. Not only could we seldom answer Russian requests for more information but there often were in some areas powerful and different rebuttals that could have been made to Russian protestations of innocence in areas of specific U.S. concern. The predictable result was that little progress was made in the first year of negotiations. This is not in any way to cast blame on the intelligence community for diplomacy's failures. It was far from clear after the first year that even the most compelling evidence would have induced the Russians to interdict the cooperation some of its experts were providing Iran.

The administration's lack of progress was frustrating to the negotiating team but it also triggered in Washington political problems for the administration. The Republicans had taken control of Congress in 1996 and followed the talks with great interest. Because of Wisner's other commitments it often was left to Timbie and me to brief various Congressional members and staff on our efforts, although Wisner and I also met with Senators Biden, McCain, and Lieberman. There were many contentious moments, particularly when the Republicans began clamoring for the Clinton administration to impose sanctions on Russia, something Clinton and his national security adviser, Sandy Berger, didn't want to do because of their broader policy objective of supporting Boris Yeltsin and Russia's fledgling democracy. Here was another example of how an administration, as had some of its predecessors, framed its nonproliferation policy against the backdrop of other competing objectives.

The other reason for the administration's reluctance to impose sanctions was that the evidentiary base was unclear regarding the complicity of Russian officials in the assistance Iran was receiving from Russia. In the Russia of the 1990s it was common for individuals and small groups to undertake all types of extracurricular and unauthorized activities for profit, a practice known as na levo ("on the left") in Russian. Whether that was the type of assistance detected by U.S. intelligence was almost impossible to answer definitively and, absent compelling proof, the Clinton administration was not prepared to make accusations against the Russian government.

Adding to the administration's political woes was an ongoing series of intelligence briefings, most at the request of Republican members in Congress, given by the CIA, on the same problems and questions they also were advising the Democratic administration. There had evolved in my judgment a faction within the senior managerial ranks at Langley that opposed the use of almost all intelligence in the negotiations and a pattern became clear that those critics seemed to be particularly eager to take the message of Russian perfidy to Capitol Hill.

After Wisner and I briefed several senators, Timbie and I were asked to give a series of briefings on the progress of the negotiations to Capitol Hill. The first time we did so was particularly unpleasant. We attempted in that briefing to paint an overly optimistic picture of what was transpiring in the Moscow negotiations. It was a mistake to do so, not only because we drew well-deserved barbs from skeptical Republicans eager to criticize any perceived administration failing but also because in Washington credibility is a precious commodity easily lost. As a career officer I had endeavored in all my interactions with Capitol Hill to avoid political posturing. After that lesson our future interactions on the Hill took on a different demeanor, resolutely, and in copious detail presenting what we were and were not accomplishing. This seemed to win us at least grudging respect from even the most vociferous Republicans.

The administration's interaction with a Congress eager to find the ammunition to justify imposing sanctions also encountered other problems. After our round of briefings, Timbie and I would receive second-hand information that CIA analysts, often on the following day, were briefing the same congressional committees, usually on the most egregious examples of Russian support to Iran. That scenario played out on several occasions and, on the surface, there was nothing improper about that. Nonetheless, within the executive branch there is a long and formal tradition that the intelligence community should not cross over into policy advocacy either for or against an administration's policies. Few candid observers would deny that this barrier has been crossed through the years on various national security issues, sometimes overtly and sometimes indirectly. My respect for the Agency's support to the delegation's preparations and actual negotiations was considerable. Conversely, I could not help but consider the possibility that a different game was being played in the halls of Congress, not only from the briefings themselves but also from the leaks to the media clearly emanating from the intelligence community regarding Russian assistance to Iran. None of this was new and the policy community in every administration was no stranger to the temptations of advancing a position through the use of leaked information. Intelligence is a critical element of policy formulation but it is no less a prized tool for policy advocacy.

In watching the Agency's presentations to Congress there also were strong suspicions among others in the White House as well as at the State Department that the CIA analysts had crossed the line into policy advocacy. By showing that the negotiations were failing the Agency would be under less pressure to bring forward sensitive sources and methods for the delegation's use. None of this can be proven and none of the negotiating team ever raised a voice in protest. The Agency's standard response when queried about why they didn't inform the White House about the briefings in advance was the noncommittal "we were just honoring legitimate requests for information" but everyone who had ever watched the process understood that how those requests were honored was of critical importance. I am confident that on my watch the executive branch never tried to influence whatever messages were presented by the CIA to Congress. As a long-serving intelligence officer I was struck throughout this process by the alternating cooperation and competition between the worlds of policy and intelligence. This was a pattern that would become even more apparent in the aftermath of the September 11 attacks, particularly as the Bush administration was formulating its policy toward Iraq.

The Clinton administration's political problems extended beyond even the bitter policy disagreements with Republicans in Congress. As noted, the Israeli government's anxiety about Iran was palpable and barely contained. Both President Clinton and Vice President Gore long had been stalwart supporters of Israel as was most of the Democratic Party. It must have been uncomfortable for the party's leaders to hear the rising chorus of criticism that the administration's diplomacy was not working emanating from both Israeli officials visiting the White House and Capitol Hill and the powerful lobbying organization, the American Israel Public Affairs Committee (AIPAC). As the White House staff officer most closely associated with this issue, I had a responsibility to maintain close professional ties to the Israeli officials assigned to their embassy in Washington. Because of the special relationship between the two countries, Israel usually posts some of its most experienced officers to Washington. My counterparts from the Israeli embassy were no exception, proving always to be exceptionally capable, very well informed, and seldom at a loss to offer suggestions for ways to foster greater Russian responsiveness to the points being made by the U.S. negotiators. In their private conversations with me it was apparent that they recognized the considerable effort being expended by Wisner's team. Nonetheless, everyone involved in the process understood that little of substance had been achieved after a year of engagement. My colleagues on the delegation shared my disappointment in not making more progress.

The second year of negotiations with the Russians saw a change in our delegation. Wisner had reached a point where his commitments to the private sector no longer could be delayed and he began phasing out of his governmental work. Robert Gallucci, a highly experienced nonproliferation expert and an important figure for the United States in the Pakistan and North Korea nuclear issues became the head of the delegation. Gallucci's quick wit and casual manner did little to mask his considerable abilities. Like Wisner,

Gallucci also was not formally in government when he was asked to head the delegation, having departed the State Department to become the Dean of Georgetown University's prestigious School of Foreign Service in Washington, DC. Despite his new academic responsibilities, Gallucci was unstinting in the time allotted to the administration's diplomatic efforts.

Under Gallucci's direction the delegation continued using cleared intelligence to make the case of Russian involvement in Iran's nuclear and missile programs. The Russian response continued to emphasize the lack of specific information from the U.S. side, which if provided, Adamov and Koptev asserted, would enable them to take more robust investigatory and enforcement measures. It was a clever negotiating tactic. Gallucci came to understand quickly that the United States was playing a losing hand as Adamov and Koptev repeatedly resorted to this same formulation of denial and requests for more information.

There was at least one stylistic change brought by Gallucci's arrival. If U.S. policy and intelligence officials shared one opinion, it was that Adamov's denials were the least credible and most disturbing. During one contentious session in Moscow, Gallucci made a long and impressive presentation of U.S. concerns about various elements of Russian nuclear cooperation with Iran. Adamov, a man of few words throughout most of our sessions, listened closely and then gave a fleeting smile of derision and in essence said through his interpreter that Gallucci was lying. Gallucci was incensed, rising from his chair as if he was about to leap over the table at Adamov. The meeting broke up shortly thereafter; it became more apparent than ever after that exchange that there was little prospect for progress.

By the time the negotiations were into their second year without measurable progress, there was a growing drumbeat among the Republicans in Congress for the administration to impose sanctions beyond the Iran-Libya Sanctions Act in August 1996. The administration still was resistant, making several high-level entreaties to Russian officials to demonstrate sufficient progress in their investigations to justify the administration arguing that a decision on sanctions should be held off.

The progress hoped for by the administration never materialized. The problem actually took a turn for the worse on July 23, 1998, when Iran flight-tested the Shahab 3 medium-range ballistic missile, capable of hitting targets to about 1,300 kilometers. The missile flew for about 100 seconds before its flight was terminated, probably for technical reasons.[6] That the first test flight probably was not fully successful because of its short flight time, a rather common occurrence in any missile's early development, was more than fully compensated by its political impact in Washington and Tel Aviv. Assistance to Iran in missile technology long suspected to have been provided first by North Korean and then Russian experts proved to be accurate. With its approximate 1,300 kilometer range, the Shahab 3, when operational, would be able to hit targets throughout the Middle East, including Israel. Prime Minister

Netanyahu's characterization of Iran posing an existential threat seemed more real than ever.

Assessing the pace and direction of Iran's nuclear program has been a continuing preoccupation of policymakers and experts for well over a decade. Some maintain that incontrovertible or absolute proof of Iran's intentions to develop a nuclear weapon still has not emerged but a broader perspective, focusing on the missile program, offers some insights into Iran's intentions. The Shahab 3 flight test was a powerful indicator of the direction of Iran's nuclear ambitions. Throughout history, every nation that has developed a long-range missile capability—as Iran showed itself to be in the process of doing with the 1998 flight test—has developed nuclear weapons. There are no exceptions. The reason to have long-range missiles is to deliver nuclear weapons to target. Every other type of warhead, such as a conventional munition, has a much smaller destructive capability and coupled with the inaccuracies of cruder missiles such as the Shahab 3, are unreliable except as terror weapons against cities, an updated version of Hitler's rocket attacks against London in World War II. Moreover, developing a long-range missile program is resource intensive, requiring a long-term commitment of substantial intellectual and financial capital. As an indicator of Iran's nuclear ambitions, more attention should be paid to Iran's missile program which even in 1998 almost certainly was more advanced than Iran's nuclear program.

Doubtless goaded by Iran's newly demonstrated Shahab 3, Israeli officials began turning up the political pressure on the Clinton administration. In late 1998 a visiting Israeli delegation came to the White House and in several separate conversations, including one in which I was the target audience, inquired about the U.S. government's possible support for an Israeli military operation against Iranian facilities. Details were never spelled out in part because the administration's immediate and forceful answer was complete rejection of the idea. The Israelis doubtless were floating a trial balloon to gauge the administration's reaction but even that act of political calculation reveals the depth of Israeli anxieties regarding Iran.

The Shahab 3 flight test, combined with the continuing lack of progress in the negotiations with the Russians and Israel's mounting frustrations, coalesced into political pressures the administration could no longer ignore on imposing sanctions against Russian entities identified as supporting Iran's nuclear and missile programs. The administration made that decision in 1999 with National Security Adviser Berger conveying the news to his Russian counterpart. The subsequent headlines caused ill will between the two countries but did no permanent damage to the bilateral relationship.

The imposition of sanctions, in conjunction with the rapidly approaching end of the Clinton administration, had the practical effect of concluding the U.S. government's sustained efforts to negotiate an end to Russian assistance in Iran. The outcome hoped for several years earlier never materialized. The administration never presented Yeltsin's government enough reason to close down, or even actively investigate, most of the types of technical assistance Russian experts were providing Iran. In a world of different political realities Yeltsin's government would not have needed such inducements; however, that world didn't exist in the late 1990s.

What were the reasons for the failure? Led by two highly skilled negotiators, backed by the complete political support of the White House, and supported by a strong interagency cast of experts, U.S. efforts were hardly lacking. One proximate cause of failure doubtless was the delegation's inability to place the most troubling and persuasive cases of Russian cooperation with Iran in front of the Russian government because of the U.S. intelligence community's desire to protect sensitive sources and methods. As noted, under different conditions that situation would have never arisen because the Russian government would have been as committed as its U.S. counterparts to ferreting out and closing down such behavior. It wasn't. The Russian government had developed long-standing and extensive trade relations with the Iranians, including the sale of conventional armaments that ran into the billions of dollars. For this and broader policy reasons related to Russia's long-term and geostrategic interests in the Persian Gulf, the Yeltsin government wasn't prepared to jeopardize its relationship with Iran, at least at the U.S. government's behest. In the end, the administration didn't give the Yeltsin government sufficient reason to seriously undertake such a change and it is far from certain there was any inducement sufficiently powerful that could have been offered by Washington.

During the Bush administration's first months in office there was no relent in Iran's nuclear and missile programmatic efforts. This is not to say that these programs progressed smoothly or without technical problems. On the contrary, Iran's developmental work in both areas proved susceptible to the almost inevitable problems that arise during highly complex scientific and technical projects, even those assisted by experienced outsiders. Iran's Shahab 3, for example, almost certainly was plagued by a series of technical problems.[7]

The new administration took little comfort from such delays. Suspicion of Iran ran high from the administration's first days in office, doubtless centered on the seemingly unshakable grip on Iran's political reins by the theocrats who had ousted one of America's most important allies in the region, the Shah, and exhibited enmity to another important ally, Israel. Other more pressing problems soon came to the fore and would provide some of the backdrop for the administration's policies toward and perceptions of Iran. Only eight months into his first term at the time of the September 11 attacks, George Bush and his administration were thrust into not only a new conflict but a new type of conflict characterized by an enemy adroit at the art of asymmetric warfare, demonstrating to a shocked administration and American public that it could inflict enormous suffering on America despite its negligible military power.

The administration concluded, in formulating a new counterterrorism and national security strategy, that it should draw a wide circle around not only terrorist organizations such as bin Laden's al Qaeda but also those nations that might support terrorism. Iran was at the top of that list. In his January 29, 2002, State of the Union address, coming just four months after the terrorist attacks against America, George Bush starkly described the emerging threats posed by Iran, Iraq, and North Korea. The president declared that, "states like these, and their terrorist allies, constitute an axis of evil."[8] Speaking before a national audience and watched by millions more abroad, the president's remarks introduced into the political lexicon a phrase that would resonate throughout the administration's tenure in office. Ayatollah Khamenei and other senior Iranians issued swift and predictable denunciations of the president's remarks, but it is unclear if Tehran's ruling circles felt that George Bush's uncompromising rhetoric was a harbinger for U.S. military action against Iran. Such calculations of possible U.S. military intervention probably were a factor in Libyan President Qaddafi's decision a year later to forgo the development of nuclear weapons, but Iran was not Libya, beginning with Tehran's far greater financial resources and military capabilities. In any event, it is likely that Iranian hardliners around Ahmadinejad interpreted those and subsequent remarks from the administration as reinforcement or justification for whatever plans they had set in motion years ago.

Events in 2002 seemed to present new indications that resources dedicated to Iran's nuclear program at least in part were intended to serve military purposes. The most alarming occurred on August 14, 2002, when the National Council of Resistance of Iran (NCRI), an Iranian opposition group, made a public claim that it had identified through well-placed and reliable Iranian government sources a "secret nuclear program." The alleged elements of that program were a heavy-water production facility at Arak (to be accompanied by a 40 MW research reactor) and a nuclear fuel production facility at Natanz. The NCRI also claimed that a front company, the Mesbah Energy Company, had been established to mislead prying eyes into the real purpose of the Arak project. The NCRI also identified four nuclear research centers at Karaj, Borab, Saghand, and Amerabad.[9] In general, reporting from dissident groups and organizations in exile must be assessed carefully. Some, not all, often attempt various tactics to discredit the ruling regime they oppose, including dissemination of false or embarrassing information. At least in terms of its accuracy, such was not the case with this reporting.

Within a month of the NCRI report, commercial satellite photography indicated that there were large construction projects underway at Natanz and also near Arak which is located about 150 miles south of Tehran.[10] To trained observers the imagery seemed to suggest that at least parts of the facilities were being constructed underground, both as a likely attempt to conceal the nature of the activity and to reduce their vulnerability to possible attack. That Iran was apparently expending considerable resources on clandestine activities with potential military application fueled international concern.

The Arak project, for example, is particularly troubling to proliferation experts. Iran reportedly had tried to purchase from China a similar, 30 MW heavy-water reactor in 1991 but the deal fell through. With the Arak project Iran now seemed to have made another effort to acquire a heavy-water reactor, this time through its own labors. Heavy water is the term for deuterium oxide. When heavy water is used in reactors it increases the efficiency of the nuclear reaction, making the breeding of plutonium much easier and less expensive than acquiring plutonium from a light-water reactor such as the one under construction at Bushehr. Heavy-water reactors have been used to support the nuclear weapons programs in Israel, Pakistan, and India. In describing the U.S. government's reaction to the revelation of Iran's projects at Natanz and Arak, State Department spokesman Richard Boucher stated at a December 13, 2002, briefing that "these facilities are not justified by the needs of Iran's civilian nuclear program."[11]

European concern about the Arak project was sufficiently high to result in a European offer to replace the Arak project with a different type of reactor which the Iranians refused. The IAEA also assessed the project with considerable skepticism. To date, none of this has deterred Iran's efforts to move forward with the project. On August 26, 2006, Iranian President Ahmadinejad inaugurated the heavy-water production plant at Arak while the research reactor remained under construction. Most experts assess that the production plant could be completed by 2009 and within a year or so begin producing enough plutonium for two to three nuclear devices.[12]

Iran's long-range missile program also continued apace. In July 2003, Iran conducted the final flight test of the Shahab 3, which began making appearances in various Iranian parades and celebrations to demonstrate Iran's growing military might. The missile's accuracy and reliability still were subjects of debate to Western technical experts but the political repercussions in Israel and throughout the region of a long-range missile being paraded through the streets of Tehran were considerable. In international politics perception can be as powerful as reality. In this case the perception and reality both seemed to indicate that Iran was becoming a growing threat to regional stability.

As Israeli threat perceptions became more acute its public rhetoric became more strident. In a November 2002 interview in the *Financial Times,* Prime Minister Ariel Sharon said Iran was the center of world terror and, as a consequence, should be the next in line for U.S. "attention" after the war in Iraq was completed. In January 2003, Project Daniel, a nongovernmental report prepared for Sharon, was explicit in its description of the various threats that a country as small as Israel faced in the Middle East, including nuclear attack. The study group, consisting of United States as well as Israeli experts, recommended that Israel be prepared to carry out preemptive attacks and covert operations against any nation's WMD facilities that might be deemed threatening.[13] In March 2003, General Moshe Ya'alon, a former Israeli Chief of Staff, said the United States, Israel, and the European community should consider launching air strikes against about fifteen suspected Iranian nuclear facilities. The following month the Israeli paper Ha'aretz reported that the Israeli ambassador in Washington was advocating regime change in Iran.[14]

Some might discount Israel's growing rhetorical broadsides as merely another piece in Tel Aviv's protracted and badly strained relations with Tehran, but Iranian developments also became of greater concern to Britain, France, and Germany, the so-called EU3, who stepped up their efforts to engage Iran in negotiations over its nuclear programs. Those talks had begun in June 2003 and took on new urgency in September 2003. For its part Iran remained resolute in maintaining that its nuclear programs and facilities, described in some detail to the IAEA in September 2003, were merely a reflection of its right to full-scale nuclear development within the terms of the NPT. IAEA Director General el Baradei had visited Iran in early 2003 and that summer his experts had issued a preliminary report based on their own visits concluding that many uncertainties still shrouded Iranian activities.

In September the IAEA increased its pressure at its General Conference in Vienna, formally stating that Iran had until the end of October to address the following areas of concern:

- Sampling at Natanz found two types of highly enriched uranium (HEU)
- IAEA inspections showed modifications to the Kalaye Electric Company
- Iran was requested to update its statement on nuclear materials since its last report

Iran was requested to explain why it had introduced nuclear materials into its pilot centrifuge at Natanz.

Iranian officials rebuffed quickly the substance and time limit placed by the IAEA, leading to the possibility of an open rift with the international organization. It was at this point that EU3's diplomacy would start to yield results. Accepting an invitation from the Iranian leadership, the EU3's foreign ministers visited Tehran in late October 2003. They seemed to have defused the looming crisis when Iran agreed to the voluntary suspension of all enrichment and reprocessing activities "as defined by the IAEA" and signed the IAEA Additional Protocol, a process of enhanced international inspections. While the Iranian government had not met the IAEA's requested timeline or responded directly to that international body, IAEA Director General el Baradei in late November signaled his approval of the deal struck with the EU3. On December 18, Iran signed the Additional Protocols but never ratified them.

The modest progress of late 2003 gave way to mounting recriminations and suspicions in 2004. A new IAEA report early that year again took the Iranians to task for lack of transparency, particularly with regard to the P-2 centrifuge designs. Suspicions were only heightened when revelations surfaced describing the scope and extent of A. Q. Khan's international network of proliferators, including the assistance they provided Iran regarding these same centrifuge designs. Iran's credibility with EU3 and IAEA continued a slow

decline, exacerbated on June 27, 2004, when Iran announced it would continue to manufacture centrifuges, contrary to its 2003 commitment to EU3
and IAEA.

The official U.S. reaction to these events was unambiguous. A clear example of Washington's growing impatience were the remarks contained in a
speech by Undersecretary of State John Bolton in late summer 2004. According to Bolton,

> Iran is pursuing two separate paths to nuclear weapons, one that would use highly
> enriched uranium for nuclear weapons and one that would use plutonium. The
> costly infrastructure to perform all of these activities goes well beyond any conceiv-
> able nuclear program. No comparable oil-rich nation has ever engaged, or would be
> engaged, in this set of activities—or would pursue them for nearly two decades
> behind a continuing cloud of secrecy and lies to IAEA inspectors and the interna-
> tional community—unless it was dead set on building nuclear weapons.[15]

The deterioration of IAEA trust in Iran also mounted in the second half of
2004 with the publication of several reports highlighting Iran's continued
obfuscation of various nuclear-related activities. Once again the EU3 stepped
in; negotiating in late November, just before an IAEA meeting that would
have been critical of Iran, what came to be described as the Paris Agreement.
The sides agreed "to begin negotiations with a view of reaching mutually acceptable agreement on long-term arrangements. The agreement will provide
objective guarantees that Iran's nuclear program is exclusively for peaceful
purposes."[16]

For a few months there seemed a glimmer of hope that Iran this time
would honor its commitments. Bush administration officials, including Vice
President Cheney and Secretary of State Rice, rather lukewarm to the EU3
efforts initially, began expressing support for their work. The United States
also agreed in March 2005 to drop its long-standing objections to Iranian
application for membership into the World Trade Organization.

Iranian politics soon became a driving factor in events over the ensuing
months. Some prospect for resolution seemed to loom with President Khata-
mi's support for the March 2005, General Framework for Objective Guarantees, which set out a four-phase plan that would included Iran's finalizing the
Additional Protocols, increased IAEA monitoring of Iranian nuclear activities
in exchange for agreed European willingness to open its energy markets to
Iran and allow Iran access to nuclear power plants. In essence, the trade of
political commitments on Iran's part in exchange for tangible European commitments was seen as badly flawed. European leaders such as Prime Minister
Tony Blair began speaking publicly of the possible need to refer Iran's
nuclear file to the United Nations Security Council for action, deeming it
essential for Iran to end all enrichment activities, something its supreme
leader was not prepared to accept. The General Framework became an almost

instant dead letter when in May 2005 Iran said it would resume uranium enrichment activities at Esfahan.

A NUCLEAR IRAN: THE ARAB VIEW

At the beginning of the Clinton administration's 1997 diplomatic push to loosen the support Russian experts were providing Iran's nuclear and missile programs, Wisner and I traveled to Egypt where we met with Egyptian President Hosni Mubarak at his summer residence. Having served as U.S. ambassador in Egypt for four years, Wisner knew Mubarak well. Our purpose in meeting the Egyptian president was to convey the U.S. government's concerns about Iran's nuclear activities and to solicit Egypt's assistance in monitoring them. Mubarak agreed to such cooperation but little apparently came of that commitment.

This incident was a reflection of both public and official indifference in various quarters of the Arab world to the scope and pace of Iran's nuclear as well as missile programs until about 2005. Although conclusive evidence is lacking to explain this attitude, Arab leaders may have calculated that mounting U.S. and European interest in Iran would be sufficient to resolve any problems, freeing the Arab states from having to take a public position critical of Tehran. Israel's nuclear capabilities, although officially shrouded as a long-standing policy by the Israeli government, probably were another factor in the reluctance of Arab states to criticize Iran, a nation patently hostile to Israel that might be pursuing capabilities to match those of the Tel Aviv government.

These nuanced assessments began changing in 2005 to 2006, albeit obliquely. Jordanian King Abdullah II began speaking publicly about Jordan's interest in a civil nuclear program. In addition to Gamal Mubarak's own public musings about Egypt's possible interest in a civil nuclear program, in December 2006 the members of the Gulf Cooperation Council (GCC)—Bahrain, Kuwait, Oman, Qatar, Saudi Arabia, and the United Arab Emirates—approached representatives from IAEA with plans for a joint civil nuclear program. Those talks continued into 2007.[17] Civil nuclear programs are fully accepted within the NPT framework but, over time, because of their inherent dual use nature they also can form the building blocks for a nuclear weapons program or at least nuclear weapons research.

There may have been other and totally unrelated factors at work as well. It is unclear if the Egyptians, Jordanians, or the GCC were driven by energy concerns that would have prompted the development of nuclear power, Israel's nuclear capabilities, or Iran's programmatic activities. At the very least it is clear from Saudi Arabia's contemplation of "leasing" nuclear weapons that at least some of the Arab nations in the region are growing increasingly restive over Iran. How the administration after Bush's deals with evolving Arab concerns and interest in nuclear technology could become one of its most important diplomatic challenges.

Another in this series of negative turns came in June 2005 with the surprise victory of Mahmoud Ahmadinejad in the Iranian presidential election. The new Iranian president would have his share of domestic problems, a number of which were exacerbated by his policy choices, but there was little ambiguity on his views regarding Iran's right to develop nuclear programs. Ahmadinejad burnished his credentials as a hard liner on the issue immediately after his election. On June 25 he stated, "It is the right of the Iranian nation to move forward in all fields and acquire nuclear technology."[18] Such statements added to the continuing disillusionment within the Bush administration, the EU3, and Israel regarding the prospects for an end to the impasse, no matter how much Ahmadinejad tried to assure that Iran's programs were consistent with the NPT.

PRESIDENT AHMADINEJAD: AN INTERNATIONAL BULLY BUT DOMESTICALLY EMBATTLED POLITICIAN?

Iranian President Mahmoud Ahmadinejad has a well-earned reputation for incendiary and heinous rhetoric in his descriptions of international events. Whether threatening to "wipe Israel off the map" or denying the Holocaust, Ahmadinejad has shown the bully's instincts in many of his remarks on foreign affairs. Iranian support to Hamas and Hezbollah, in addition to its nuclear ambitions, has burnished the image of the Iranian government as pursuing an aggressive, and to some, extreme set of policy preferences. This combination of assertiveness and defiance has made Ahmadinejad a highly popular figure in some parts of the Muslim world. While his often inflammatory and extemporaneous remarks may conceal underlying nuanced calculations regarding their effects on various international audiences, there is little doubt but that Ahmadinejad also swims in troubled domestic waters where his political standing is far from absolute.

As a former mayor of Tehran, by far Iran's largest and most important city, Ahmadinejad might have been expected to develop a modicum of political skills. In one respect he demonstrated these skills by his unexpected ascension to the Iranian presidency in August 2005, a position second only to that of supreme leader Ayatollah Khamenei. Portraying himself as a populist committed to addressing Iran's considerable domestic woes, beginning with high inflation and equally high unemployment, Ahmadinejad defeated the better known and former president Ayatollah Rafsanjani.

That political high-water mark was followed by a series of political gaffes almost from Ahmadinejad's first days in office. Similar to the purges of Iranian professionals in the 1980s, he fired nearly 20,000 bureaucrats, the backbone of Iran's administrative cadre, while eschewing any efforts to ally himself politically with the traditional conservatives, Khamenei's powerful supporters. Campaign promises notwithstanding, Ahmadinejad offered few, if any, solutions to Iran's economic woes that persist despite Iran's considerable oil wealth that often is spent on subsidizing gasoline prices and inefficient public works projects.

Foreign investment has slowed considerably, doubtless in large measure because of Ahmadinejad's foreign policies. Unemployment shows no signs of abating while food and housing prices continue to rise by at least 15 percent to 20 percent annually. Iran's economy has visible and important fault lines.

This litany of problems has taken a toll on the Iranian president's domestic popularity which hovers around 35 percent. His unpopularity was reflected in the December 2006 elections for the clerical Assembly of Experts who advise the supreme leader. Candidates associated with Ahmadinejad were soundly defeated, although Parvin Ahmadinejad, the president's sister, won a seat on the Tehran City Council along with forty other women.

For the president, the election results sparked a round of sharp criticism of both his domestic and foreign policies. Throughout December, a state-run radio ran programming debating the hard line taken by Ahmadinejad on the nuclear question. In January 2007, a small majority in the Iranian parliament formally criticized his handling of Iran's festering economic and unemployment prob- lems. Soon thereafter, *Jomhouri Eslami*, a newspaper that supports Khamenei, went public with the view that Ahmadinejad had managed the nuclear issue poorly and that his efforts to tout that program at every turn in part was intended to distract from his mismanagement of the economy. Within Iran, Ahmadinejad's oft-chanted mantra that atomic energy is Iran's inalienable right has become the punch line in a series of jokes. As the paper's editorial pointed out, "Anything that is repeated more than necessary instead of strengthening the will, leads to dismissal. The fact that in every speech in every city you talk about nuclear energy does not seem to be the right strategy." Shortly thereafter, a second editorial in the popular newspaper *Hamshari* opined that an "effective strategy" on the nuclear issue was needed before the cost to the country became too high.[19] At least for the short-term it appears that Ahmadinejad has lost some of Khamenei's support and confidence but in the complex currents of Iranian politics it may be too soon to know the long-term effect of this sparring on Iran's president.

Other statements by the new Iranian president only fueled those concerns. During an October 25, 2005, speech to a group of 4,000 Iranian students at a program titled "The World Without Zionism," Ahmadinejad said, "The estab- lishment of the Zionist regime was a move by the world oppressor against the Islamic world.... The skirmishes in the occupied land are part of a new war of destiny.... As the Imam said, Israel must be wiped off the map."[20] Reac- tion from Israel was pointed and swift; Prime Minister Sharon called for Iran's expulsion from the United Nations while the United States and various European nations rose in vociferous protest at the Iranian president's incendi- ary remarks. Undaunted by such broad condemnation, or perhaps energized by it, Ahmadinejad proceeded to deny the Holocaust in a December 2, 2005, speech at a Muslim summit. Political rhetoric, even at its most inflammatory, often is targeted for different audiences and for different purposes and, some- times, can be more alarming that a nation's intended course of action. Such was not the case here. Ahmadinejad's remarks can only be described as at such variance from civil discourse—or what passes for it at times among nations—that complete rejection of its message was the only credible response from the West and Israel. Perhaps more alarming was the prospect that the president of a major nation in the region had a messianic vision of politics that he might attempt to carry out.

Nonetheless, Ahmadinejad was Iran's president and there was little prospect of that changing in the near-term. His combative stance extended to an increasingly confrontational posture in response to the EU3 and IAEA's repeated requests for Iranian transparency in its nuclear work. In the last half of 2005 Iran announced it would restart its enrichment process, setting up a confrontation with EU3 in early 2006. At that time the Europeans concluded that their efforts to negotiate a resolution to the Iran problem had stalled due to a "documented record of concealment and defeat."[21] Shortly thereafter, in March 2006, the United Nations Security Council became directly involved in the controversy, noting that it had serious concerns about Iran's record of not complying with IAEA requests. U.N. Security Council Resolution 1696 also was passed at that time, calling on Iran to end its enrichment work by the end of August 2006. Ayatollah Khamenei responded by stating that the Security Council was a paper factory for issuing worthless and ineffective orders. Iranian nuclear-related activities did not cease as a result of the U.N. demand, setting up a new level of diplomatic confrontation on December 23, 2006, when Security Council Resolution 1737, sponsored by France, the United Kingdom, and Germany, passed unanimously.

The product of months of diplomatic wrangling between the United States, Russia, and China over whether and how to impose sanctions, Security Council Resolution 1737 was a watershed, marking the first time sanctions had been imposed on Iran by that international body for its nuclear and missile programs. The resolution called on Iran to suspend all enrichment-related and reprocessing activities; work on all heavy-water related projects, including research and development; and all states were directed to refrain from providing any technical or financial external assistance to those activities.

The sanctions were not as punitive as some in the Bush administration might have desired. Nonetheless, the international community had formally said that Iran's activities, empty promises and unsatisfactory explanations, could no longer be ignored. Because the resolution draws on Article 41 of Chapter VII of the U.N. Charter, military force is not permitted as a means of enforcing the resolution. Rather, economic sanctions have been imposed, centered on freezing the assets of organizations and individuals associated with Iran's nuclear and missile programs. The following Iranian organizations engaged in nuclear-related activities of concern to the United Nations were cited in the resolution:

- Atomic Energy Organization of Iran
- Mesbah Energy Company

- Kala Electric
- Pars Trash Company
- Farayand Technique
- Defense Industrial Organization
- 7th of Tir

The following Iranian organizations engaged in missile-related activities of concern to the United Nations were cited in the resolution:

- Shahid Hemmat Industrial Group
- Shahid Bagheri Industrial Group
- Fajr Industrial Group

The U.N. Security Council Resolution 1737 also cited various Iranians associated with the above organizations and named Major General Yahya Rahim Safavi, Commander-in-Chief of the Iranian Revolutionary Guards Corps as involved in both programs.[22]

Reactions to the U.N. Security Council decision fell along predictable lines. Iranian spokesmen derided the action while maintaining that Iran's inalienable right to develop nuclear technology could not be impinged. Official U.S. and Israeli commentary expressed satisfaction with the action while underscoring the need for Iranian compliance and continued IAEA vigilance with Iran's programmatic activities. Vitaly Churkin, Russian Ambassador to the United Nations, whose country had spent months opposing and attempting to slow progress on the sanctions resolution, highlighted in his assessment of the resolution that Iran would have the sanctions lifted if it complied with the U.N. Security Council demands.

Regardless of Russia's differing perspectives and emphasis, U.N. Security Council Resolution 1737 put the international community's relationship with Iran on a different footing. At the same time, virtually all observers recognized that the sanctions lacked the scope or power to compel any favorable change in Iran's behavior as Iranian actions demonstrated. Iran still remained defiant after the imposition of the sanctions, refusing to halt its nuclear activities, carrying out more developmental work for the Shahab 3 missile. Ahmadinejad poured oil on the political flames swirling around Iran's recalcitrance, saying in late February 2007, that "Iran has worked the technology to produce nuclear fuel and Iran's movement on this path is like a train on a one-way track with no room for stopping, reverse gear or braking."[23] The statement drew a round of criticism even from some Iranian factions seeking a peaceful resolution to the problem, but they were powerless to restrain Iran's equally provocative actions a month later, when the Iranian Revolutionary Guard Corps (IRGC) seized fifteen Britons—eight sailors and seven marines—conducting operations in what the British government maintained were Iraqi waters near Iran. The hostages were released as an "Easter present" to the British government in early April 2007.

On March 24, 2007, a new round of sanctions was imposed unanimously under U.N. Security Council Resolution 1747.[24] The new sanctions add to the first sanctions list an additional fifteen individuals and thirteen organizations, including the state-owned Bank Sepah and IRGC, the elite military force that operates separately from other parts of the armed forces. Iranian arms exports are banned but curiously, arms imports were not addressed. Russian President Putin and Chinese President Hu Jintao both underscored the importance of Iran responding to the underlying reasons for the Security Council's actions. Those actions and remarks did nothing to bring any change in Iran's nuclear policies which in April 2007 announced that it had enriched uranium on an industrial scale.[25]

There has been little in Iran's actions or pronouncements to suggest a crisis isn't in the offing. Sparked by remarks from President Bush and Vice President Cheney that "all options were on the table" regarding U.S. policy choices for dealing with Iran's nuclear program, reports and rumors had circulated through Washington for several years that the administration was considering a military strike against Iran. Unconfirmed reports in 2005 surfaced from the German news agency DDP that CIA Director Porter Goss in late December 2005 asked Turkish Prime Minister Erdogan to provide Turkish support for a possible air attack against Iran.[26] Such reporting gathered momentum in 2006 and early 2007 as Iran's defiance of the Security Council became more pronounced. Seymour Hersh, one of America's most accomplished investigative journalists, wrote an article in the *New Yorker* magazine describing Air Force planning for strikes against Iran and parallel efforts by U.S. Special Forces to initiate contacts with various Iranian minority groups throughout the country.[27] Secretary of Defense Robert Gates, among others, denied that the administration had plans for any imminent military action, but not all international observers were convinced, probably beginning with the ruling theocrats in Tehran. The deployment to the Persian Gulf of the aircraft carrier USS John Stennis and a supporting naval battle group joined the USS Eisenhower carrier battle group, representing a doubling of U.S. naval firepower in the region and doubtless conveying a different signal to Tehran than the statement issued by Secretary Gates.

Political rhetoric at times can be both powerful and at other times deliberately vague. The Bush administration had been describing the evolving Iranian threat as "unacceptable" for at least several years, an assessment interpreted by many as conveying a readiness to undertake some type of concerted action. Would those actions be limited to supporting U.N. Security Council Resolutions? As Iran continued to defy the international community, the increasingly-likely answer seemed to be no. What is the range of policy options that might be under consideration by the administration?

Options for Ending the Iranian Nuclear Threat

DOES IRAN PLAN to use nuclear technology to develop nuclear weapons? After years of debate and growing suspicions, the international community, as reflected in U.N. Security Council Resolutions 1737 and 1747, has shown its strong suspicions about Iran's nuclear intentions. Iran has carried out so many legally questionable activities for so long and concealed them from international scrutiny on so many occasions while developing a parallel long-range missile program that the only logical explanation is that Iran is seeking a nuclear weapons capability and the means of delivery. The Security Council's first, modest steps to compel Iranian compliance with its resolutions almost certainly will fail. For the Bush administration, the question that has consumed and confounded it since early in its first term has been the development of a policy likely to bring success against a regime of seemingly unremitting hostility toward and contempt for the international community. In this policy context success can be defined as an end to Iran's efforts to produce, either through enrichment or reprocessing, sufficient quantities of fissile material to make a nuclear device. In addition, and consistent with other discussions in this book, policies and programs would continue to work to ensure that Iran (as well as other nations) did not acquire those materials directly through external sources. Because the current U.N. approach of mild economic sanctions is unlikely to lead to this outcome, we will turn our attention to the other options available to the United States to end the Iranian threat.

Prior to taking up that question directly, it is instructive to inquire into two related issues, Iranian threat perceptions and the current (as of early 2007) state of its nuclear program. In so doing we encounter immediately an underlying element of uncertainty in assessing both issues. U.S. intelligence supporting policy debates on Iranian motives and technical developments is often incomplete and sometimes inaccurate. It is not a question of lack of resource commitment on the part of the intelligence community; the collection and analytic resources dedicated to this problem are extensive, although they perhaps are reduced because of the requirement to support U.S. military operations in Iraq. Nonetheless, the entire history of U.S. efforts to assess and formulate responses to proliferation in Pakistan, North Korea, and Iran is littered with intelligence assessments that widely missed the mark. Because of this intelligence shortfall, some policy questions on Iran have to draw too heavily, in my judgment, on a variety of open or unclassified sources, including Iranian governmental pronouncements, reporting from dissident groups bitterly opposed to the theocratic government, and classified liaison reporting from cooperative states in the region, all with their own national interests at stake. Sources of this type doubtless have utility and on numerous occasions have served policymakers well. But such sources also have obvious analytic limitations. Policymakers have the prerogative of picking and choosing what unclassified and classified sources they will emphasize in their deliberations; the problem arises, particularly when assessing broad questions of Iranian intent and plans, when multiple or sensitive sources are not available to factor into the policy mix. For the foreseeable future policymakers will be faced with the likely prospect that many of their deliberations will not be informed or guided by consistently reliable and comprehensive insights into Iran.

The consequences for regional stability of Iran's acquiring a nuclear weapon have been presented in the previous chapter. Is it appropriate now to assess Iran's threat perceptions? What does the region and world look like from Tehran? What shapes its threat perceptions? Lacking definitive information for the reasons cited above, some recent events in Iran's history offer some speculative comments. Iran's long and bloody battle with Iraq remains burned into Iranian thinking, not only for the losses of Iranian military and civilian personnel, estimated as being in the tens of thousands, but also because of Iraq's use of chemical weapons that, in Iranian eyes, were never criticized by the international community. Prior to Israel's successful 1981 attack against the Iraqi Osirak reactor, in 1980 the Iranians had attempted a similar attack, albeit unsuccessfully. Iran is not a stranger to both the potential of and threats posed by weapons of mass destruction (WMD).

On the whole, Iran's theocratic rulers hold uncompromisingly strident views of America and Israel but they have often been pragmatic, not irrational, in choosing courses of action to protect Iran's security interests—an assessment that juxtaposes with President Ahmadinejad's often grotesque and vituperative statements. For example, when confronted with disadvantageous military circumstances, Iranian rulers have not engaged in suicidal actions. At the outset of its war with Iraq in 1980, Iranian political rhetoric called for the war continuing until Saddam Hussein was removed from power or soundly defeated. However, as Iranian losses mounted from a series of Iraqi victories, the Iranian leadership correctly assessed its predicament and sued for peace, dropping its broader political objectives concerning Hussein. Regarding Israel, the Iranian approach has been to avoid direct confrontation with its regional adversary. To be sure, Tehran has supported actively its proxy, Hezbollah, which has caused considerable trouble for the Israeli political and military establishments. At this point, however, the Iranian leadership does not appear to seek a major conflict or direct confrontation with the still highly capable Israeli armed forces. In this context, Iranian military planners doubtless are fully conversant with the views of some in the Israeli political and military leadership regarding their advocacy of preemptive attack against Iranian nuclear and missile facilities. Iran's considerable expenditure of the resources required to construct various nuclear-related facilities underground and locate them throughout the country almost certainly stems in large measure from that concern.

For the Iranian leadership, the presence of U.S. military forces in the region likely is a source of even deeper concern. Ironically, U.S. military operations that toppled the Iraqi regime of Saddam Hussein, Iran's bitter foe, and its prosecution (with NATO) of hostilities against the Taliban in Afghanistan, another Iranian foe, have been far from detrimental to Iranian strategic interests in the Middle East. Nonetheless, the presence of a large number of weary but now battle-hardened U.S. forces in an adjoining country, along with the growing U.S. naval presence in the Persian Gulf, can't be ignored in any strategic assessment undertaken in Tehran. In addition, the U.S. Air Force's global ability to strike targets quickly and powerfully with precision-guided munitions launched from aircraft, along with its inventory of highly accurate long-range cruise missiles, is a constant reminder that the U.S. military remains the most potent fighting force in the world.

Despite, or perhaps because of this strategic calculus, Iran's chosen path has been defiance of the international community, pursuing military capabilities, although not yet fully developed, as a possible counterweight to U.S. presence in the region. What is absent from this equation, however, is that Iran's nuclear and missile programs have a lineage that extends in time much further back than the Bush administration's invasions of Iraq and Afghanistan. Iran's nuclear and missile programs in no way can be seen as a retort to the current or past administration; there are too many factors that have been in play for too long. As such, it is impossible to ignore the growing body of evidence that Iran has harbored a consistent and long-term strategy to become a nuclear weapons state.

If this assessment is accurate, the timeline for Iran's possible acquisition of a nuclear device becomes a critical issue for policymakers. Again, myriad uncertainties surround this question. Since at least the early 1990s, U.S. and Israeli policymakers, intelligence analysts, military commanders, and nongovernmental experts have devoted considerable attention to this issue but often have been wide of the mark. For example:[1]

- Early 1991: Israeli officials claim that Iran with Pakistan's assistance could make a bomb by the end of the decade.
- January 1995: U.S. Defense Secretary William Perry says Iran may be less than five years from having a weapon.
- 1996: Israeli Prime Minister Shimon Peres says Iran may develop nuclear weapons within four years.

- 2002: Central Intelligence Agency Director George Tenet says Iran is seeking long-range ballistic missiles and WMD and probably will have them by 2015. According to Tenet, Iran may be able to produce enough fissile material indigenously by the end of this decade for a nuclear weapon.
- January 2005: Meir Dogan, head of the Israeli intelligence service Mossad, says Iran's program is almost at the point of no return, claiming that once Iran has succeeded in enriching uranium that it is "home free."
- June 2006: Director of National Intelligence John Negroponte says Iran could have a nuclear bomb between 2010 and 2015.

Iran may not succeed quickly in mastering the intricacies of fissile material production, but that is a very risky position to take as a basis for policy positions. The easiest and fastest route for Iran to cross the nuclear threshold, which it apparently has not done as of early 2007, would be to acquire a sufficient amount of fissile material from another nation, either through purchase or illicit diversion. In this scenario Iran might fabricate a nuclear device within approximately twelve to twenty-four months of the actual acquisition of the fissile material. The timelines associated with the other routes to a nuclear device—Iran's indigenous enrichment and reprocessing programs—also don't lend themselves to precise estimates. The reprocessing route, dependent to a considerable extent by progress at the Arak facility, could possibly produce enough plutonium to make two to three bombs by 2009 to 2010 at the earliest.

David Albright, president of the Institute for Science and International Security, in mid-2006 applied his considerable insights as a former International Atomic Energy Agency (IAEA) inspector to the development of what he describes as two worst-case scenarios for Iran to obtain highly enriched uranium.[2] According to Albright and Hinderstein, those paths would be a clandestine centrifuge enrichment capability and a "breakout" centrifuge enrichment capability. Noting the many technical uncertainties surrounding these estimates such as the level of Iran's centrifuge development in the face of some IAEA reporting unresolved technical problems in mastering that technology, their assessments can be summarized as follows:[3]

- In the clandestine scenario, construction of a secret plant, if it had commenced in early 2006, probably wouldn't be completed before the end of 2007. From that point it would take at least one year to produce sufficient highly enriched uranium (HEU) for a nuclear device. After that, converting the components into a weapon would take an additional few months, putting the earliest date for Iran to cross the nuclear threshold at 2009.
- In the breakout scenario, Iran continues its efforts to install 3,000 centrifuges in its production-scale plant. Without major delays this could be completed by 2009 or 2010. At that time the centrifuges could be reconfigured to make HEU, which then would require a few months at least of additional work to weaponize or convert the HEU into a nuclear device. Successful completion of a "breakout" program could be 2009 to 2010.

If Albright and Hinderstein are correct, the international community still has some time to pursue a combination of diplomatic initiatives and various forms of sanctions to change Iranian behavior. Iran's obstructionism and deceit yield few reasons to believe that it would be prepared in the immediate future to slow or stop the nuclear and missile activities that resulted in the imposition of U.N. sanctions. Nonetheless, every effort should be made to formulate a comprehensive effort from the United States and its European partners. Concurrently, it must be recognized that an Iranian nuclear reversal along the lines chosen in the past by South Africa, Brazil, or Argentina seems highly unlikely. Recognizing that diplomacy and the first rounds of mild Security Council sanctions seem increasingly unlikely to succeed, policymakers would have a set of options, short of resorting to military operations, which can be summarized as:

- Toughened economic and financial sanctions, possibly accompanied by increasing political isolation for the regime.
- Negotiation of a comprehensive agreement that addresses Iranian security concerns in return for an end to the threatening elements of the Iranian nuclear and missile program.
- Regime change, presumably the result of internal political upheaval rather than the even more difficult process of attempting to effect change from outside the country, although regime change also could be a desired outcome of a U.S. attack against Iran. General regime change could be accompanied by efforts to induce or, if necessary, forcibly remove key Iranian scientists from their work.

Because there is no reliable methodology for confidently assessing the efficacy of any set of nonmilitary options until their implementation is underway, various government officials and experts have been looking closely at the prospects for carrying out military operations against Iranian nuclear and missile facilities. Israel was successful in carrying out an air strike in 1981 against the Iraqi reactor at Osirak, but that model also provides scant guidance for the consideration of any similar operation against Iran. Osirak was one target, in the middle of the desert and above ground. In Iran, an attacking nation or coalition would confront multiple targets located in various parts of the country. Many of them are partially or completely buried underground, while others are located in or near population areas. Iran is determined that its assets will not suffer the fate of the Iraqi reactor, at least not without the expenditure of enormous effort from the attacker.

A review of the history of similar decisions shows that on most occasions nations have been reluctant to carry out preemptive attacks against those actively pursuing or developing a nuclear weapons program. Note the following examples:[4]

- During World War II the Allies spared no effort in repeatedly trying and in 1944 succeeding, to destroy the Norwegian Norsk Hydro plant that was producing heavy water for Nazi Germany.

- There are indications that at the onset of the Cold War President Truman was made aware that a preemptive U.S. attack against the Soviet Union might succeed in preventing the Soviet Union from developing nuclear weapons. Truman would not approve such an attack.
- In the early 1960s, U.S. policymakers again contemplated such an option to prevent Chinese acquisition of nuclear weapons. President Johnson sided with those in his administration who argued that even if successful, such an attack would only buy the United States some time while strengthening Chinese resolve to ultimately develop nuclear weapons. China joined the nuclear club in 1964.
- India was cognizant of at least the outlines of Pakistan's nuclear weapons development program by the late 1970s to early 1980s. Confronted with the uncertainties of whether a military strike against Pakistan would be successful in slowing or halting its nuclear ambitions, as well as uncertain whether Pakistan would respond with attacks against India's nuclear facilities, the Indian government chose to eschew a preemptive attack.
- In 1994 the Clinton administration contemplated military options against North Korea for its clandestine nuclear weapons development efforts, finally settling on the diplomatic track of the Agreed Framework.

Mindful of this history of generally avoiding direct military confrontation, does the Iranian case support the path of preemption? In the worst case scenario where all other options had yielded unsatisfactory results, the United States and possibly other governments would have to confront the terrible choice of either resorting to force or acquiescing in Iran becoming a nuclear weapons state. It is a choice that might well have to be made in favor of military action given the profound and long-term implications of Iran in possession of nuclear capabilities. In March 2006, National Security Adviser Stephen Hadley stated, "The doctrine of preemption remains sound and must remain an integral part of our national security strategy."[5] Prior to any decision to conduct military options, policymakers would have to resolve, or at least try to work through, a political Rubik's Cube of military and political problems. There would be myriad challenges in planning and executing the attack, problems caused by the attack in the international community, and Iranian responses to the attack.

The challenges of choosing the military option begin at the outset; namely, determining with the highest level of confidence possible, a comprehensive target list. As noted, many Iranian facilities are at least partially buried and there remains the possibility that Iran has developed clandestine facilities unknown to U.S. or Israeli intelligence. Beyond those uncertainties, there exist at least several dozen clearly identified nuclear-related targets, including those on the U.N. sanctions list that, at a minimum, would have to be attacked for there to be a reasonable chance of significantly slowing Iran's programmatic activity. Each target likely would have multiple aim points to raise the attacker's odds of inflicting significant damage. Whether this limited target set would be chosen in place of a broader and more ambitious attack against Iranian missile, chemical, and biological facilities, for example, is unknown but doubtless would be considered by military planners. Some of them would contend that it is unwise to leave Iran with other weapons that it could use in retaliation against a U.S. attack. In addition to the primary and possibly large target set, the attack likely would begin as have others in the past with attacks against air defense and air force assets to "clear a path" for penetrating bombers such as the B-2 stealth aircraft. Other assets, such as the B-52 long-range bomber, likely would launch cruise missiles from outside Iranian air space.

In strictly military terms, the U.S. Air Force and Navy, if so ordered, could plan through the Joint Chiefs of Staff and successfully execute an attack with those parameters. This is the type of warfare at which the U.S. military excels. Iran's air defenses are based for the most part on aging Soviet-era surface-to-air missiles that U.S. active and passive countermeasures could readily defeat. Iran's Air Force also would be hard-pressed to significantly disrupt or even significantly degrade a major U.S. air attack.

More problematic is what constitutes success beyond the capability to put weapons on targets. It is at this point that the "fog of war" poses a series of challenges for U.S. military planners. They readily acknowledge that one of the most difficult challenges for the U.S. military is destroying or severely damaging underground facilities.[6] Iran has had many years to plan and carry out the construction of numerous underground facilities such as at Natanz and Arak supporting critical elements of its nuclear program. Within the U.S. inventory there exist various types of "bunker busting weapons" such as the BLU-28 and BLU-116. Their effectiveness would be determined largely by their accuracy as well as the type and amount of hardening carried out by Iranian military planners.

Even if the attack itself succeeded in inflicting something close to the desired levels of damage, how long would be the resulting delay before Iran could or would begin rebuilding? For example, if Iran required three years to build an enrichment facility, is it reasonable to assume that it would take at least that long do so again? A logical answer is yes, but it also could be argued that in the aftermath of a U.S. attack that Iran would undertake a crash program to accelerate construction. For example, Iran might make the strategic decision to concentrate its remaining resources into a crash program to build one or perhaps a few nuclear devices. Frank Barnaby, a physicist associated with Oxford Research Group, in early 2007 developed three scenarios by which Iran could carry out a crash program in retaliation against a military attack:[7]

- Iran could use stored, fresh nuclear fuel to produce HEU in a small centrifuge facility as one way to fabricate a nuclear device.
- Iran could chemically remove plutonium from irradiated reactor fuel elements from Bushehr or Arak, if either remained operational, and use it to fabricate a nuclear device.
- Iran could assemble new centrifuges and produce HEU. Iran may have stored additional centrifuges in secure locations. Countries sympathetic to Iran in the aftermath of an attack also could be an external source of centrifuges.

Conversely, it is possible that a crippling preemptive attack would convince the Iranian leadership that the expenditure of resources to reconstitute those facilities would be fruitless if it judged the United States would carry out another attack. Any answers to the questions surrounding Iran's reconstitution capabilities are fraught with uncertainties. What is certain, however, is that the experience gained and knowledge learned by a large cadre of Iranian scientific and technical experts cannot be destroyed in military operations.

Another set of issues surrounds the ultimate purpose of the attack. While Iranian nuclear, missile, and, possibly, other military assets would be attacked, would the current or succeeding administration consider striking targets such as the Iranian Revolutionary Guard Corps, the regime's staunchest supporters, in hopes of effecting regime change? How would the Iranian public react to such attacks? Iran in some ways is a tragedy, its people struggling to join the twenty-first century while trapped in a system of government that lionizes the Middle Ages. The Iranian populace, some 70 million strong, is descendant of a great civilization. Today's Iran also is a young nation whose population has a median age of about twenty-four; the United States, often described as a young country, has a median age of about thirty-seven. Iran's youth has considerable potential but it has lived under the repressive and oppressive yoke of a brutal regime since 1979. It deserves better but what would emerge in the aftermath of a U.S. "decapitation attack" is impossible to predict. The Iranian public may well loathe its current government, but a spark of nationalism also could emerge from any attack on its soil, propping up what many inside the country may well view as a discredited regime. The theocrats immediately would portray any U.S. attack, even if supported by the United Nations, as proof positive of the continuing crusade of the West against the Muslim world. The way to regime change, if it is to occur at all, likely will require sustained, subtle, and thoughtful measures, a substantial challenge for any U.S. administration governing in a fractious and demanding political environment with presidential elections on the horizon.

The response in the international community also would take many forms. Within Arab governments there likely would be a muted but genuine sigh of relief if Iran's nuclear and missile programs suffered significant setbacks. Concurrently, among the general populace in those countries there should be expected considerable unrest at what will doubtless be perceived as the United States again inflicting its will on the Muslim world. Would Sunnis and Shi'as set aside their bitter differences and find common cause in confronting the infidels? Would such common sentiments translate into renewed terrorist attacks against the United States or Israeli interests in the region, even if there was no Iranian instigation for such attacks?

Prior to any attack would the United States alert Russian officials of its plans? Russia is a particular challenge to any consideration to use force because its strategic interests in Iran are considerable. Vocal disapproval from Moscow would add political complications but not necessarily impede military operations against Iran. For this and various other political reasons it would be preferable for the United States to have the formal support of the United Nations for military action. The sanctions imposed by the U.N. Security Council in December 2006 and March 2007 do not authorize the use of force against Iran as a means of enforcing them. New Security Council authorization for the use of force would be very difficult, perhaps impossible, to secure for the same reason; Russia and probably China might well refuse to support such an authorization. Even if their political support was forthcoming, any Security Council resolution supporting the use of force almost certainly would not include approval for the forced overthrow of the Iranian regime. Nonetheless, receiving U.N. support is sufficiently desirable that every effort should be expended in reaching international consensus. Nonetheless, failure to acquire that support should not be the determining factor in any U.S. decision.

Any use of force against Iran inevitably triggers a cascade of political and diplomatic challenges for which the current or next administration must be prepared well in advance. Those challenges will arise as much from within the United States as abroad. The American public, weary of the war in Iraq and now broadly skeptical of the rationale for fighting it, would be wary to support a military operation against Iran, no matter how justified that difficult undertaking might be. The current U.S. Congress also almost certainly would be skeptical of a military operation short of a direct Iranian provocation. From this perspective alone U.N. authorization of the use of force would assist the administration's case considerably.

Iran's response to unilateral U.S.- or multilateral U.N.-approved military action could take multiple paths whose timing would be difficult to judge. There also is a dearth of reliable information suggesting which set of options Iran might prefer to undertake. Nonetheless, it is possible to describe the broad outlines of those options. The first set would incorporate various options for directly attacking U.S. interests and assets. Targets could include U.S. warships operating in the Persian Gulf or the use of mines against U.S. naval assets. In the first Gulf War the USS Princeton and USS Tripoli were struck by mines and the Iranians are doubtlessly aware of this vulnerability although the U.S. Navy certainly is as well. Iran also could consider increasing its efforts to carry out or support increased attacks against U.S. forces in Iraq. The United States also maintains a large permanent presence in the Gulf of military bases in Kuwait, Oman, and Qatar. Israel would be another likely target for Iranian retaliatory measures. Those measures might include renewed hostile actions by Hezbollah against northern Israel, or military strikes against Israel directly if Iran still had the means to do so following the initial attack.

Tehran might use oil as a political or economic weapon, but its effects are far from certain. Iran could attempt to close oil traffic, for example, through the Strait of Hormuz although the U.S. Navy doubtless would be prepared for that contingency. Iran exports on a daily basis slightly more than 5 percent of the world's oil, a sufficient amount to shake oil markets where the price of crude oil almost certainly would spike after the initial attack. The Strait of

Hormuz is the transit route for oil flowing from other nations as well. In early 2007 the price of light crude oil was about $65 per barrel; the price of that same barrel of oil easily could move past the $100 per barrel mark and perhaps well beyond it if Iran could successfully disrupt even for a short period the transport of oil through the Strait. Soaring energy prices doubtless have considerable potential to harm not only the United States but the global economy, an outcome unlikely to yield much support for an embattled Iranian regime. Moreover, although there would be sharply rising oil prices resulting from an Iranian cutoff of its oil exports and a resulting increase in the price of crude oil produced in all exporting nations, Iran would stand to lose a considerable amount of revenue by its action. Oil revenue is estimated to provide about 60 percent of Iran's national budget, a substantial percentage that Tehran might not be able to forgo for any sustained period of time.[8]

Finally, would Iran attempt to carry out military strikes or undertake covert operations against Arab states in the region friendly to the United States such as Qatar? Adel Assadinia, a former Iranian diplomat and Council-General in Dubai who fled his country after becoming a whistleblower against corrupt officials, claims that in the event of an attack against Iran there exists a plan for trained "sleeper cells" to be activated for the purpose of fomenting unrest against America in the Gulf states.[9] Whether this represents Tehran's strategic planning or not, the biggest surprise in confronting Iran militarily likely would be if there was no surprise in its actions.

If the United States is committed to its declaratory policy that it is unacceptable for Iran to acquire nuclear weapons, within a few years it may well have to confront the option of resorting to military force. This policy option, unappealing in many ways, would unleash myriad unpredictable consequences, many of them potentially negative for the United States and its allies. Nonetheless, the inescapable reality is that a nuclear-armed Iran would present the international community with a set of far more negative, and, as discussed above, well understood, consequences. Today's Iran is too dangerous and unpredictable to allow it to join the nuclear club without the expenditure of every resource at the international community's command. Given America's current bitter experience in Iraq, could it summon the political will and support to commit to such a dangerous and complicated undertaking?

To avoid the dilemma of choosing war or acquiescence to Iranian ambitions, is it possible for the United States and international community to craft a series of comprehensive and primarily economic pressures that would induce changes in Iranian behavior? Such an approach, to have optimal chance of success, would have to be multilateral, particularly in the support accorded it by those with strategic interests in the region such as Russia as well as the presumably more supportive European Union members. France and Germany, for example, are Iran's largest trading partners and without their uncompromising support an expanded sanctions regime almost certainly is doomed to failure. Comprehensive sanctions, in contradistinction to the U.N. Security

Council's agreement to impose modest sanctions in late 2006 and early 2007, would aim to impart significant blows to the most critical parts of the Iranian economy, its oil and gas industry.

History provides only some modestly useful, and certainly not definitive, insights into the prospects for success of a strengthened sanctions regime. Since the Carter administration, various U.S. presidents, including presidents as politically diverse as Ronald Reagan and Bill Clinton, have used executive orders and supported legislation that imposed unilateral sanctions of various types on Iran. Other nations, as well as the U.N. Security Council, have imposed other sanctions. These sanctions and the strategies behind them have not been sweeping in intent and nature. As a result, to date the international community has been unsuccessful in bringing about any fundamental or even perceptible change in Iran's nuclear or missile programs. The accumulated record offers little support to those who believe that sanctions are effective in preventing a determined and well-financed country from acquiring nuclear weapons. Predictably, in their many public comments, Iranian spokesmen paint a picture of defiance and ridicule at the effect of sanctions. For example, in the face of the looming first set of U.N. Security Council sanctions in late 2006, Iranian Minister of Economic Affairs and Finance, Davud Danesh-Jafari, asserted that Iran's economy could comfortably withstand sanctions, in part by using an Economic Stabilization Fund established in the 1980s.[10]

In the face of this overall negative assessment, there may be some bright spots. Imposing sanctions has not always resulted in policy failures. A closer examination shows that over time, the accumulated weight of various sanctions has had at least some negative effect on the Iranian economy. For example, U.S. pressure has been increasing on international banks that for years have dealt with Iran. U.S. State Department and Treasury officials have conducted quiet discussions with as many as forty banks and international financial institutions, including the major banks UBS, Credit Suisse, and HSBC, resulting in the cut off or cut back of their relationships with various Iranian entities.[11] As a result, Iran's ability to finance projects for its critical but aging petroleum industry infrastructure is being compromised. For other Iranians, bank credit previously used to finance imports is no longer available or also severely curtailed, necessitating advance payments for many imports.[12]

At least one source that has received little attention in U.S. policy circles also suggests that in their private assessments Iranian officials might be far more concerned about the imposition of a strong sanctions regime than conveyed in their public pronouncements. According to an article in the *Weekly Standard* (September 2006), the foreign affairs and defense commission of the Majlis, the Iranian parliament, issued a classified one hundred-page report on the impact on the Iranian economy of sanctions. The report was sent to President Ahmadinejad and other senior Iranian officials.[13] The article claims the Majlis report was leaked to the influential French newspaper *Le Monde*.[14] The authenticity of the report attributed to the Majlis hasn't been corroborated, but if genuine, it paints a sobering picture of the structural weaknesses in the Iranian economy, often overlooked in some circles in the West, as well the fragility of Iran's financial situation.

As holder of the world's second largest gas and oil reserves in which global demand for energy is seemingly insatiable, Iran's long-term financial picture, at first blush, appears bright. In addition to those described in the above-cited reports, there are underlying problems in Iran's economy that paint a different picture. Despite its abundant oil and gas resources, Iran imports most of the refined products it uses, including gasoline whose price is highly subsidized. Commensurate with the demands of its growing population, Iran's demands for gasoline and other petroleum-refined products are increasing by about 10 percent per annum, putting added pressure on the oil sector. Consequently, a comprehensive embargo on Iranian imports of those commodities could take a heavy toll on the economy. In addition to targeting the Iranian oil and gas sector and the other recently imposed Security Council sanctions, future sanctions actions should target key elements of the regime's support, beginning with the Iranian Revolutionary Guard Corps, which, in addition to its well-known security responsibilities, finances much of its work through various commercial transactions.

Perhaps more important, the Majlis report conveys recognition and perhaps even alarm that disruptions in Iran's economy could trigger widespread social unrest. "It is important to delay any measures which could affect the population because of the risk of instability."[15] The report goes on to say that in the face of sanctions Iran "would be forced to modify its national priorities, and to devote the bulk of its resources to preventing major social upheaval."[16] The Majlis report provides powerful ammunition for giving expanded sanctions an opportunity to take effect.

For an expanded and potentially effective sanctions regime to be put in place will require unstinting European support. U.S. trade with Iran is inconsequential because of Washington's long-standing unilateral sanctions. Japan and China see Iran as a source of energy. Russian support would be desirable but Moscow's trade and geopolitical interests in Iran, along with its approach to the U.N. Security Council sanctions debates, make it an unlikely participant in an aggressive sanctions strategy. Under these conditions we have to focus our gaze on Europe. Germany, Italy, France, the United Kingdom, and the Netherlands provide Iran vital investments and bank credits. Germany is particularly important to Iran; some two-thirds of Iranian industry relies on German parts.[17] Even as the Iran situation worsened, and as Britain, France, and Germany (the EU3) were observing at close range, European trade with Iran rose by 29 percent from 2003 to 2005 to about $15 billion.[18] Even as German political leaders including Chancellor Angela Merkel were emphasizing the Iranian threat, German exports to Iran fell by only 6 percent in 2006 from the previous year.[19] Those figures hardly breed confidence in Europe's willingness to alter its commercial relationships with Iran. A major test case of that willingness will come in late 2007 but once again possible tradeoffs are involved. A final decision then is likely to be taken in favor of moving ahead with the huge Nabucco pipeline project by which gas from Iran, and elsewhere in the region will be shipped west to Baumgarten, Austria. The $6 billion project, led by Austria's OMV Corporation, could begin construction in 2008 and completed by 2010 to 2011.[20] Iran's stake in the project is considerable, accounting for about half of the estimated 30 billion cubic meters capacity of the completed pipeline. Because of the substantial European financial stakes involved, as well as the fact that the pipeline is viewed by many in Europe as a way to reduce European dependence on Russian gas exports, there doubtless would be strenuous resistance to modifying the project by limiting or ending Iranian participation in it. Is Europe prepared to take such a position and is the U.S. government prepared to encourage it to do so?

The readily apparent problem with this approach is that sanctions take time to work. Given that Iran may be within a few years from acquiring a nuclear weapon if it continues at its present pace, that timeline provides the international community with a clear indication that the window could close quickly on whatever opportunity it has for imposing effective sanctions that might compel a change in Iranian behavior.

The other problem is the effect of comprehensive sanctions on Western economies. In an economically interdependent world, severe limits on Iranian energy exports, including a reduction or cutoff of Iranian oil and gas supplies, would impose some amount of pain on the economies and public in Europe, Asia, and the United States. Are national governments prepared to expend the political capital required to convince their citizens that they should accept some financial discomfort for the greater good of trying to keep Iran from becoming a nuclear weapons state?

Despite their limitations, on balance comprehensive sanctions are useful and, barring a seismic shift in Iranian policies, should be incorporated into the Bush administration's existing unilateral strategy and the U.N. Security Council's current multilateral sanctions strategy. The only incentive offered by a comprehensive sanctions regime is that the sanctions presumably would end if Iran's egregious behavior regarding its nuclear and missile programs ends. Is there a different diplomatic approach, backed by a new multilateral security arrangement that has not been pursued by the Bush administration or any of its predecessors? Is it possible to use the hard lessons of the Iranian case to develop a new strategic framework for nuclear nonproliferation that addresses the problems at the nation-state level, the so-called rogue nations, and subnational groups such as Islamic fundamentalists?

PART THREE

Policy and Programmatic Recommendations

Toward a New Strategic Framework for Nuclear Nonproliferation: Policy Recommendations

SINCE THE DAWN of the nuclear age every U.S. administration has wrestled with various approaches to containing the spread of nuclear weapons. Much of the international community shares that goal, reflected in the establishment of the International Atomic Energy Agency (IAEA) which today plays an important role in monitoring nuclear proliferation activities. Various international legal instruments have been negotiated, adopted, and abided by dozens of nations, including the Nonproliferation Treaty (NPT), establishment of the Zangger Committee, and the Nuclear Suppliers Group. The U.N. Security Council and various nations have used applied sanctions as a means to modify or compel changes in states pursuing the acquisition of nuclear weapons. Innovative steps, ranging from the U.S. government's Proliferation Security Initiative (PSI) to Ted Turner's commitment (joined more recently by Warren Buffett) of considerable private resources through the Nuclear Threat Initiative (NTI), an organization located in Washington, DC, which carries out programmatic and educational activities related to nonproliferation, are laudable. The creativity and effectiveness of the NTI demonstrate the role nongovernmental organizations can play, not only in assessing and speaking out on various proliferation issues—their traditional functions—but in taking an active role in nonproliferation projects. In toto, the international community, often with the United States in the lead, has dedicated significant political, financial, and intellectual resources to the problems of nuclear proliferation.

One of the often overlooked but most positive statements that can be made about the often fractious nature of international politics since the dawn of the nuclear age is that nuclear weapons have been not been used by one nation against another since the end of World War II. In addition, nations that have pursued nuclear weapons such as South Africa, Libya, Argentina, and Brazil have abandoned their pursuits for assorted reasons of national interest. North

Korea may follow the same path, although final judgment awaits additional actions by Pyongyang. Other nations such as those in the former Soviet bloc, Ukraine and Kazakhstan, also turned away from nuclear weapons even when they could have maintained them after the breakup of the Soviet Union. These are significant achievements that contribute directly to nuclear security.

These positive outcomes are only part of the international landscape which has been darkened by the nuclear weapons programs in India, Pakistan, North Korea and, almost certainly, Iran. With a mixed record of successes, failures, and the prospect that some nations in the Arab world will be tempted by the nuclear genie if Iran crosses the nuclear threshold, it is appropriate to inquire whether it is possible to develop a new strategic framework for nuclear non-proliferation that would significantly reduce our continuing nuclear insecurity. If we are to do so we should first see the fault lines in the existing nonproliferation regime.

A persistent theme running through the history of nuclear nonproliferation efforts is that the priority of those efforts has been sacrificed on the altar of various competing and often short-term national and international objectives. In an era of Islamic fundamentalism accompanied by nations whose interest in acquiring nuclear weapons is barely contained, a cornerstone of U.S. policy for any future administration should be that halting the proliferation of nuclear weapons (as well as other weapons of mass destruction [WMD]) is its highest national security priority. Any compromise of that standard, as has occurred frequently in the past, runs an unacceptably high risk of fostering nuclear insecurity. The Bush administration, as well as its predecessors, has chanted this mantra but the bureaucracy working for the president often has failed to implement his priorities without being held accountable. Ways to address that problem constitute the focus of the concluding chapter.

The second lesson is that unilateral actions by any nation, including the United States, at best have a modest record of success in favorably resolving some of the most serious proliferation problems. There are exceptions, but not many. A multilateral but significantly modified approach that continues to draw heavily on the United Nations and supported by the IAEA will be an important element in any strategic framework for nuclear nonproliferation. As we will see shortly there is another way of harnessing a multilateral organization in a common approach to nonproliferation.

As we will soon observe, there remain occasions when the United Nations fails or refuses to take what U.S. or foreign governmental officials deem appropriate action against a proliferator. A strategy centered on multilateral cooperation does not remove the prerogative for unilateral action; it only presumes that multilateral approaches should be given preference, whenever practicable, to support national policy objectives. Each proliferation case also has unique elements, beginning with the nation or terrorist organization pursuing nuclear weapons, its location, strategic objectives, and the implications for other nations in the region. For example, in the Iran case there is little doubt but that the delays and ultimately modest set of sanctions imposed by the U.N. Security Council can be attributed to the strategic interests of Russia and China. Russia has extensive trading and strategic interests in Iran. China has a compelling interest in ensuring the reliability of energy supplies for its growing economy and likely sees that policy goal as much more important than ending putative Iranian WMD programs that, even if successful, would not threaten it anyway. In an international system where self-interest and sovereignty continue to predominate, future U.S. administrations will continue to confront the likelihood that it will bear special burdens for resolving proliferation problems. An integral component of the strategy for doing so likely will require the continuing embrace of the Bush administration's strategy of preemption.

For this reason a sobering assessment of the performance of multilateral organizations must be addressed before ascribing too much faith in their future potential and promise for taking on the most pressing proliferation problems. The April 2007 resolution of the hostage crisis in which fifteen British sailors and marines were forcibly detained for two weeks by Iranian forces while on routine patrol in Iraqi waters underscores the point that in the early twenty-first century national interests still often trump, and frustrate, the call for collective action against unwarranted aggression. In the British hostage case neither the European Union nor the United Nations contributed much to the Blair government's efforts to end the seizure peacefully. Under European law, the Britons are citizens of Europe, not just England. According to a *Washington Post* commentator, Britain asked the European Union to threaten to freeze a year of exports, some $18 billion, to Iran. The European Union refused to do so.[1] The United Nations Security Council proved of equally modest support for the United Kingdom, expressing only its "grave concern" about the situation.[2] These examples are at significant variance to the desirability of placing more, not less, reliance on the international community.

As the British hostage crisis illustrates, no perfect answer exists as to what constitutes the best mix of unilateral or multilateral approaches for any particular event or problem, particularly as they apply to Iran. In the current international system, the United States for the foreseeable future likely will have the widest-ranging interests in stopping the spread of various WMD and, as such, will have to be prepared to take unilateral action. The paradox is that at a time when U.S. influence and credibility have been reduced in the Middle East by its military adventures, the options for effective unilateral actions have been diminished. For this reason, it may increase its reliance on multilateral instruments to support its policy objectives, as it has done regarding Iran in turning to the U.N. Security Council to augment the Bush administration's unilateral sanctions strategy. Nonetheless, where the United States can still unilaterally and effectively act is through the application of military power, the last resort of policy.

Is there a middle ground between formal multilateral approaches and U.S. reliance on its own resources? One of the most important insights offered by the success of the PSI is that it is possible to draw on the common interests of large segments of the international community in a common approach to nonproliferation. Furthermore, that cooperation was solidified not through the United Nations system or complex legal instruments such as those taken to great heights by the European Union but rather through the broad recognition among nations that they were not powerless to interdict the spread of WMD. The PSI in years to come may be seen as a harbinger of a new model for international cooperation on nonproliferation problems.

There is no "magic bullet" for policymakers in the United States or elsewhere whose application will ensure success either against Iran or the next nation seeking membership in the nuclear club. Nonetheless, there are a series of measures, some modest and some more sweeping in nature, that, if taken together, form the elements of a strategic framework for preventing the spread of nuclear weapons. This framework does not dispense with existing approaches but, in acknowledging their individual and collective limitations, attempts to revise, improve, and build on them. Although other elements could be added to the framework, my intention here is to present those with the highest potential for addressing significant shortfalls in the current nonproliferation regime.

Modifications to existing approaches are essential but insufficient. Along with improvements in the existing nuclear nonproliferation regime, new security relationships that enhance deterrence against those in possession of WMD also should be considered as well. A new strategic framework for nonproliferation can and should become a centerpiece of U.S. foreign policy. A number of U.S. allies around the globe share many of the same policy outlooks on nuclear nonproliferation as their Washington counterparts, suggesting that elements of the strategic framework have value for them as well.

The first element of the new strategic framework is leadership within the United States regarding the future testing of nuclear weapons. The Department of Energy (DOE) is charged with ensuring the integrity of the U.S. nuclear stockpile, a program called stockpile stewardship. One of the central elements of that program has been to determine and certify to the Department of Defense that U.S. nuclear weapons are reliable. For decades the U.S. scientific community has understood at least the theoretical reliability problems associated with weapons that remain in storage for extended periods, sometimes decades. In a crisis or national emergency, U.S. policymakers and military commanders require confidence in these weapons. Until the 1992 decision made by President Clinton to stop all U.S. nuclear testing, the United States from time to time throughout the Cold War would detonate nuclear weapons first, in above ground tests, and later, underground tests of their reliability. Significant advances in computer modeling have rendered the need for future testing virtually obsolete. In 1999, the Clinton administration sought to join other nations in ratifying the Comprehensive Test Ban Treaty (CTBT) but the Senate refused to do so at the time. This oversight should be rectified by Senate ratification of the CTBT at the earliest possible opportunity. Doing so would make it politically harder, but would not prevent, any nation from conducting its own nuclear tests.

The second element of the new strategic framework would be the unanimous adoption by all IAEA members of the Additional Protocol. After the 1991 Gulf War, international inspectors in Iraq uncovered considerable evidence that Saddam Hussein's nuclear scientists, working in conjunction with A. Q. Khan's proliferation network, had made significant strides in developing a clandestine nuclear program. This called into question the IAEA's ability to detect in a timely fashion such programs, exposing the limits of the safeguards program. In the wake of this widely acknowledged problem, which highlighted North Korea's own clandestine actions during this period, the decision was made to augment existing safeguards procedures with new and more stringent measures.

What emerged from the effort which dates to 1993 is the Additional Protocol, a series of voluntary measures agreed to by nations consenting to provide additional information on their nuclear programs while allowing greater access to both declared nuclear facilities as well as sites deemed suspect by the IAEA. Driven to action by the lessons learned in dealing with Iraq and North Korea, the primary impetus for the Additional Protocol is how best to uncover in a timely way undeclared facilities. On its face, the Additional Protocol is a useful step in addressing this fissure in the IAEA's safeguards work. For it to be fully effective it will have to overcome two limitations. First, the political will of the IAEA will be critical if an aggressive series of inspections, which can include environmental sampling at suspect sites to detect traces of radioactive materials, is to be carried out. The IAEA, as an international body, acts with consensus and one of the criticisms leveled by some in the Bush administration is that building consensus for concerted action is anathema to timely action. The second limitation is that the voluntary nature of the Additional Protocol has resulted in seventy-eight nations of the IAEA's roster of 144 members putting the procedures into place (as of March 2007) but nations of greatest proliferation concern such as Iran have signed but have not ratified the Additional Protocols, leaving the IAEA with significantly reduced access to Iranian facilities. For example, after the passage of U.N. Security Council Resolution 1747 regarding Iran, the IAEA requested that cameras be placed in the underground uranium enrichment facility at Natanz but the Iranians refused the request.[3] Only Iran can break this logjam but shows little inclination to do so.

As a recognized nuclear weapons state, the United States is quite low on any IAEA interest list for applying the inspection provisions of the Additional Protocol. Nonetheless, the Clinton administration signed the Additional Protocol in June 1998 and in March 2004 the Senate ratified the Additional

Protocol at the urging of President Bush. However, implementing legislation is still required from Congress to trigger formal entry into force of the U.S. political commitment. That legislation was proposed in 2004 by Senator Richard Lugar but still languishes. Perhaps a Congress controlled by the Democratic Party will take up this legislation which would be a useful demonstration of U.S. support for the IAEA's role in monitoring nuclear programs of concern.

The third element of the new strategic framework also places the IAEA in a central role. Efforts to secure nuclear materials in various nations have lagged badly. One of the shortfalls in the international community's work has been that such work, when it is carried out, is not required to meet any internationally agreed on standards. The DOE nuclear material security program to install rapid and comprehensive security upgrades packages at Russia's Rosatom sites is largely the product of experience gleaned from similar efforts to secure the U.S. nuclear stockpile. U.N. Security Council Resolution 1540 mandates all states to provide "appropriate effective" security for their nuclear materials. The practical meaning or detailed guidance on how to implement that phrase has never been fully spelled out. At a minimum, the IAEA should be asked by the Security Council to develop a set of universally applicable security standards that could resist external attack as well as insider efforts to divert materials.

The fourth element returns the onus for action to the industrialized and wealthy nations, known as the G8.[4] At the June 2002 G8 Summit in Kananaskis, Canada, a G8 initiative for a Global Partnership was announced, committing the G8 members to preventing terrorists from acquiring or developing WMD, missiles, or related equipment and technology.[5] The G8 countries pledged $20 billion over the next ten years to fund projects. About half of that funding would come from the United States (most of it from already planned funding levels for existing programs) with most of the initial projects located in Russia, with its vast and still often unsecured WMD stockpile.[6] The G8 members agreed on six principles to prevent terrorists from gaining access to WMD or related materials:[7]

1. Promote multilateral treaties that help prevent the spread of weapons, materials, and know-how.
2. Account for and secure these items.
3. Promote physical protection of facilities.
4. Help detect, deter, and interdict illicit trafficking.
5. Promote national export and transshipment controls.
6. Manage and dispose of nuclear, biological, and chemical weapons materials.

It is hard to overestimate the potential importance of the G8's commitment of such substantial resources to nonproliferation problems. Its leadership in this area is precisely what should be expected of a group whose combined gross domestic products account for about 65 percent of the world's economy.

In addition, since the original partnership was announced, another thirteen countries have joined the partnership, including Norway, Poland, Switzerland, Finland, the Netherlands, Australia, Belgium, the Czech Republic, New Zealand, the Republic of Korea, Denmark, Sweden, and Ireland.[8]

As it moves to the second half of its ten year commitment, the partnership will need to address two areas of concern. The first is the focus of many of the first projects, which have clustered around nuclear submarine dismantlement and chemical weapons destruction. Chemical weapons destruction is a worthy endeavor; but disposing of the nuclear reactors of submarines is more problematic from a proliferation standpoint. For years the Russian military has been soliciting international support for this work, emphasizing that fuel rods from its aging nuclear submarine fleet might be vulnerable to theft. That scenario is possible, but many nonproliferation experts long have seen the submarine reactor problem as much more of an environmental problem for Russia resulting from leaking reactor cores than a nonproliferation problem. Projects related to securing Russia's vast stocks of nuclear materials merit higher funding priority. From a broader perspective, as of July 2006, the last official report on the progress being made by the original G8 contributors, only $3.5 billion out of the pledged $20 billion has been expended on projects.[9] The rate of G8 contributions needs to be accelerated and increased substantially.

The fifth element of the strategic framework is a fundamental revision of the process by which the U.N. Security Council imposes sanctions. Under current practices, consideration of sanctions is carried out on a case-by-case basis subject to protracted and often bitter debate among Security Council members, each with its own perspectives and interests. As demonstrated by the various positions of Security Council members regarding the timing and extent of sanctions they would agree to impose against Iran, the result has been the passage two U.N. Security Council resolutions whose greatest value is in their symbolism rather than their content. Pierre Goldschmidt, a former IAEA senior official, has called for modifying the way in which the Security Council imposes sanctions.[10] For Goldschmidt, the preferred U.N. Security Council method would be the passage of a legally binding requirement by which any nation later deemed by the IAEA to be in noncompliance with its NPT obligations would be subject automatically to a set of previously agreed on sanctions.[11] This approach would ensure that there is no protracted debate on the type of sanctions to be imposed; they would be triggered immediately on Security Council receipt of an IAEA report of noncompliance with a state's NPT obligations. Whether nations would be prepared to agree in advance to an appropriately broad set of sanctions is problematic. Nonetheless, Goldschmidt's idea has the advantage of recognizing that the Security Council's current case-by-case approach to sanctions is not very satisfying or effective and therefore needs to consider a fresh approach if it is serious about maintaining its credibility.

The sixth element addresses the nexus between energy and security. For Russia, Great Britain, and other nations, nuclear power is playing an increasingly prominent role in meeting their present and future energy requirements. While it may serve as one approach to meeting global energy demands, civil nuclear power, as discussed throughout this book, also provides a direct path to nuclear weapons development. Scientists have spent decades working on the problem of developing and deploying what is referred to as "proliferation resistant reactors." A proliferation resistant reactor results from the adoption of reactor and fuel cycle concepts that would make it more difficult to divert civilian nuclear fuels to weapons purposes.[12] One of Russia's leading scientists, academician Yevgeny Velikhov, director of the prestigious Kurchatov Institute in Moscow, has been touting ways to turn this technology concept into reality for at least a decade. Scientists in the United States and elsewhere have conducted separate but similar research. If nuclear energy is going to figure more prominently in meeting future global energy needs, increased international cooperation is required to move forward on an international standard for proliferation resistance. Such cooperation could be led by the United States and Russia working in concert but should be open to scientists from other nations.

A strategy of cooperative engagement, rather than previous confrontational approaches, is the seventh element and option for U.S. and international nonproliferation policymakers. Historically, proliferation problems have been addressed by a specific set of policies such as sanctions or focused diplomatic efforts to negotiate an end to the troubling behavior. On rare occasions, such as the 1994 Agreed Framework with North Korea, the United States incorporated broader economic and political elements into its strategy for resolving the North Korean nuclear problem by offering oil for certain North Korean actions related to its nuclear program. The Agreed Framework remained viable for a number of years and the Bush administration's recent strategy toward North Korea has shown elements of a similar approach.

The broad expansion of political and economic policy tools in the service of nonproliferation objectives is attractive for several reasons. Unlike political isolation or economic sanctions which seek to compel changes in a nation's behavior, a strategy of engagement offers positive inducements for nations to moderate their behavior. In the Iran case the following would be some of the preconditions before entering into such negotiations. First, the strategy would have to be multilateral in its approach. The U.S.-Iranian bilateral relationship at this time is so dominated by mutual distrust that any meaningful agreement between the antagonists is highly unlikely. Moreover, Iranian president Ahmadinejad has proven himself to be so puerile and discredited in his personal dealings with parts of the international community that any approach to Iran should bypass him and focus on the supreme leader, Ayatollah Khamenei. In the past, Khamenei has evinced a policy pragmatism that seeks ways to strengthen Iran's strategic position without confrontation, a flexibility rarely demonstrated by Iran's president. According to one former U.S. government official, in early 2003, "the Iranian Foreign Ministry sent Washington a detailed proposal for comprehensive negotiations ... the document acknowledged that Iran would have to address concerns about its weapons programs and support for anti-Israeli terrorist organizations."[13] The Bush administration apparently did not pursue the offer for reasons that remain shrouded in mystery.

The process of even beginning a sweeping dialogue with Iran would be exceptionally difficult. It is likely that Ahmadinejad would seek to rally his supporters against such an approach. Nonetheless, as described in the boxed display in Chapter 5, Ahmadinejad's political standing in Iran is far from unassailable. There would be other hurdles to overcome as well. Further complicating the prospects for success is the disjointed and often opaque nature of Iranian politics. The nuclear program almost certainly is controlled by hardline elements in Iran, beginning with the Iranian Revolutionary Guard Corps (IRGC), and it is far from assured that they could be induced to support a negotiated end to their cherished nuclear and missile programs, the centerpiece of any exchanges. In this respect Iranian public opinion also may not be supportive of Western attempts to reach such an accommodation. Many young Iranians clearly yearn for better relations with and understanding of the West. On balance, they seem to have much less of the revolutionary zeal that still marks the attitudes of many older ruling theocrats as well as President Ahmadinejad. At the same time, the Iranian public views nuclear power—and perhaps even nuclear weapons—as the right of a great and historic civilization.[14]

Keeping these caveats in mind, we can explore the case for positive engagement. With the support of the U.N. Security Council and U.N. Secretary General Ban ki-Moon, a comprehensive strategy regarding Iran would be presented. It would be appropriate for Britain, France, and Germany (the EU3) to be involved in this presentation because of its past engagements with Iran. There also would have to be the direct engagement of the U.S. Secretary of State as critical parts of the proposed solution require U.S. commitments. The ultimate goal of the offer would be an end to Iran's most troubling programmatic activities in exchange for security guarantees that would render moot any Iranian claims that it needs WMD. The offer to Iran would include:

- An end to all multilateral and unilateral sanctions.
- The restoration of diplomatic relations between Iran and the United States.
- A commitment that force would not be used against Iran for its past activities.
- International assistance would be provided to develop and modernize its energy infrastructure.
- The Bushehr power plant would be completed and begin operation without delay or interference.

In exchange for these steps, Iran would commit to:

- End all nuclear fuel cycle activities.
- Ratify the Additional Protocol.

- End its long-range missile program and allow verification.
- End support for, including funding to, terrorist organizations.
- Support a negotiated resolution to the Arab-Israeli conflict.

The eighth and final element of the new strategic framework centers on the means of enhancing deterrence against nations that cross the nuclear threshold. Iran is the near-term and obvious target for a strategy that specifically incorporates deterrence as one of its constituent parts. Despite the efforts of the United States and the United Nations, Iran may succeed in becoming a nuclear weapons state. The implications would be profound for the entire Middle East; Iran's foreign policy options would increase markedly and, of equal importance, the Sunni Arab nations may feel compelled to develop their own nuclear capabilities. No one can predict the likelihood of this chain of events happening, but the inherent dangers of other nations in the Middle East considering the nuclear option should cause the next administration grave concerns.

One way to reduce the risk of a nuclear-armed Middle East would be for the West to offer security guarantees to any nation in the region forswearing nuclear arms. In simplest terms the offer would call for immediate military support to any nation in the region attacked by a nuclear weapons state. While this offer almost certainly would hold little appeal to Israel, already a nuclear weapons state and wholly unprepared to trade its existing capabilities for guarantees, the offer might be effective for the Arab states. Such a pact already exists between France and Qatar. For various political reasons it is unlikely that any offer from the United States alone would be embraced in Riyadh or Cairo.

There exists, however, another approach that might be more palatable to Arab sensitivities. Since its inception the North Atlantic Treaty Organization (NATO) has stood as a deterrent against aggression. Its original purpose, to deter and, if necessary, respond to an attack against Europe by the Soviet Union, has been overtaken by history's march. NATO remains a formidable military organization, however, and there is no reason why its mission could not be modified to incorporate a focus that looks to the South, not the East.

The creation of a NATO-Middle East Security Arrangement (NAMESA) would be a constant reminder to Iran that the price of aggression, if it were to become a nuclear weapons state, would be exceptionally high. United States power projection capabilities would remain the bulwark of any military force that might be called on to confront Iran but it would be supported by its NATO partners. NAMESA would be a collective security arrangement open to any NATO member or Middle East nation willing to commit its military resources or manpower, in times of crisis or war, to the defense of any nation in the Middle East threatened by a nuclear state. In anticipation that Iran may also succeed in developing long-range missiles capable of reaching European targets, NAMESA would not ignore future European defense requirements.

In this context support also is merited for U.S. plans to install a limited number of ballistic missile defense interceptors and radars in several European countries.

Central to the question of such an ambitious partnership is the precise nature of the commitment being made by the NATO members. As pointed out by the authors of a thoughtful article on the future of NATO, Article 5 of the North Atlantic Treaty stipulates that an attack on one member is to be regarded as an attack on all members.[15] Is it realistic to expect that Norway or Italy, for example, would send troops to fight or die in the Middle East? Under NATO's current provisions, those countries and other members would have the choice, not the obligation, to do so as the Treaty currently only calls for each member to take "such action as it deems necessary." Article 5 has only been invoked once, after the events of September of 11, 2001.[16] Nonetheless, all NATO countries contributed to the U.S.-led efforts to expel Iraq from Kuwait in 1990.[17] On balance, and setting aside the U.S. role, NAMESA's creation probably would not result in a vast military coalition arraigned against Iran in a time of crisis. However, a few of the more prominent European nations might contribute to such a multilateral force, a potentially useful political signal, particularly when melded with U.S. capabilities, to any Iranian aggression.

The always present Israeli-Arab suspicions also would have to be worked out in advance before NAMESA could be established. Recognizing that the Arab states would be highly unlikely to join any collective endeavor of which Israel was a part, the United States and Israel could reach what is sometimes referred to as a side agreement providing for comparable U.S. bilateral support to Israel.

Is NATO up to the task? In recent years it has taken on an out-of-area mission in Afghanistan, formally leading the International Security Assistance Force (ISAF), and relieving some of the responsibilities that otherwise would have been borne by U.S. military forces already stretched thin in Iraq. NATO also has operated for training purposes in Iraq and supported the African Union in Darfur. While the individual fighting abilities of the NATO members varies considerably—there is a general falloff of European NATO military capabilities once one moves past the British and German militaries—NATO represents not just an eclectic fighting force but also the political will of twenty-six members with vested political and economic interests in Middle East stability. Global threats require solutions that transcend regional organizations. NATO can become a powerful symbol of the possibilities inherent in using existing capabilities in innovative ways.

Toward a New Strategic Framework for Nuclear Nonproliferation: Programmatic Recommendations

THIS BOOK HAS put forth the proposition that within the U.S. government there exists a set of programs and policy choices that, if effectively applied, could significantly reduce the risk of nuclear or radiological attack against this nation and its allies. There are examples of notable and important programmatic successes, including efforts by the Department of Defense (DOD) in the 1990s to dismantle large numbers of Soviet-era strategic weapons and the successes by the Department of Energy (DOE) in the early years of the Bush administration to enhance the security of large amounts of poorly secured nuclear and radiological materials in Russia. Similarly, the Clinton and Bush administrations devoted considerable diplomatic effort designed to slow or halt the nuclear ambitions of North Korea and Iran and to assist Pakistan in enhancing the security of its nuclear stockpile.

Despite considerable bipartisan political support, the appropriation of billions of dollars for the nonproliferation programs, fifteen years of effort, the political leadership and shared views of the nuclear proliferation threat by Presidents Clinton and Bush, America remains highly vulnerable to nuclear or radiological attack. If our political leaders and the American public judge this situation to be unacceptable, the critical question becomes what realistic and available remedies are at hand to reduce our nuclear insecurity.

DOE's semi-autonomous National Nuclear Security Administration (NNSA) over the past several years has so badly mismanaged its nonproliferation programmatic responsibilities and misled the Congress while doing so that it has forfeited the privilege of playing a leading role in U.S. governmental efforts to secure nuclear and radiological sources. Because of the size of DOE NNSA's extant nonproliferation programs—approximately $1.5 billion annually—there is but one option for making a fundamental change in location of the programs. DOD is the only other organization in the U.S.

government with a proven track record of running large nonproliferation or threat reduction programs successfully. The overall size of the Pentagon's Defense Threat Reduction Agency suggests it could absorb, without undue disruption, the transfer of DOE's programs. The work being done at DOD is so similar to that at DOE in fundamental ways, beginning with comparable missions, that maintaining these programs in separate departments with different managerial philosophies is patently inefficient. Program consolidation also would provide an opportunity to present the Russian security establishment one U.S. organizational point of contact for all threat reduction work with the exception of the small programs run through the State Department which are well run and need not be relocated.

Transferring the DOE programs also provides a logical opportunity to realign them so that they work synergistically. For example, in the first part of this decade the nuclear security programs working at Russian nuclear sites were under the same managerial roof as the Second Line of Defense (SLD) program working at Russian borders. Those programs should be rejoined, at least the part of SLD still working in Russia.

The DOE radiological security program has fallen on such hard times that it requires special attention. IAEA officials have spoken to me and others privately on this issue, expressing considerable disappointment that the department has squandered the momentum and good will built up during the program's initial years. The 2007 Government Accountability office (GAO) report on DOE's work in this area concurs. As discussed in a previous chapter, the radiological threat is so pervasive that the program's pace and scope should be accelerated rapidly with appropriate funding levels if proper management can be identified.

The transfer of programmatic responsibility to DOD would, of necessity, include the reassignment to the Pentagon of at least some of the current DOE federal, contract, and laboratory personnel familiar with the current workings of the NNSA programs. Without proper management and oversight from the beginning, the inevitable job scramble of programmatic relocation could result in the same ineffective managers doing the same jobs and simply changing their place of employment. To limit this occurrence, Congress, whose support would be required for the transfer of responsibilities, could insist that no current DOE manager in the senior executive ranks would be eligible to run his or her transferred program although they could become deputies to a new cadre of program leadership taken from outside the current DOE ranks.

One of the first tasks for DOD would be to assess the appropriate level of resources for programmatic work in Russia. As described elsewhere, vast amounts of fissile and radiological material remain poorly protected at many Russian sites. Nonetheless, the Russian economy, under President Putin's ambitious leadership, has made impressive strides and is much more capable of assuming at least part of the considerable financial burden for security upgrades. A new administration might consider reviewing with its Russian counterparts the financial aspects of this cooperation. Can Russia, for example, contribute more funding to its own critical nuclear material programs given its growing oil wealth? Doing so would free up current U.S. resources earmarked for work at nuclear sites that could then be shifted into the radiological security work.

Once accomplished, the transfer of what in organizational terms is one of the DOE NNSA's two primary missions raises easily answered questions about the continued viability of that organization. Created in 1999 to 2000 by the Congress through legislation whose purpose was to establish an organization that would address the chronic and reckless indifference to protecting nuclear security at some DOE laboratories—particularly Los Alamos National Laboratory and Sandia National Laboratory—the NNSA has utterly failed in the carrying out the tasks that led to its creation. Underscoring this point, in late 2006 Energy Secretary Samuel Bodman publicly sacked NNSA Administrator Linton Brooks, using a blistering press announcement to fire Brooks for failing to successfully bring badly needed and long overdue change to the security culture at the national laboratories. As NNSA Administrator, Brooks was the same official who had impeded the proper management of the international threat reduction programs under his authority while tolerating the managerial abuses of some senior officials.

Brooks' forced departure, albeit an overdue and wholly necessary decision, comes too late to redeem NNSA. After seven years of bureaucratic existence, much of it spent in aimless floundering suffused with indifferent senior leadership, NNSA has been a failed experiment. With the transfer of its international programs to DOD, NNSA's other key missions, safeguarding the U.S. nuclear stockpile and overseeing navy nuclear programs can revert to their former organizational location wholly within the department known as Defense Programs. The NNSA can and should be abolished.

Because the NNSA has proven incapable of managing the U.S. national laboratories under its purview, sweeping changes are required at DOE; moreover, the DOE national laboratory system also must come under review. Throughout the Cold War, the DOE laboratories have served U.S. national security interests well and with distinction. However, with the collapse of the Soviet Union the requirement has ended for a nuclear arsenal sized against the Soviet threat. This is not to imply in any way that the United States should abandon its possession of nuclear weapons and a robust nuclear capability. On the contrary, decisions were taken in March 2007 for a "reliable, replacement warhead" to ensure the safety and security of the U.S. nuclear stockpile for decades to come.

In its assessment of current trends and developments, this book has endeavored to show that we live in a world of diverse and significant security threats that also easily could increase in complexity in the years ahead. As a result, for the foreseeable future nuclear weapons need to remain an essential element of U.S. military capabilities. Nonetheless, maintaining and modernizing those capabilities does not require indefinite continuation of the entire Cold War national laboratory structure. The Lawrence Livermore National Laboratory in California, once under DOE authority, now primarily supports the Department of Homeland Security, proof that the laboratory system can be significantly modified to serve important and evolving U.S. national security priorities. Still, more needs to be done.

For reasons related primarily to political expediency, the Clinton and Bush administrations have shared a revulsion for taking on the broader questions of the future direction of the national laboratory system. A bipartisan Commission—one of Washington's favorite bureaucratic tools for addressing unpleasant situations—comprised of respected national security experts should be formed with the mission of reviewing the future missions of the national laboratories and recommending whether significant cost savings could be realized by downsizing or merging several of the laboratories. A bipartisan Commission presumably also would consider the most effective ways to harness the world-class scientific expertise resident at the labs to more effectively serve not only emerging national security requirements but pressing domestic requirements in such areas as health care. Some of this is already happening but the efforts are scattered with little strategic focus. This national debate is long overdue and should no longer be postponed because it could pose uncomfortable decisions for our political leadership. The resulting streamlined and refocused system of national laboratories would have clearly defined missions and probably reduced personnel size and would be able to continue the critical nuclear-related missions for which they were created while taking on new missions.

Executive and legislative branch actions needed to carry out these changes are essential but insufficient. Robust congressional oversight of the threat reduction programs has been badly lacking for years. A handful of congressional staffers and fewer members of Congress can identify the most critical programs in any of the executive branch departments or describe in reasonable detail their missions, leadership, accomplishments, or internal shortfalls. In fairness, the GAO, when given the opportunity, often does a thorough job of assessing the progress and problems of the nonproliferation threat reduction programs, producing considerable anxiety, for example, among DOE managers when a planned inspection or audit is announced. However, the GAO lacks the resources and mandate to carry out investigations of all the most important threat reduction programs annually, a level of review that is mandatory if Congress is to exercise effective oversight. The Material Protection, Control, and Accounting (MPC&A) Program, with its critical mission for enhancing U.S. security against nuclear terrorism, is a prime example. Prior to its 2007 review, the GAO's most recent comprehensive review of the program was 2003, a lengthy delay during which time many negative elements were introduced into the program. Congress faces the pressing challenge of deciding how much oversight it wants to impose on the complex and critically important threat reduction programs which are managed in some cases by individuals with poor track records.

Regardless of congressional action to enhance its oversight responsibilities, the executive branch also has duties to enhance the interagency coordination and management of the threat reduction programs entrusted to its care. Within the National Security Council Staff structure, the White House foreign policy, and national security apparatus, there are individuals, usually senior career officers or political appointees with similar levels of experience, who oversee the government's nonproliferation and counterterrorism programs. In practical terms, their authority is derived from the governing style of the administration, beginning with the president and his national security adviser. During Bill Clinton's second term, for example, National Security Adviser Sandy Berger was highly supportive of his staff and encouraged its active engagement in shaping programmatic and policy initiatives. In contrast, George Bush's management style, reflected in the approaches to the National Security Council staff directed first by Condoleezza Rice and then Stephen Hadley, Bush's national security advisers, was to have that staff largely serve as a coordinating body, taking a much less active role in leading the interagency, resolving disagreements, or proposing new initiatives in comparison to their predecessors.

Despite their differences in approach for working with the interagency, both administrations did not take sufficient or consistent measures to oversee, direct, and hold accountable those managing the established threat reduction programs that form the backbone of U.S. nonproliferation efforts. As a result, inefficiencies and needless slowdowns in program execution have been tolerated while benchmarks of success were never demanded or, for those that existed, assessed independently on a continuing basis.

The Bush administration, more so than the Clinton administration, endeavored to develop policy oversight and guidance for its nonproliferation programs with the creation of the Proliferation Strategy Policy Coordination Committee chaired by an NSC Senior Director. The GAO in a January 2005 report noted that improved coordination of the U.S. government's various biological security programs was evident. However, it found major gaps in the coordination of other major nonproliferation programs. Its conclusion was that "DOD and DOE strategic plans for threat reduction and nonproliferation programs are not integrated and do not address U.S. programs worldwide." No governmental guidance was identified, for example, for the critical border security programs. Clearly, the administration's well-conceived plan for coordination is not working.[1]

The threat reduction programs, so critical to U.S. national security, can achieve accelerated and improved performance levels and so can the White House's oversight of these programs. A useful first step would be the establishment of a nonproliferation coordinator or "czar," reporting directly to the National Security Adviser. Ideally, that individual would be a person of national stature able to command the respect of an often recalcitrant bureaucracy. Perhaps even more importantly, that individual would be empowered to exercise significant authority over the size and priorities of the threat reduction budgets. Those budgets are developed traditionally within the individual departments with limited White House or Office of Management and Budget (the president's budget office) input at the end of the executive branch's budget formulation process. That process does not afford enough time for thorough review, debate, and decisions regarding budgetary priorities.

A senior official with ongoing program oversight accountable only to the president and his national security adviser could affect substantial change in this often unwieldy process because his primary responsibility would be to ensure the best possible management of the threat reduction programs. That individual also would coordinate his work with that of the ambassadors assigned to international organizations such as the IAEA, ensuring that the entire interagency capabilities of the U.S. government are considered and brought to bear at those organizations that are so critical to U.S. national security interests. Depending on the personal style of our ambassadors, that type of coordination occurs but it is far from being a universal standard. However, under the current system some U.S. ambassadors, particularly those with continuing career interests at the State Department, are fully engaged in representing the State Department interests and priorities, at times to the detriment of the interests and capabilities of the other executive branch departments. This is far from a universal criticism; recent U.S. ambassadors to the IAEA, including Ken Brill and Greg Schulte, have been exceptionally supportive of the U.S. interagency and its work in Vienna. A White House "czar" would have as his first duty the interests of the entire interagency. Implementing a set of recommendations for reforming and reorganizing the U.S. government's work and oversight of its threat reduction programs would make a significant and lasting contribution to enhancing America's security against the threats described in this book. The changes proposed herein are broad and to some, probably heretical, or just too challenging to a number of entrenched interests and ways of doing business. Bringing about such changes will require the sustained commitment of the next president and whatever Congressional majority emerges from the 2008 elections. The American public has every right to expect this level of engagement on such critical questions from its elected representatives. Still, more must be done.

This study has emphasized the U.S. government's international programmatic responses to nuclear and radiological threats, but those problems are so broad that even the U.S. government's considerable resources require augmentation in many areas. At a time when the underlying threats have not abated and critical U.S. programs are failing to execute their missions, it becomes even more critical to leverage the resources of the international community. An old Russian proverb says one soldier does not make a battlefield. Today's battles require the support of the international community, not just a few nations or "soldiers." One approach to enhancing the international community's cooperation would be in securing radiological sources. DOE's efforts in this regard are lagging badly as shown in the GAO Report. The IAEA has demonstrated considerable leadership in this area and it should be encouraged to continue doing so. Drawing on its own assessment of the needs of the international community, the following recommendations are a good starting point for enhancing the IAEA's mission:[2]

- It should develop a coordinated overall international strategy for the provision of assistance to nations where high-risk vulnerable sources are used, stored, or transported based on each nation's needs. This may include assessments of the nation's existing regulatory and legislative control of sources.
- The international strategy also could have a regional flavor. As demonstrated by its role in expediting U.S.-Russian cooperation in this area, the IAEA has shown itself highly useful in bringing together nations committed to working together in securing radioactive sources. For example, a regional initiative led by the IAEA in the Middle East would send a strong signal that the international community will take the strongest possible measures to secure radioactive sources in this politically volatile region.
- The IAEA also can promote research and development, in cooperation with national laboratories such as the development of international measures that will minimize the consequences of malevolent use.

Concluding Observations: Finding Political Solutions to Security Problems

THE THREATS TO our security posed by nuclear and radiological terrorism do not exist in a political vacuum. Rather, they unfold as part of a broader mosaic of global problems roiling much of the international community. Terrorist attacks that are conceived in the Middle East or Asia, organized and planned in Europe, and intended to be carried out in the United States, for example, underscore the global nature of today's security threats. Law enforcement and intelligence professionals in the United States and overseas have applied their skills successfully in disrupting many such attacks. But enhancing our security requires a broader approach as well. As former British Prime Minister Tony Blair wrote in early 2007, "We will not win the battle against global extremism unless we win it at the level of values as much as that of force."[1]

What are the elements of a strategy to win the war against Islamic fundamentalists? While Osama bin Laden and his ideological mentor Ayman al-Zawahiri have offered the United States and Europe cease-fire agreements, there is no reason to believe that either individual is prepared to eschew violence against the United States or the West. In their eyes the West is the cause of the alleged wrongs perpetrated against Muslims for decades. For this reason alone, and there are many others, confronting Islamic fundamentalism as well as rogue nations and their interest in acquiring nuclear and radiological weapons is likely to be a long-term fixture in our security calculations. As a result, the demand for resources to counter these threats, both personnel and financial, will continue to be considerable, even after the war in Iraq is resolved. Regardless of how one judges the various policy choices made by the Bush administration in its counterterrorism strategy, there can be no debate regarding the size and scope of the resources committed by the U.S. government. It has been unprecedented. The American public has been willing to support the commitment of those resources for many elements of U.S. domestic and foreign counterterrorism policy, including sweeping changes in the U.S. government's structure organization represented by the creation of a Department of Homeland Security, changes in the intelligence community, and military operations in Afghanistan, but reserved its deepest criticism for the application of resources in Iraq. The challenge confronting the next administration will be to develop a comprehensive, sustainable, and broadly supported series of policy options that maximize the effectiveness of our resources. Here are a few ways that can be accomplished.

Relative to its expenditures on military operations, the U.S. government spends a pittance on its public diplomacy. In the context of developing a comprehensive counterterrorism strategy, a coordinated, global diplomatic initiative merits rapid and broad resource expansion and political support. This initiative would build on but greatly expand the work being done by presidential confidant and senior State Department political appointee Karen Hughes, an admitted novice at international diplomacy. The U.S. government has many skilled career diplomats; but it is not clear if they are being employed as creatively as possible for this task.

To do so requires the development of at least two major diplomatic tracks. The first would be a major initiative to restore U.S. credibility throughout the Middle East and Asia, not so much by touting Washington's avowed belief that the entire Middle East can be transformed politically, but by conveying a larger message, with presumably broader appeal, about America's commitment to a core set of universal values of respect for human rights and the dignity of the individual.

It wasn't so long ago that there was virtually a global outpouring of support and empathy for America after the attacks of September 11, 2001. Much of that good will has been hemorrhaged by the choices made in the ensuing period by the administration, not only in its invasion of Iraq but its slow response to investigating, ending, and holding senior officials accountable for the prison scandal at Abu Ghraib and its embrace of the Central intelligence Agency's tactics of rendition, the secret movement and extreme interrogation of suspected terrorists. Whether or not one agrees with the rationale for invading Iraq, our subsequent actions have placed us on the moral defensive in much of the Muslim world.

The sad irony is that Islamic fundamentalists and their religious extremism represent the true unmistakable threat to the lives of millions across a region that these extremists would presume to rule. It is their intolerance and "values," if that word can be applied credibly, that offer little, if anything, to meet the social or educational needs of the peoples in the region. If anyone should want to envision the type of society that would be created by Islamic fundamentalists they only need recall the brief period of Taliban rule in Afghanistan. Women were persecuted relentlessly, relegated to wholly subservient societal roles, while educational opportunities for the young centered almost exclusively on teaching a radical interpretation of the Koran. The dawn of the twenty-first century, with all its manifest problems, also bears witness to many positive developments in health care, education, global communication, technology, and science. Recognizing that vast areas of deprivation still exist and that the opportunities of a new century surely have not been felt equally across the globe, more people in more parts of the world are living better lives than ever before. The world, albeit in fits and starts, is moving forward. In contrast, Islamic fundamentalists reject modernism, preferring to turn back the clock 500 years. Why we fight should be as much about the protection of values and the defense of civilization as it might be to enhance U.S. influence in strategically important lands or secure abundant supplies of oil. Diplomacy can lead the way and that diplomatic initiative should harness the skills not only of the U.S. diplomatic corps but also U.S. counterparts in the United Kingdom, elsewhere in Europe, Japan, and other nations who share democratic and humanitarian values.

A useful first step in this approach would focus on those moderate Arab nations in the region, including Jordan, Egypt, and Saudi Arabia. To repeat, the diplomacy advocated here, which should be augmented by Arab language broadcasting, does not lecture or tout the inherent superiority of the American version of democracy. History shows that democracy can be imported successfully but exporting it is far more difficult. Rather, this diplomatic track would emphasize the bankruptcy of radical extremism and the benefits for millions who refute it in terms of a quality of life that reflects the chosen values and desires of those citizens living in an age of considerable opportunity. Their path to democracy, if and when that unfolds, surely will look considerably different than what has evolved over centuries in the West.

The Bush administration has taken some positive steps in conveying U.S. support for the opportunities present in moderate and forward-thinking governments with the establishment of three Arabic language broadcasting centers.

1. Radio Sawa, the Middle East Radio Network, commenced broadcasting in March 2002. It offers music and news aimed at those fifteen to twenty-nine years old. Separate programming targets Iraq, Jordan, and the West Bank, the Persian Gulf, Egypt, and Morocco.
2. Al-Hurra, the Middle East Television Network, was launched in February 2004. It provides news, current affairs, and entertainment programming twenty-four hours-a-day, seven days per week to twenty-two countries.
3. Al-Iraqiya, the Iraqi media network, was originally set up in March 2003 by the Department of Defense. It has been expanded to include two national radio channels and two national television channels.

These are important examples of creative public diplomacy. Each broadcast center has its limitations but each apparently also has found a more than respectable market share among various Arab audiences. Moreover, the programming offered by these networks is a powerful counter to the editorial slant of broadcasting entities such as al-Jazeera with its often anti-American messages.[2]

The expanded use of public diplomacy presumes at least a modicum of support from moderate Arab governments. To date their support for U.S. efforts has been strong. But there also are other underlying political realities throughout the region. The strongest and most obvious is the desire of these regimes to remain in power. Corruption and indifference to the needs of the governed by long-ensconced rulers in the region far too often have been hallmarks of these so-called moderate regimes. Hosni Mubarak has ruled Egypt since October 1981 and seems intent in handing over the reins of power to his son. Dynastic rule also is the hallmark of the Saudi ruling family. Are these styles of government swimming against the tide of history, particularly in a region clamoring for societal change? U.S. interest in shaping, to the extent possible, the direction of inevitable change is considerable, leading to the requirement for a second diplomatic approach.

The U.S. government should match its public critique of the hollowness of religious extremism practiced by Islamic fundamentalists with a quieter but no less powerful message to the ruling parties in the moderate Arab states. That message would center on the reality that the grievances held by many in their societies contribute to the extremism in the region. From the outside we may view the appellation "moderate governments" as appropriate in a geopolitical context but for millions of citizens within those countries there is a perception that the ruling elites far too often have been impervious to genuine change, neglecting both their citizen's needs and grievances. There is danger, as history has shown repeatedly, for any government that commits the fundamental blunder of not providing for the basic needs of its citizens. In Egypt, for example, the political gains of the Muslim Brotherhood should be viewed with alarm by those committed to the status quo ante, not necessarily because the Brotherhood will come to power overnight but because it represents a different vision of Egyptian society and how to reform it than that offered by President Hosni Mubarak and those who have supported and benefited from his protracted rule. Mubarak's response has been to revert to old patterns of governing; his government is planning to modernize Egypt's constitution by banning all parties based on religion, such as the Muslim Brotherhood. How does Washington assess the long-term prospects that by this legal sleight-of-hand the Muslim Brotherhood will vanish from the political scene?

Similar examples are easy to find throughout the region. In Jordan a law has been passed that allows journalists to be jailed for vague forms of slander. In February 2007, ten intellectuals in Saudi Arabia were jailed for signing a petition calling for the House of Saud to consider a transition to constitutional monarchy.[3]

Under these circumstances the second diplomatic track for the U.S. government revolves around the message that U.S. support for those moderate governments requires concerted efforts on their part for political and economic reform. Today the highest priority of many ruling parties in the region is to remain in power at almost any cost. U.S. officials long have recognized this obvious dynamic, but as Secretary of State Rice has acknowledged, past U.S. policy in the region has been to trade democracy and support for democratic values for security but it has not achieved either. U.S. policy must convey in the strongest possible terms that the long-term viability of those ruling in the moderate parts of the Arab world will most likely result from good governance, respecting its citizens while endeavoring to provide them suitable political and economic opportunities. U.S. assistance programs, again in financial terms a small percentage compared to the amount committed to U.S. military operations, should be increased commensurate with the progress made in those nations to show their responsiveness and willingness to change.

Political problems require a political approach that reflects nuance and sophistication as well as the last resort—application of force. The threat of radical fundamentalism almost certainly will remain a preeminent challenge to U.S. national security for the foreseeable future. As such, a credible military capability will remain a critical element of U.S. policy against terrorism. The war in Afghanistan is necessary and should be prosecuted vigorously. Regardless of the outcome of the fighting in Iraq, the United States will continue to have enemies and must be prepared to defend against them. Nonetheless, military force as the sole or even predominant instrument of policy offers little promise of resolving the long-term and underlying political challenges that lie ahead. As described elsewhere in this book, radical fundamentalism poses a direct and continuing threat to such moderate, secular, and generally pro-Western Arab regimes such as Saudi Arabia, Egypt, and Jordan. To underscore this point, those nations, while struggling with their internal problems, also have been the unwilling hosts of bloody terrorist attacks. In addition, the Shiite-dominated radical government in Iran, if it were to succeed in achieving its nuclear ambitions, would be viewed in the Sunni Muslim world as a threat every bit as real, if not more so, than Israel. Already we have seen hints in the Egyptian political leadership that it would respond to Iranian nuclear capability by considering the pursuit of its own nuclear capabilities. Whether this rhetoric would be backed up by such a policy choice is unclear at this time. What is clear, however, is that the United States faces a series of political challenges in the Middle East that call for a broader set of diplomatic engagements, backed by expanded and creative assistance programs.

The importance to U.S. policy interests of Pakistan and Russia, albeit for different reasons, merits the particular attention of the next administration. Pakistan's complex security and political environment have been discussed and need not be repeated. What remains is an understanding of how—and whether—the next administration will be able to influence in any meaningful way Pakistan's future development. The Bush administration has maintained pressure on President Musharraf's government to aggressively expand its efforts to pursue and neutralize al Qaeda and Taliban elements operating along the Pakistan border. One positive sign of Pakistan's responsiveness was the arrest in February 2007 of Mullah Obaidullah Akhund, a leading Taliban strategist. That development stands in juxtaposition to other examples of Pakistan taking only modest steps to control its virtually lawless border areas.

What lies behind the headlines should be the focus for the next administration. For every such highly publicized arrest there are thousands of young Pakistanis receiving religious training in the madrassas system that fosters new hatred for the West, developing the next generation of terrorists. The Pakistani public school system also deserves criticism. Throughout Pakistan, only 52 percent of primary-school-age pupils attend school and nearly one-third will drop out. Only 22 percent of girls above age ten complete primary school, compared to 47 percent of boys.[4] For those who make it to the school-house door, conditions there are hostile to learning as demonstrated by poor teachers, few textbooks, and badly overcrowded conditions. The result is a daily lesson for a generation of students that reinforces that extremist message that the Pakistani government and the opportunities it offers its youth merit no support. Pakistan has become an international breeding ground for terrorists and, on balance, President Musharraf has not done enough to reverse this course with his security and social policies. Growing domestic pressures on his rule will severely challenge the staying power of his regime.

For Washington the challenge is to develop a set of policy options that offers some opportunity for change within Pakistan or at least supports those capable of bringing change. In today's Pakistan, Musharraf is viewed in Washington's policy circles as a known quantity and "the only game in town," the one political force who can maintain a relatively pro-Western political orientation. That assessment explains much of the $10 billion in assistance provided by Washington to Pakistan since September 11, 2001. Most would concede that Musharraf has shown strong survival skills and an ability to navigate Pakistan's dangerous political landscape. Nonetheless, that perspective, at least as a basis for policy, looms as badly short-sighted. Musharraf rules as a result of a military coup; the ages echo with the lesson that even when military rulers are able to maintain power for a protracted period they almost always implode in a sea of popular clamoring for change. Self proclaimed "enlightened military ruler" may be one of political science's most obvious oxymorons.

The next administration need not feel compelled to automatically support ongoing military rule for fear that any regime change could throw Pakistan into the hands of an Islamic fundamentalist ruler. It can, and should, support and urge President Musharraf to support the establishment of democratic practices, beginning with free elections, that could lead to genuine reform in Pakistan. The outcome would be far from certain but there may be reasons for cautious optimism. In 2002, the last major election in Pakistan, religious political parties won just 11 percent of the vote.[5] More recently, in fall 2006, a nation-wide poll showed only slightly more than 5 percent in parliamentary elections would vote for the main religious party, Muttahida Majlis-e-Amal.[6] Even if the apparent political strength of radical elements in Pakistan is more intense than deep within Pakistan society, the election of even a highly capable president committed to steering Pakistan on a course of moderation would face enormous challenges. Few would doubt the interest of radical fundamentalists, perhaps including elements within the Inter-Services Intelligence Agency (ISI), in seizing the reins of power through any means if given the opportunity to do so. Reports from Pakistan in spring 2007 described a new terrorist tactic within Pakistan: the use of suicide attacks in the relatively stable areas of the country and threatening the English-language schools with more violence.[7]

Should presidential elections occur, possibly in late 2007 or early 2008, U.S. policymakers would have to make their total commitment to supporting the government emerging from that process, a distinct shift from past U.S. policies that at times were rooted in short-term policy objectives at the expense of Pakistan's long-term development. Musharraf's military rule offers little chance of bringing about fundamental change in Pakistan and, absent countervailing evidence, the next administration should use that assessment as the guiding principle behind its bilateral relations with Islamabad. Appreciating that Pakistan's long-term security is closely tied to the continuing flow of U.S. economic and military assistance, Islamabad will observe closely Washington's growing relationship with India.

Another set of policy choices flows from the opportunities for the United States to improve its bilateral relationship with Russia. Vladimir Putin's presidency in many ways has stood in marked contrast to the policies Boris Yeltsin supported through much of the 1990s. Putin has proven himself to be an intelligent and tough-minded defender of what he clearly sees as Russia's traditional interests, particularly in what Russians describe as the "near abroad." Large elements of Putin's current foreign policy are the product of an apparently planned and concerted effort to restore Moscow's role as a major force in international affairs. That role in recent years often has not coincided with U.S. preferences, either in terms of Moscow's lukewarm support for meaningful sanctions against Iran, the use of oil as a political weapon against Ukraine and Georgia, or opposition to U.S. efforts to place ballistic missile defense assets in certain European countries. Putin's domestic policies also have reflected choices that have alarmed U.S. policymakers and expert observers alike as he has steered a steady course toward what most in the West would describe as greater political authoritarianism.

Only Russia can determine its fate and U.S. capacity to influence that course seems marginal or indirect at best. For example, Russia, the most Slavic of nations in lore, faces the reality of a rapidly expanding Muslim population. In Moscow alone the number of Muslims is estimated at over two million and across Russia's vast expanses there are an estimated fourteen to twenty million Muslims, mostly living in southern Russia. Those numbers represent a sizable percentage in a nation of only 145 million people and whose overall numbers are declining.[8] Vladimir Putin is aware of the political challenges and strategic implications of these figures as the long-running and bloody war in Chechnya is a battle against Muslims trying to break free of Kremlin rule.

There also is a more-nuanced element behind the presence of a large Muslim community in Russia's midst that Putin also appreciates. In 2003, during a visit to Malaysia, Putin declared that Russia was a Muslim power which hoped to influence Muslim affairs.[9] Historically, Russia's rulers would seldom be described as demonstrating an admirable record of tolerance toward various minority groups. Old habits change slowly. The international Muslim Brotherhood, for example, remains banned in Russia. Nonetheless, there is an interesting dynamic unfolding the way Muslim groups are being accepted into Russian society even while Chechnya remains a festering sore for both the Kremlin and the Muslim world. In Kazan, Tatarstan's capital, the city's kremlin houses a mosque while the local imam maintains a positive relationship with his Orthodox counterparts. The number of mosques throughout the region has risen to 1,300 from about twenty a generation ago.[10] In the often sharp give-and-take of Russian politics, these trends may be easily reversed. Alternatively, they also may lead to an unexpected alliance, perhaps with anti-Western overtones, between Orthodox Russia and its Muslim minority. For those in the U.S. government policy and intelligence communities charged with developing effective counterterrorism policies, these possibilities loom as the subtle and difficult-to-answer problems that are the most vexing but perhaps the most important.

Yet, Russia's size and strategic location make it too important to ignore. The next administration would do well to realize that the United States has its own significant interest in working with Russia in the areas of counterterrorism and nuclear nonproliferation. The Bush administration has pursued some of these areas and President Putin has responded in several positive ways. Putin understands the threat Islamic fundamentalism poses to his country no less clearly than his counterparts in the West. Mutually shared interests may serve as a sufficient basis for a satisfactory relationship between the two former antagonists. Nonetheless, it is in U.S. interests to do better. In this respect few could describe the Bush administration's policies toward Russia as either attentive or imaginative. The Russians recognize the value of symbolic gestures and one of the most powerful signals the Bush administration or its successor could send would be an end to the Cold War trappings represented by the 1970s Jackson-Vanik restrictions on trade. Lifting Jackson-Vanik will not serve as a panacea for the broader set of concerns harbored by both sides but it will show that Washington is taking a fresh approach to the bilateral relationship. In addition, since President Putin is scheduled to leave office not long before the Bush administration departs office, an opportunity awaits those on both sides who favor something better than the current uneasiness between the two nations.

There are many ways to reduce the nuclear insecurity hovering over the United States and its allies. Some of those remedies are derived from innovative and global cooperation among nations and organizations with common interests. Ironically, the battle against Islamic fundamentalists has in many ways sparked previously unimagined cooperative efforts. Still other approaches are derived from the myriad U.S. government programs established to address various parts of the problem. This combination of policies and programs has made us safer but skewed priorities; the lack of a sense of purpose also has undermined much of what should have been accomplished to this point on behalf of the American public. We are not yet safe. In the face of relentlessly determined opponents the American public is not powerless. Its government and outside experts understand how to dramatically reduce the threat of nuclear and radiological attack. What has been lacking too often has been the will and the sense of urgency to do so. The American public can and should raise its powerful voice to its representatives in the legislative and executive branches with the message that given the stakes involved only their best efforts are acceptable.

Is the threat as real as described in this book? George Tenet, in his book *At the Center of the Storm*, provides perhaps the best answer. He writes, "We have learned that it is not beyond the realm of possibility for a terrorist group to obtain nuclear weapons. I have often wondered why this is such a hard reality for so many people to accept ... nuclear terrorism remains now a terrifying possibility and extraordinarily hard to stop ... the terrorists are endlessly patient ... one mushroom cloud would change history. My deepest fear is that this is exactly what they intend."[11]

Notes

INTRODUCTION

1. Dana Priest, "Tenet Warns of Al Qaeda Threat," *Washington Post*, February 25, 2004, A1. DOE estimate used by the Material Protection, Control, and Accountability program.

2. Graham Allison, "Tick, Tick, Tick," *Atlantic Monthly*, October 2004, 35; available at www.theatlantic.com/doc/200410/allison.

3. David Albright, "Al Qaeda's Nuclear Program: Through the Window of Seized Documents," Nautilus Institute, Special Forum 47, Berkeley, CA, November 6, 2002.

4. Ibid.

5. "Osama bin Laden's Mandate for Nuclear Terror," www.jinsa.org/articles/html, posted January 10. 2004.

6. Ibid.

7. See www.fas.org/irp/threat/terror.

8. Greg Gordon, "Experts: U.S. Unprepared for Nuclear Terror Attack," McClatchy Newspapers, March 1, 2007; available at www.homelessonthehighdesert. wordpress.com/2007.

9. Anna M. Pluta and Peter D. Zimmerman, "Nuclear Terrorism: A Disheartening Dissent," *Survival* 48, no. 2 (2006): 62.

10. Ibid., 61.

11. Ibid.

12. Ibid., 62.

13. Ibid.

14. Graham Allison, *Nuclear Terrorism: The Ultimate Preventable Catastrophe* (New York: Times Books, 2004), 3.

15. DOE estimate used by the Material Protection, Control, and Accountability program.

16. See, for example, the IAEA report at www.iaea.org/News Center/News/2007/Georgia.

17. "Moscow Lashes Out at Georgia as Uranium Plot Thickens," *New York Times*, January 27, 2007, A4.

18. Ibid.

19. Ibid.

20. Matthew Bunn and Anthony Wier, "Securing the Bomb 2006," http://www.nti.org/e_research/stb06webfull.pdf.

21. Ibid.

22. Allison, *Nuclear Terrorism*, 15.

23. See GAO Report GAO-07-347R, "Combating Nuclear Smuggling: DNDO Has Not Collected Most of the National Laboratories' Results on Radiation Portal Monitors in Support of DNDO's Test and Development Program," www.gao.gov.

24. Dr. Peter Zimmerman, personal communication with author, December 2006.

25. See the nuclear events database at www.iaea.org.

CHAPTER 1

1. See Clinton Letter on Weapons of Mass Destruction, November 14, 1994, at www.nautilus.org/dprkbriefingbook.

2. For the text of Executive Order 12938, see www.disastercenter.com/laworder/12938/htm.

3. An excellent source of information on global military forces is *The Military Balance* (London: Routledge [published for the International Institute for Strategic Studies], 2007).

4. Information derived from Richard Rhodes, "Living with the Bomb," *National Geographic*, August 2005, 104.

5. Graham Allison, *Nuclear Terrorism: The Ultimate Preventable Catastrophe* (New York: Times Books, 2004), 72.

6. Ibid.

7. Ibid.

8. On the history of the Nunn-Lugar Program, see www.nti.org/scripts/nunn+lugar.

9. Ibid.

10. See the discussion of the Russian-American Nuclear Security Advisory Council at www.ransac.org/documents/search/nunnlugar.

11. See www.ndf.org/Mission.

12. An excellent source of information on Operation Sapphire is www.geocities.com/wshingleton/swords.html.

CHAPTER 2

1. Report Card on DOE's Nonproliferation Programs by the Secretary of Energy's Advisory Board. Executive Summary, January 10, 2001, www.seab.energy.gov/publications/rpt.

2. For the text of NSPD-17, see www.fas.org/irp/offdocs/nspd/nspd-17.html.

3. Speech given by Baroness Margaret Thatcher in London, England, October 1, 2002.

4. See www.gao.gov.

5. Notra Trulock, *Code Name Kindred Spirit: Inside the Chinese Nuclear Espionage Scandal* (San Francisco: Encounter Books, 2002).

6. DOE senior managers, personal communication with author, February 2006.

7. Matthew Bunn and Anthony Wier, "Securing the Bomb 2006," http://www.nti.org/e_research/stb06webfull.pdf.

8. Ibid.

9. Ibid.

10. Ibid.

11. Ibid.

12. Sam Roe, "America Faces Bigger Risk than Agency Claims," *Chicago Tribune*, January 29, 2007, 9.

13. Ibid.

14. Ibid.

15. See www.usinfo.state.gov/products/pubs/proliferation.

16. Remarks by John R. Bolton at the Proliferation Security Initiative meeting, Paris, France, September 4, 2003; available at www.usinfo.state.gov/products/pubs/proliferation.

17. An excellent source of information on the BBC China operation is contained in Gordon Correra, *Shopping for Bombs: Nuclear Proliferation, Global Insecurity, and the Rise and Fall of the A. Q. Khan Network* (New York: Oxford University Press, 2006).

18. Ibid., x.

19. "Disarming Libya: WMD," U.S. Congressional Research Service Report, April 22, 2004.

20. See www.state.gov/t/isn/rls/fs/75845.htm.

CHAPTER 3

1. Dr. A. J. Gonzalez, personal communication with author, September 2005.

2. Graham Allison, *Nuclear Terrorism: The Ultimate Preventable Catastrophe* (New York: Times Books, 2004), 31.

3. John Sudnik, "Dirty Bomb Attacks: Assessing New York City's Level of Preparedness from a First Response Perspective" (master's thesis, Naval Postgraduate School, 2006).

4. Peter Bergen, *The Osama bin Laden I Know* (New York: Free Press, 2006), 242.

5. A. J. Gonzalez, "Security of Radioactive Sources: Threats and Answers," in *Security of Radioactive Sources: Proceedings of an International Conference Held in Vienna, Austria, 10–13 March 2003, Organized by the International Atomic Energy Agency* (Vienna: International Atomic Energy Agency, 2003), 37–38.

6. "Radiological Dispersion Devices," Human Health Fact Sheet, August 2006, prepared at Argonne National Laboratory, www.ead.anl.gov.

7. "U.S.-Russia Collaboration in Combating Radiological Terrorism," National Research Council, 2006; executive summary available at www.nap/edu/catalog.php?record_id 1801.

8. Sudnik, "Dirty Bomb Attacks."

9. Department of Homeland Security official, conversation with author, January 25, 2007.

10. Daniel Benjamin and Steven Simon, *The Next Attack: The Failure of the War on Terror and a Strategy for Getting It Right* (New York: Times Books, 2005), 13.

11. Gonzalez, "Security of Radioactive Sources," 48.

12. Ibid., 49.

13. Representatives from Rostekhnadzor, conversation with author, May 2002.

14. Nikolai Agapov, conversation with author, May 2002.

15. "U.S.-Russia Collaboration in Combating Radiological Terrorism," 14.

16. Peter Zimmerman, "The Smoky Bomb Threat," *New York Times*, December 19, 2006, A33.

17. Ibid.

18. Ibid.

19. May Jordan, "Britain Asks 48 Nations to Help Test for Polonium," *Washington Post*, January 12, 2007, A10.

20. Ibid.

21. Zimmerman, "The Smoky Bomb Threat."

22. "DOE's International Radiological Threat Reduction Program Needs to Focus Future Efforts on Securing Highest Priority Radioactive Sources," January 2007; available at www.gao.gov.

23. Ibid.; see executive summary.

CHAPTER 4

1. Joseph Nye, "Nonproliferation After North Korea," *Washington Post*, November 5, 2006, B7.

2. Samina Ahmed, "Pakistan's Nuclear Weapons Program: Moving Forward or Tactical Retreat?" Kroc Institute Paper no.18, February 2000.

3. Pervez Musharraf, *In the Line of Fire* (New York: Free Press, 2006), 274.

4. Ibid., 286–87.

5. Bill Powell and Tim McGirk, "The Man Who Sold the Bomb," *Time*, February 14, 2005, 25.

6. Gordon Correra, *Shopping for Bombs: Nuclear Proliferation, Global Insecurity, and the Rise and Fall of the A. Q. Khan Network* (New York: Oxford University Press, 2006), 6.

7. Ibid., 8.

8. Ibid., 14.

9. Ibid., 27.

10. Powell and McGirk, "The Man Who Sold the Bomb," 28–29.

11. Correra, *Shopping for Bombs*, 13.

12. An excellent source of information on the Nonproliferation Treaty is the Web site of the Center for Nonproliferation Studies, www.cns.org.

13. See the National Security Archives at George Washington University at www.gwu.edu/usarchiv.

14. Quoted in Seymour Hersh, *The Samson Option* (New York: Random House, 1991), 210.

15. Correra, *Shopping for Bombs*, 21.

16. Nye, "Nonproliferation after North Korea."

17. Zbigniew Brzezinski, "Reflections on Soviet Invasion of Afghanistan," memo dated December 26, 1979; available at www.mtholyoke.edu/acad/intrel.

18. Peter Grier, Faye Bowers, and Ovais Tohid, "Pakistan's Nuclear Hero, World's No.1 Nuclear Suspect," *Christian Science Monitor,* February 2, 2004, 1.

19. Correra, *Shopping for Bombs*, 41.

20. David Albright and Corey Hinderstein, "The Centrifuge Connection," *Bulletin of the Atomic Scientists* 60, no. 2 (March/April 2004): 63.

21. Carnegie Endowment for International Peace, "A. Q. Khan Nuclear Chronology," *Issues Brief* 8, no. 8 (September 7, 2005): 1.

22. Robert Gates, *From the Shadows* (New York: Simon and Schuster, 2006), 320.

23. Excellent background material on this period is contained in Steve Coll, *Ghost Wars: The Secret History of the CIA, Afghanistan, and Bin Laden from the Soviet Invasion to September 10, 2001* (New York: Penguin, 2004).

24. Gaurav Kampani, "Proliferation Unbound: Nuclear Tales from Pakistan," Center for Nonproliferation Studies, February 23, 2004; available at www.cns.org.

25. Carnegie Endowment for International Peace, "A. Q. Khan Nuclear Chronology."

26. Ibid.

27. Musharraf, *In the Line of Fire*, 289.

28. See "Pakistan Nuclear Weapons," www.globalsecurity.org/world/pakistan/nuclear.

29. Sartaj Aziz, speech delivered to the Asia Society in New York City, October 1998; available at the Asia Society Web site, www.asiasociety.org.

30. Seymour Hersh, "The Cold Test," *New Yorker*, January 27, 2003.

31. Correra, *Shopping for Bombs*, 79.

32. Ibid., 49.

33. For information on Pakistan's nuclear weapons program and capabilities, see www.nti.org.

34. Larry Niksch, "North Korea's Nuclear Weapons Program," Congressional Research Service Report to Congress, October 5, 2006.

35. Graham Allison, "Tick, Tick, Tick," *Atlantic Monthly*, October 2004; available at www.theatlantic.com/doc/200410/allison.

36. Correra, *Shopping for Bombs*, 92.

37. Glenn Kessler, "New Doubts on Nuclear Efforts by North Korea," *Washington Post*, March 1, 2007, A1.

38. Powell and McGirk, "The Man Who Sold the Bomb," 29.

39. Dianne E. Rennack, "India and Pakistan: U.S. Economic Sanctions," Congressional Research Service Report to Congress, February 3, 2003.

40. Ibid.

41. Correra, *Shopping for Bombs*, 145–46.

42. Musharraf, *In the Line of Fire*, 290.

43. Deb Riechmann, "Bush 'Taken Aback' by Musharraf Comment," Associated Press, September 22, 2006.

44. Richard Armitage, interview on PBS *Frontline*, July 20, 2006, www.pbs.org/wgbh/pages/frontline/taliban/interviews/armitage.html.

45. David Albright and Corey Hinderstein, "Unraveling the A. Q. Khan and Future Proliferation Networks," *Washington Quarterly*, Spring 2005, www.twq.com/05spring/docs/05spring_albright.pdf.

46. *The 9/11 Commission Report: Final Report of the National Commission on Terrorist Attacks upon the United States* (New York: W. W. Norton, 2003), 369.

47. Daniel Benjamin and Steven Simon, *The Next Attack: The Failure of the War on Terror and a Strategy for Getting It Right* (New York: Times Books, 2005), 47.

48. Musharraf, *In the Line of Fire*, 292.

49. Benjamin and Simon, *The Next Attack*, 105.

50. Correra, *Shopping for Bombs*, 114.

51. The text of the speech is contained in "Disarmament Diplomacy," *Acronym Institute*, January/February 2004, www.acronyminstitute.org.uk/dd/dd75/75news02.htm.

CHAPTER 5

1. "Getting Ready for a Nuclear Iran," October 2005, www.strategicstudiesinstitute.mil.army.

2. Gordon Correra, *Shopping for Bombs: Nuclear Proliferation, Global Insecurity, and the Rise and Fall of the A. Q. Khan Network* (New York: Oxford University Press, 2006), 68.

3. Ibid., 69.

4. Ibid., 71.

5. "Getting Ready for a Nuclear Iran."

6. For an overview on Iran's ballistic missile programs, see Center for Defense Information, "Iran's Missile Flight Tests," July 1, 2004, www.cdi.org.program/document.cfm.

7. Consistently excellent analysis of Iran's nuclear and missile programs has been carried out by Anthony H. Cordesman of the Center for Strategic and International Studies in Washington, DC. On the Shahab 3, see his 2004 work "Iran's Developing Military Capabilities," www.iranian/News/2004/December/csisiranmilitary/December 2004.pdf.

8. For the text of the 2002 State of the Union address, see www.whitehouse.gov/speeches.

9. See Alireza Jafarzadeh, "New Information on Top Secret Projects on Iranian Regime's Nuclear Programs," August 14, 2002, www.iranfocus.com/modules/news/article.php?storyid.

10. One of the most comprehensive uses of commercial satellite photography to monitor the Iranian nuclear program has been carried out by David Albright, president of the Institute for Science and International Security; see the Index of Satellite Imagery at www.isis-online.org.

11. See www.globalsecurity.org/wmd.

12. Ibid.

13. For an overview of Project Daniel, see www.acpr.org.il.

14. Farhang Jahanpour, "Iran's Nuclear Threats: Exploring the Politics," June 2006, www.oxfordresearchgroup.org./uk/publications.

15. Bolton's remarks, dated September 13, 2004, are found at Near East Report, www.iranwatch.org/privateviews/aipac.

16. Cordesman, "Iran's Developing Military Capabilities."

17. "Gulf States Have the Right to Nuclear Energy: UN," April 13, 2007; available at www.einnews.com.

18. "Ahmadinejad: Iran Will Continue Nuclear Program, Does Not Need U.S. Help," Iran Republic News Agency, June 26, 2005, www.iran-daily.com/1385/2596/html/index/htm.

19. Naghmeh Sohrabi, "Iran: Where a Tomato Is Not a Tomato," March 27, 2007, www.brandeis.edu/centers/crown.

20. "Ahmadinejad: Wipe Israel Off Map," October 26, 2005; available at www.aljazeera.net.

21. Cordesman, "Iran's Developing Military Capabilities."

22. "Security Council Imposes Sanctions on Iran for Failure to Halt Uranium Enrichment," December 23, 2006, www.un.org.news/press/documents.

23. "Ahmadinejad Says No Brake on Iran's Nuclear Drive," February 25, 2007; available at www.France24.com.

24. "UN Toughens Sanctions Against Iran, Adding Arms Embargo," March 24, 2007; available at www.un.org.news/press/documents.

25. Thomas Shanker, "Security Council Votes to Tighten Iran Sanctions," New York Times, March 25, 2007, A1.

26. "Is Washington Planning a Military Strike?" December 30, 2005; available at www.spiegel.de/international.

27. Seymour Hersh, "The Iran Plans," New Yorker, April 17, 2006.

CHAPTER 6

1. Anthony H. Cordesman and Khalid R. Al-Rodhan, "Iranian Nuclear Weapons: The Uncertain Nature of Iran's Nuclear Program," working draft, April 12, 2006; available at www.csis.org. On the Negroponte assessment, see "Iran Bomb within Next Ten Years," June 18, 2006; available at www.bbc.co.uk/2/hi/MiddleEast.

2. David Albright and Corey Hinderstein, "When Could Iran Get the Bomb?" Bulletin of the Atomic Scientists 62, no.4 (July/August 2006): 26.

3. Ibid., 31.

4. Bennett Ramberg, "The Preemption Paradox," Bulletin of the Atomic Scientists 62, no. 4 (July/August 2006): 48.

5. Quoted in Sam Gardiner, "The End of the Summer of Diplomacy," Report for the Century Fund; available at www.tcf.org/list.asp?type.

6. See, for example, Cordesman and Al-Rodhan, "Iranian Nuclear Weapons."

7. Frank Barnaby, "Would Airstrikes Work?" March 2007; available at www.oxfordresearchgroup.org.uk/publications.

8. International Monetary Fund, "Staff Report for the Article IV Consultation," www.imf.org/external/publications/ft/scr2006.

9. Colin Freeman, "Iran Poised to Strike in Wealthy Gulf States," *Sunday Telegraph*, March 5, 2007, www.telegraph.co.uk/news/main/jhtml?xmlnews/2007/03/04/wiran04.xml.

10. "Economic Sanctions Ineffective: Experts," August 1, 2006; available at www.mehrinews.com/en/archive.

11. Robin Wright, "Iran Feels Pinch as Major Banks Curtail Business," *Washington Post*, March 26, 2007, A10.

12. Ibid.

13. Olivier Gutta, "Sanctions Against Iran Would Work," *Weekly Standard*, February 19, 2007, 27.

14. Laurent Zecchini, "L'Embargo: Qui Fait Peur?" *Le Monde*, January 20, 2007.

15. Gutta, "Sanctions Against Iran Would Work."

16. Ibid.

17. Matthias Kuentzel, press conference in Berlin, March 23, 2007; available at www.realite-EU.org.

18. Ibid.

19. Ibid.

20. Ibid.

CHAPTER 7

1. Charles Krauthammer, "Britain's Humiliation—and Europe's," *Washington Post*, April 6, 2007, A21.

2. Ibid.

3. George Jahn, "Doubts Remain Over Iran's Nuclear Claims," April 10, 2007, www.boston.com/news/world/Europe/articles/2007/04/10/russia_doubts_iran_nulcear_claims/.

4. The Group of 8 (G8) is an international forum for discussions and decisions by the heads of government (presidents and prime ministers) of the United States, the United Kingdom, Russia, Germany, Italy, Japan, Canada, and France. The member countries take turns hosting an annual meeting.

5. See Fact Sheet for Strengthening the Global Partnership at www.sgpproject.org/resources.

6. Ibid.

7. Ibid.

8. See the Global Partnership Scorecard 2006 at www.sgpproject.org/publications/GPscorecard2006.

9. Ibid.

10. Pierre Goldschmidt, "Priority Steps to Strengthen the Nonproliferation Regime," Carnegie Endowment Outlook Paper no. 33, January 2007; available at www.carnegieendowment.org/publications.

11. Ibid.

12. An excellent overview on the topic is found in Harold Feiveson, "The Search for Proliferation-Resistant Nuclear Power," *Journal of the Federation of American Scientists* 54, no. 5 (September/October 2001).

13. Flynt Leverett, "The Gulf between Us," *New York Times*, January 24, 2006, 19.

14. An excellent discussion of the perceptions of the Iranian public and political leadership regarding nuclear issues is contained in Ray Takeyh, *Hidden Iran: Paradox and Power in the Islamic Republic* (New York: Times Books, 2006):139–53.

15. Ivo Daalder and James Goldgeieer, "Global NATO," *Foreign Affairs* 85, no. 5 (September/October 2006): 112.

16. Ibid.

17. Ibid.

CHAPTER 8

1. "Weapons of Mass Destruction: Nonproliferation Programs Need Better Integration," Government Accountability Office Report 05-157, January 2005; available at www.gao.gov.

2. A. J. Gonzalez, "Security of Radioactive Sources: Threats and Answers," in *Security of Radioactive Sources: Proceedings of an International Conference Held in Vienna, Austria, 10–13 March 2003, Organized by the International Atomic Energy Agency* (Vienna: International Atomic Energy Agency, 2003), 55-56.

CHAPTER 9

1. Tony Blair, "A Battle for Global Values," *Foreign Affairs* 86, no. 1(January/February 2007): 79.

2. Richard A. Clarke, ed., *Defeating the Jihadists: A Blueprint for Action* (New York: Century Foundation Press, 2004), 94–95.

3. "Regression Analysis," *The Economist*, March 17–23, 2007.

4. "Teachers, Don't Leave Them Kids Alone," *The Economist*, April 7–13, 2007.

5. Mark Mazzetti, "One Bullet Away from What?" *New York Times*, March 11, 2007, sec. 4, 1.

6. Ibid.

7. Carlotta Gall, "Islamic Militants in Pakistan Bomb Targets Close to Home," *New York Times*, March 14, 2007, A1.

8. "A Benign Growth," *The Economist*, April 7–13, 2007.

9. Ibid.

10. Ibid.

11. George Tenet, *At the Center of the Storm: My Years at the CIA* (New York: HarperCollins, 2007), 279–80.

Selected Bibliography

"Ahmadinejad: Wipe Israel Off Map." Available at http://www.aljazeera.net, accessed October 26, 2005.

Albright, David, and Corey Hinderstein. "The Centrifuge Connection." *Bulletin of Atomic Scientists*, March/April 2004.

———. "Unraveling the A. Q. Khan and Future Proliferation Networks." *Washington Quarterly*, Spring 2005.

———. "When Could Iran Get the Bomb?" *Bulletin of the Atomic Scientists*, July/August 2006.

Allison, Graham. *Nuclear Terrorism: The Ultimate Preventable Catastrophe*. New York: Times Books, 2004.

Azhar, Saeed, and Steve LeVine. "Nuclear Scientist Denied Knowing bin Laden." *Wall Street Journal–Europe*, November 5, 2001.

Baker, Howard, and Lloyd Cutler. "A Report Card on the Department of Energy's Nonproliferation Programs with Russia." U.S. Secretary of Energy Advisory Board, January 2001.

Baker, Peter. "Pakistani Scientist Who Met bin Laden Failed Polygraphs, Renewing Suspicions." *Washington Post*, March 2, 2002.

Benjamin, Daniel, and Steven Simon. *The Age of Sacred Terror: Radical Islam's War against America*. New York: Random House, 2003.

———. *The Next Attack: The Failure of the War on Terror and a Strategy for Getting It Right*. New York: Times Books, 2005.

Bergen, Peter. *Holy War, Inc.: Inside the Secret World of Osama bin Laden*. New York: Free Press, 2001.

———. *The Osama bin Laden I Knew*. New York: Free Press, 2006.

Blair, Tony. "Our Values—and Theirs." *Foreign Affairs*, January/February 2007.

Bodansky, Yosef. *Bin Laden: The Man Who Declared War on America*. Roseville, CA: Prima, 2001.

Bonner, Raymond, and Craig S. Smith. "Pakistani Said to Have Given Libya Uranium." *New York Times*, April 19, 2004.

Broad, William J., David Rohde, and David E. Sanger. "Inquiry Suggests Pakistanis Sold Nuclear Secrets." *New York Times*, December 22, 2003.

Brzezinski, Zbigniew. *Power and Principle: Memoirs of the National Security Advisor, 1977–1981*. New York: Farrar, Straus and Giroux, 1985.

Bunn, Matthew, and Anthony Wier. "Securing the Bomb 2006." Available at http://www.nti.org/securing the bomb2006, accessed March 7, 2007.

Burke, Jason. *Al Qaeda: The Story of Radical Islam*. London: I. B. Taurus, 2003.

Christopher, Warren. *Chances of a Lifetime*. New York: Scribner, 2001.

Clarke, Richard A. *Against All Enemies: Inside America's War on Terror*. New York: Free Press, 2004.

———. *Defeating the Jihadists: A Blueprint for Action*. A Century Foundation Task Force Report. New York: Century Foundation Press, 2004.

Clinton, William. *My Life*. New York: Knopf, 2004.

Coll, Steve. *Ghost Wars: The Secret History of the CIA, Afghanistan, and bin Laden from the Soviet Invasion to September 10, 2001*. New York: Penguin, 2004.

Cooper, Helene, and David E. Sanger. "Strategy on Iran Stirs New Debate at White House." *New York Times*, June 16, 2007.

Cordesman, Anthony H. *Iran's Developing Military Capability*. Washington, DC: Center for Strategic and International Studies, 2005.

Cordesman, Anthony H., and Khalid Al-Rodhan. *Iran's Weapons of Mass Destruction*. Washington, DC: Center for Strategic and International Studies, 2006.

Correra, Gordon. *Shopping for Bombs: Nuclear Proliferation, Global Insecurity, and the Rise and Fall of the A. Q. Khan Network*. New York: Oxford University Press, 2006.

Cowell, Alan, and Steven Lee Myers. "British Accuse Russian of Poisoning Ex-KGB Agent." *New York Times*, May 23, 2007.

Cullison, Alan. "Inside Al Qaeda's Hard Drive." *Atlantic Monthly*, September 2004.

Cullison, Alan, and Andrew Higgins. "Computer in Kabul Holds Chilling Memos." *Wall Street Journal*, December 31, 2001.

Daalder, Ivo H., ed. *Beyond Preemption: Force and Legitimacy in a Changing World*. Washington, DC: Brookings Institution Press, 2007.

Day, Kathleen. "Sting Reveals Security Gap at Nuclear Agency." *Washington Post*, July 12, 2007.

El Baradei, Mohamed. "Towards a Safer World." *The Economist*, October 16, 2003.

Esposito, John L. *Unholy War: Terror in the Name of Islam*. Oxford: Oxford University Press, 2002.

Fathi, Nazila. "Iran Says It Can Enrich Uranium on an Industrial Scale." *New York Times*, April 10, 2007.

Fielding, Nick. "Bin Laden's Dirty Bomb Quest Exposed." *London Times Online*, December 19, 2004.

Friedman, Thomas. "Iran Arrests Grandma." *New York Times*, May 30, 2007.

Gaddis, John. "Bush's Security Strategy." *Foreign Policy*, November/December 2002.

Gates, Robert. *From the Shadows: The Ultimate Insider's Story of Five Presidents and How They Won the Cold War*. New York: Simon and Schuster. 1996.

Hersh, Seymour. "The Cold Test." *New Yorker*, January 27, 2003.

————. *The Samson Option: Israel's Nuclear Arsenal and American Foreign Policy.* New York: Random House, 1991.

Hsu, Spencer S., and Walter Pincus. "U.S. Warns of Stronger Al Qaeda." *Washington Post*, July 12, 2007.

Hymans, Jacques E. C. *The Psychology of Nuclear Proliferation: Identity, Emotions, and Foreign Policy.* Cambridge: Cambridge University Press. 2007.

International Atomic Energy Agency. "Action Plan to Protect against Nuclear Terrorism." March 2002. Available at www.iaea.org/news/center/features/nuclear_terrorism/index.shtml.

International Institute for Strategic Studies Dossier. *Iran's Strategic Weapons Programmes.* London: Routledge, 2005.

Jacobson, Michael. *The West at War.* Washington, DC: Washington Institute for Near East Policy, 2006.

Katona, Peter. *Countering Terrorism and WMD: Creating a Global Counter-terrorism Network.* London: Routledge, 2006.

Kaye, Dalia Dassa, and Frederic M. Wehrey. "A Nuclear Iran: The Reactions of Neighbours." *Survival*, Summer 2007.

Keppel, Gilles. *The War for Muslim Minds: Islam and the West.* Cambridge, MA: Harvard University Press, 2004.

Kristof, Nicholas D. "A Nuclear 9/11." *New York Times*, March 10, 2004.

Lewis, Bernard. "Time for Toppling." *Wall Street Journal*, September 27, 2002.

————. *What Went Wrong? Western Impact and Middle East Response.* Oxford: Oxford University Press, 2002.

Lipton, Eric. "A Nuclear Ruse Uncovers Holes in U.S. Security." *New York Times*, July 12, 2007.

Mitchell, Richard. *The Society of the Muslim Brothers.* New York: Oxford University Press, 1993.

Musharraf, Pervez. *In the Line of Fire: A Memoir.* New York: Free Press, 2006.

"Muzzling Dissent and Moving to a War Footing." *The Economist*, June 30, 2007.

Niksch, Larry. "North Korea's Nuclear Weapons Program." Congressional Research Service, October 5, 2006.

The 9/11 Commission Report: Final Report of the National Commission on Terrorist Attacks upon the United States. New York: W. W. Norton, 2003.

Nye, Joseph. "Nonproliferation after North Korea." *Washington Post*, November 5, 2006.

Perkovich, George. *India's Nuclear Bomb.* Berkeley: University of California Press, 2000.

Pluta, Anna M., and Peter D. Zimmerman. "Nuclear Terrorism: A Disheartening Dissent." *Survival*, Summer 2006.

Pollack, Kenneth. *The Puzzle Palace.* New York: Random House, 2004.

Rhodes, Richard. "Living with the Bomb." *National Geographic*, August 2005.

Richardson, Louise. *What Terrorists Want: Understanding the Enemy, Containing the Threat.* New York: Random House, 2006.

Riechmann, Deb. "Bush 'Taken Aback' by Musharraf Comment." Associated Press, September 22, 2006.

Rohde, David, and Amy Waldman. "Pakistani Leader Suspected Moves by Atomic Expert." *New York Times*, February 10, 2004.

Russell, Richard. *Weapons Proliferation in the Greater Middle East.* Oxford: Routledge, 2005.

Sagan, Scott. "Keeping the Bomb Away from Tehran." *Foreign Affairs*, September/October 2006.

Sanger, David E. "Nuclear Scientists in Pakistan May Have Links to Al Qaeda." *New York Times*, November 28, 2001.

———. "Inspectors Cite Big Gain by Iran on Nuclear Fuel." *New York Times*, May 15, 2007.

Security of Radioactive Sources: Proceedings of an International Conference Held in Vienna, Austria, 10–13 March 2003, Organized by the International Atomic Energy Agency. Vienna: International Atomic Energy Agency, 2003.

Shanker, Thomas. "Security Council Votes to Tighten Iran Sanctions." *New York Times*, March 25, 2007.

Shenon, Philip. "Terror Suspect Says He Wants U.S. Destroyed." *New York Times*, April 13, 2002.

Sudnik, John. "Dirty Bomb Attacks: Assessing New York City's Level of Preparedness from a First Response Perspective." Master's thesis, Naval Postgraduate School, 2006.

Takeyh, Ray. *Hidden Iran: Paradox and Power in the Islamic Republic.* New York: Times Books, 2006.

Talwar, Puneet. "Iran in the Balance." *Foreign Affairs*, July 2001.

Tenet, George. *At the Center of the Storm: My Years at the CIA.* New York: HarperCollins, 2007.

———. Testimony of the Director of Central Intelligence before the House and Senate Intelligence Committees, October 17, 2002.

Timmerman, Kenneth R. *Countdown to Crisis: The Coming Nuclear Showdown with Iran.* New York: Three Rivers Press, 2006.

Trulock, Notra. *Code Name Kindred Spirit: Inside the Chinese Nuclear Scandal.* San Francisco: Encounter Books, 2002.

Tyler, Patrick E. "Libyan Stagnation a Big Factor in Qaddafi Surprise." *New York Times*, January 7, 2004.

Warrick, Joby. "Tunneling Near Iranian Nuclear Site Stirs Worry." *Washington Post*, July 9, 2007.

White House Press Office. *The National Security Strategy of the United States.* Washington, DC: Government Printing Office, 2002.

Wit, Joel, Daniel Poneman, and Robert Gallucci. Going Critical: The First North Korean Nuclear Crisis. Washington, DC: The Brookings Institution Press, 2004.

Wright, Robin. *The Last Great Revolution: Turmoil and Transformation in Iran.* New York: Oxford University Press, 2001.

———. "Slowdown Seen in Iran's Nuclear Program." *Washington Post*, July 10, 2007.

Zimmerman, Peter D. "The Smoky Bomb Threat." *New York Times*, December 12, 2006.

Index

About the Author

JACK CARAVELLI is one of America's leading experts on nonproliferation and nuclear terrorism. He is a Senior Visiting Fellow at the U.K. Defence Academy and a Visiting Professor at Cranfield University. He was Deputy Assistant Secretary at the U.S. Department of Energy (2000–2003), and he served on the White House National Security Council (1996–2000), where he was the president's principal advisor for nonproliferation policies and programs involving Russia and the Middle East. He began his governmental career in 1982 at the Central Intelligence Agency. Caravelli is a Chatham House Fellow and a member of the advisory board of Oxford University's Pluscarden Program on Intelligence and Terrorism.